Asset Protection through Security Awareness

T0293610

Asset Protection through Security Awareness

Tyler Justin Speed

CRC Press
Taylor & Francis Group
Boca Raton London New York

CRC Press is an imprint of the
Taylor & Francis Group, an **informa** business

AN AUERBACH BOOK

CRC Press
Taylor & Francis Group
6000 Broken Sound Parkway NW, Suite 300
Boca Raton, FL 33487-2742

First issued in paperback 2019

© 2012 by Taylor & Francis Group, LLC
CRC Press is an imprint of Taylor & Francis Group, an Informa business

No claim to original U.S. Government works

ISBN: 978-1-4398-0982-2 (hbk)
ISBN: 978-0-367-38181-3 (pbk)

Library of Congress Cataloging-in-Publication Data

Speed, Tyler Justin.
    Asset protection through security awareness / Tyler Justin Speed.
        p. cm.
    Includes index.
    ISBN 978-1-4398-0982-2 (hardback)
    1. Computer networks--Security measures. 2. Information technology--Security measures. 3. Business enterprises--Security measures. I. Title.

TK5105.59.S643 2011
658.4'78--dc23   2011045952

**Visit the Taylor & Francis Web site at
http://www.taylorandfrancis.com**

**and the CRC Press Web site at
http://www.crcpress.com**

Contents

Introduction

Welcome to *Asset Protection through Information Security*. This book is intended to inform the reader about the ins and outs of protecting your organization's network from a high-level perspective. This book is meant to provide a basic oversight of topics surrounding the issue of computer security, such as privacy concerns, access controls, risk management, and more. Each chapter delves into a new topic, and gives a brief overview of how best to provide security for that issue. Throughout the book, the topic of security awareness is woven into the text, inasmuch as the most cost-effective and meaningful method of providing security in any organization is increased awareness among the employees.

Assumptions

This book was written with the assumption that the reader has a basic working knowledge of computers. No networking experience is necessary, although such experience will expedite the process of deepening the reader's understanding of the concepts presented within the text. Absolutely no programming knowledge is required, nor are any coding examples reviewed in the text. It is also assumed that the reader has at least an interest in networking, asset protection, computers, or computer security.

Why Was This Book Written?

In most organizations, there exists a gap between management and technicians tasked with providing security to network systems. This "gap" is a gap of both technical language and understanding of compliance issues. Management personnel understand the need for compliance, but generally lack the technical language necessary to ensure their networks are in compliance. Technicians live in a world of technical language, but don't generally concern themselves with compliance unless moved to do so by management. This book is intended to fill this gap between technicians and management, by providing a common ground of understanding for both. Whether you are a manager or technician, this book sits in the middle ground where both can meet and discuss important security topics.

For Whom Is This Book Intended?

If you work for an organization and are entrusted with any level of protection of organizational assets, this book is for you. The assets you may be entrusted to protect might be customer data, networking equipment, or employee information, to name just a few assets this book attempts to cover.

What Is Not Covered in the Text?

As mentioned, this is not a book for coders, but was written as a primer on the subject of security management principles and not as a highly technical and detailed volume. Therefore it does not discuss how to eliminate buffer overflows, or how to design and implement an intrusion detection system. Readers may therefore discover what they consider to be holes in this book, because not every topic under the security sun is discussed, but that was never the intention. Although this book does discuss practices surrounding security management, it is not intended to be read as a complete tome of knowledge on the subject. There are countless volumes dedicated to the topic of security, and this is only one of them. Within each security topic, dozens of books could be written to the nth degree of detail.

What Is Information Security?

Information security is the study of protecting an organization's data from harm. What is constituted by *harm* will vary from one network to the next, but an accepted measurement of what constitutes protected data is the assurance of four characteristics. The first three are summed up in a common framework known as the CIA triad, and the fourth characteristic is nonrepudiation (see Figure 1).

The common framework used by information security professionals to describe what is necessary for successful computer security is the CIA triad: the three requirements of confidentiality, integrity, and availability. All three are necessary for any file to be considered protected. In addition to the CIA triad, nonrepudiation plays a large role in information security. The following discussions of the CIA triad and nonrepudiation illustrate the need for all four components of security.

Confidentiality

Confidentiality is the assurance that information is accessible only by authorized users. Confidentiality is lost when secure information is disclosed to, or observed by, an individual who is otherwise unauthorized to have access to the information. Because confidentiality can be broken either by unauthorized disclosure or visual exposure, both digital and physical means of securing it must be considered.

CIA Triad + Nonrepudiation

CONFIDENTIALITY
In order to be considered secure, data must be kept away from competitors and unauthorized users. Confidentiality ensures data isn't viewed by such users.

INTEGRITY
Data can be easily corrupted. Integrity is the level of certainty that the data is the same as when it was created. In addition to continuous file integrity, the files should be obtained and managed ethically, with integrity.

AVAILABILITY
Whether your data is complete or not, an organization must be able to access critical data. If data is inaccessible, it lacks availability and is no good.

NONREPUDIATION
Data should be stored in such a manner as to ensure anybody accessing the data can be verified. For instance, each user should have a unique ID and login password to make certain more than one person cannot access the same account. In this manner, only one person can be held accountable for any given digital activity on the network.

Figure 1   The CIA Triad

Digital means of securing confidentiality are as varied as the networks upon which the information is stored. Access controls, password management, firewalls, network intrusion detection systems, antivirus software, network monitoring, and public key infrastructure policies all work together to help ensure confidentiality.

Physical means of securing confidentiality include locking file cabinets, secure rooms, physical deterrents such as fences and other perimeter barriers, passkeys, security checkpoints, physical keys, security guards, and any other means to keep unauthorized users from accessing systems and files. Something as simple as the installation of a monitor screen so passersby cannot view what's on a computer screen would be considered a measure toward protecting confidentiality.

Integrity

The second portion of the CIA triad is integrity. Integrity, in regard to computer security, means both a state of completeness, and the adherence to a code of accepted ethics or morals. If a file is transmitted from one user to another, checksums can be used to determine if the file is complete. Integrity also speaks to the ethical validity of a file. If a file is ill-gotten, or stolen, it lacks a level of integrity.

Availability

Even if a file's confidentiality and integrity are maintained, it must be available in order for it to be of any value to its owner. A file can exist on hard drive with its integrity intact, and still be considered unavailable. If a word processing file extension is deleted, it cannot be opened. Even when most files are deleted, they are still fully stored on a hard drive, with integrity, but they are just no longer accessible due to the lack of the needed file pointer. Another possible scenario for files that meet confidentiality and integrity, but fail availability, is any situation wherein a hard drive is stolen and contains an encrypted file. The file may be complete, so the integrity of the file is intact. It is also encrypted, and therefore it meets the requirements for confidentiality; however, in this scenario, because the hard drive was stolen, the file would not meet the requirements for availability.

Nonrepudiation

Another key factor of complete security is the issue of nonrepudiation. Nonrepudiation is the creation and follow-through of security controls, policies, and procedures in such a manner as to eliminate the possibility of repudiation of culpability from a malicious user. The concept of nonrepudiation is violated in many organizations whenever a user's password is given to a user and also stored in a notebook or database by the user's boss. If the user's login is used to log into the system and cause damage to the network, a user could reasonably repudiate the claims that he was responsible, inasmuch as more than one person has access to his login credentials.

1

CREATING A CULTURE OF SECURITY AWARENESS

You have strengths and weaknesses. These come from your position. Your position comes from your knowledge of the situation.

Sun Tzu

Protecting Corporate Assets

The goal of corporate security is to protect the organization's assets. When most people think about assets, they naturally think of possessions of the physical realm. These possessions may include real estate, facilities, manufacturing equipment, automobiles, desks, computers, chairs, tools, and more. These tangible assets are used to accomplish the daily operations of the organization, and leveraged to finance new projects. They are measurable in terms of value and directly affect the bottom line of an organization. For the sake of this book, these assets are referred to simply as physical assets.

Perhaps even more valuable than physical assets are the ideas and data that help keep organizations competitive and efficient. These ideas can include new designs from engineering, proprietary production methods and procedures, sensitive company financial data, customer contact information, and employee records. Any piece of information that is beneficial to the organization is an asset. Likewise, any sensitive data that would cause damage to the organization if seen by outside entities should be considered as assets worthy of protection. For the sake of this book, these assets are referred to simply as informational assets.

Types of Protective Measures

TECHNICAL MEASURES
Hardware or software measures directed at providing digital protection for data contained on the organization's network. Firewalls, cryptographic algorithms, antivirus programs, etc. are all considered Technical Protective Measures.

PHYSICAL MEASURES
Barriers and monitoring equipment designed and implemented to prevent direct physical harm to the physical network equipment upon which the organization's data is kept. Fences, security cameras, backup systems, automobile barriers, security guards, etc. are all considered Physical Protective Measures.

PERSONNEL MEASURES
Policies and procedures, which are directed at instructing everyone within the corporation, including employees from senior management to the end users, on proper computer and network operations, in regards to inputting, managing, and securing all critical data.

Figure 1.1   Protective Measures

Protective Measures

Both physical and informational assets need to be protected from internal and external threats. It is interesting to note that regardless of which type of asset an organization is trying to protect, the approach to protecting them is very similar. Because we live in a physical world, everything, even data, will exist in its most basic form at a physical level. Engineering designs, human resource records, customer service notes, production methods and procedures, all exist in the physical realm. Therefore, it is important to implement technical protective measures, physical protective measures, and personnel protective measures (see Figure 1.1).

Technical Protective Measures

First on the list of means for protecting networks and data are technical protective measures. Let us consider technical protective measures to include any measure directly dealing with the transfer of digital data, including digital firewalls, network intrusion detection systems, antivirus programs, network traffic sniffers, penetration testing,

Ten Steps for Promoting Security Awareness

ACKNOWLEDGE SECURITY ISSUES
Analyze the current state of the organization to determine and make a list of what security issues currently face the organization.

ACCEPT RESPONSIBILITY
Organization's cannot simply ignore security issues, but must accept responsibility and own the process from the beginning to the fruition of a Security Plan and provide proper training.

ASSESS RISK
Without performance of a clear risk analysis, the creation of Security Policies will have no good foundation.

CRAFT SECURITY POLICIES
Using the Risk Assessment as a guide, the organization should build appropriate security policies to protect the organization while safeguarding the organization's finances.

TRAIN AT ALL LEVELS
Make sure all employees are aware of the expectations and requirements for their position in the organization.

CREATE BENCHMARKS
These benchmarks will be central to appropriately monitoring the successes and opportunities for improvement within the organization, and should be clearly established before any audits are performed.

PERFORM SECURITY AUDITS
Auditing the security functions of an organization are key to staying on track.

ENCOURAGE SECURE OPERATIONS
Don't simply provide negative consequences for employees who breach established security protocols, but also be sure to provide incentives for those personnel who appropriately implement the required security procedures.

ASSEMBLE A SECURITY TEAM
The organization's security team should be inclusive of people from all portions of the organization, but everyone on the team should have a solid understanding of network security operations.

PLAN FOR DISASTER
Have backups and contingency plans in place for major systems to ensure minimal down time in the event of a disaster.

Figure 1.2   Promoting Security Awareness

backup media, cryptographic measures, forensic software applications used to retrieve deleted or destroyed data, and wireless encryption, just to name some of the measures a company can implement. These are all necessary, but are inadequate without their cousins, physical protective measures and personnel protective measures (see Figure 1.2).

Some information technology (IT) professionals are excellent at making certain their networks have the latest technical protective measures in place. These technicians pride themselves on how few viruses have successfully invaded the network, and are gurus of network security. Security patches are regularly installed, and networks are constantly monitored. There is no activity on the networks that goes unnoticed by the eyes of these IT professionals.

Although these IT professionals are excellent at keeping digital data secure from would-be cyber criminals, there is sometimes a dearth of actual physical security. So great can the lack of physical and personnel security be, that sometimes all of the digital fortress buttressing accomplished by the IT personnel only serves to provide an illusion of security, when in reality the networks are wide open to attack by internal threats.

Physical Protective Measures

When we stop to remember stored data are simply ones and zeros, it is quickly understood that all data are physical. These ones and zeros are all stored on physical hard drives, which need to be physically protected from external and internal attacks. Sensitive company records must be kept on databases, which will usually reside in a physical server room. Secure walls, ventilation, fire suppression systems, doors, and locks are among some of the requirements for properly securing an organization's server room. Without proper physical security in place to stop unauthorized individuals from accessing the server room, the databases contained on the server hard drives are as good as public knowledge. The same goes for the computers, routers, monitors, and other physical parts of the network infrastructure. It doesn't matter how good the firewall installed at a network's gateway to the Internet is; if a computer's disk drive is not physically protected, an unauthorized user can easily upload malicious software directly onto any one of the computers from inside the gateway, and all data contained therein will be compromised.

Personnel Protective Measures

Personnel protective measures deal with what can sometimes be the greatest risk to an organization's network, the end users of the network and computers. Whether through incompetence, poor training, genuine mistakes, or truly malicious intent, end users wield an amazing amount of power over the networks on which they work. Through the design and implementation of good policy, many of the threats posed by end users can be mitigated, managed, transferred, and, in isolated cases, completely eliminated.

Mitigating Risks Associated with Personnel   There will always be a level of risk associated with hiring someone and allowing him or her access to an organization's network. Accepting this risk is a part of doing business, however, managers can mitigate some of this risk by requiring employees to complete a thorough pre-employment process. This process should include several items to improve the chances of success. First, the interview should include a skills assessment test, to make certain the incoming employee has mastered at least the minimum skillset required for employment. In addition, if the employee has achieved that minimum level of skill, it can be safely assumed she will be able to learn more, and further training as required by her job will not be in vain.

In addition to a skills test, a background check is a good idea for anyone who could possibly come into contact with a computer. A background check should be considered an absolute must for any employee who will be handling money, employee health records, or customer credit card information. There are many companies specializing in providing low-cost background checks with near immediate results, so cost and time should not be a consideration when deciding to implement this step of the hiring process.

Another frequently forgotten and neglected aspect of hiring is the checking of references. If references are listed by an incoming employee, call them. If references are not given, ask for at least three, and then follow up by checking them out. If references are not provided when requested, don't hire the person. It is better to regret not hiring someone who "felt" like a good fit, than to hire someone and find out later he has seriously jeopardized the security of your organization. Many security issues can be avoided by thoroughly vetting incoming employees, so whatever other security choices are made at your organization, make absolutely sure these are strictly adhered to, without exception.

Managing Risks Associated With Personnel   Managing threats includes proper security training, implementing continual reviews of processes, and regularly scheduled auditing of security systems.

Once an incoming employee is properly vetted, the next step in her process as a newcomer to your organization should be training. Training should not only include how to perform the requirements of a job, but should also include a complete review of the organization's security policies. Wherever appropriate, security should be discussed and woven into each facet of an employee's job.

Transferring Risks Associated with Personnel   One of the options when managing risk is the transference to another entity. This transference of risk usually occurs in one of two ways. Either the authority over and responsibility for key processes are given to another entity, or insurance is purchased. For instance, third-party firms specializing in customer service can handle incoming calls and issues from customers. Human Resource consultants can be hired to handle many of the HR concerns of corporations, such as providing HIPAA-compliant health record management for employees. Accounting firms are available to provide fiscally responsible and security compliant handling of company financials. Manufacturing companies hire third-party vendors to build components and subcomponents of products to lower overhead costs, but they also realize security benefits associated with having fewer internal employees directly interfacing with the company networks.

Eliminating Risks Associated with Personnel   Firing an employee who is known to present a specific threat to the security of a company and its assets is one method of eliminating a single threat. However, because people are dynamic, the requirements for dealing with personnel-related risks will vary from day to day, but cannot ever be fully eliminated.

A Culture of Security Awareness

It is the belief of the author that if true security is to be realized in any organization, a culture of security awareness must be encouraged at all levels, from the top down. Regardless of the industry in which an organization operates, there are trade secrets, personnel information, customer information, and proprietary data that must be protected. At virtually every level of operation, people must be careful to protect the assets and interests of the organization they serve. This care will most effectively be derived from a workforce whose culture includes an awareness of security issues.

Creating or altering a work culture is not as difficult as it may seem. Knowledge is at the core of building a workforce aware of security issues. The facts regarding organizational assets and the potential risks facing them should be known by employees using and interfacing with those assets. Once this knowledge and care pervades every facet of the organization, employees will find themselves immersed in a culture of security awareness.

Education Is Key

Perhaps the most effective security measure one can put into place is simply educating employees about the inherent risks associated with any given activity. Making the workforce aware of information security issues is an essential cornerstone of a holistic approach to securing an organization's data. Similar to educating production workers about machinery and processes that may cause damage to the product or harm employees when misused, educating today's workforce about the inherent risks of simply using a computer will give employees the necessary tools to keep company and personal information from harm. Once aware of these risks, people will be more mindful of the potential harm, and will be forced to change their habits in order to be more circumspect.

Creating the Culture

Every organization has its own unique culture, language, and methods of operation. In order to infuse every level of an organization with security, the culture must adapt to embrace new and potentially difficult ideas and policies. There are several steps and layers necessary to create and maintain a culture of security awareness through the ranks of an organization. These steps include:

1. Acknowledging security issues
2. Accepting responsibility
3. Assessing risk
4. Crafting security policies
5. Training at all levels
6. Creating benchmarks for success
7. Security audits
8. Encouraging secure operations
9. Building a security team
10. Planning for disaster

Acknowledging Security Issues

Part and parcel of fostering a culture of security awareness is the acceptance of the real dangers facing anyone whose computer is connected to the Internet. It is no secret that the simple act of connecting a computer to the Internet immediately places all of its contents in peril of being compromised. Every computer that has a connection to the Internet is already sitting on the front lines of our cyber defenses. Our world will only continue to become increasingly interconnected via the Internet as time marches onward. The vast majority of businesses will eventually suffer considerable financial loss due to a cyber attack. This financial loss will be realized in costs associated with sidelining labor into fixing inoperative software applications, filtering e-mails, and reformatting systems, among many other reactive measures. The reality of being attacked by a cyber criminal is a very real and present threat that faces any network today.

The recognition of this threat is evidenced by the birth of entirely new industries dedicated to the protection of data. Several billions of dollars a year, in fact, are spent on securing networks and protecting proprietary information contained within company networks. Entire corporate departments are dedicated to securing data; academic programs that focus on computer protection have been created; and books such as this one have been written; all toward the end of helping organizations, end users, programmers, and anyone who otherwise comes into contact with the Internet keep their digital assets safe. The sooner we all accept the fact that the responsibility of protecting these assets lays within our own hands, the sooner our information will be secure from the myriad threats that face us whenever we interact with the Internet.

Accepting Responsibility

At first blush, it may seem self-evident that protecting the data on our own computers does and should fall within our own realm of responsibility. Although some may see accepting this responsibility as a foregone conclusion of owning a computer, the world of information security is such an abstract and unique phenomenon that it deserves a bit more attention and thought.

Physical Security Versus Information Security   If we stop and think about the physical world, we will quickly realize that we really play a much smaller role in protecting ourselves there than we do in the digital world. Police officers, military personnel, and the entire combination of societal and governmental assistance are at our sides whenever we step outside our homes. We usually don't worry about being attacked while in public because we live in a generally lawful society, which does not allow for rampant violence and physical intrusion into each other's lives. If we are ever unlucky enough to be the victim of a physical assault, our court systems are designed around and capable of understanding and dealing with physical crime. In addition to the structures of laws and the executive enforcement of those laws, there is a strong social aversion to such unlawful physical behavior. In most cases, if someone accosted you at a grocery store without cause, strangers would rush to your aid in some form or another. They might assist by trying to stop the attacker; they might follow the attacker to his or her car and write down a license plate number for the police to handle later; or they may simply offer you condolences and assistance in getting things together after the attack.

The Unseen Digital World   This same societal structure within which we can feel relatively secure in the physical world simply does not exist in the digital world. This is primarily because the digital world is essentially unseen. Attackers can attack at random and with anonymity. The technology used to attack is fairly new and always changing, so there is even a chance laws may not exist to prosecute digital criminals when and if they are caught. Even if the criminal is caught, which is highly unlikely, and even if there are laws on the books that apply to the crime committed, the criminal may not be in the same country as the victim, and could avoid prosecution altogether. This is the elusive, anonymous, and frustrating world of digital crime. Organizations and individuals cannot rely upon social structures, laws, or other existing barriers to protect their data. Instead, the responsibility for protecting data must be accepted by the owners of the data. Once responsibility of protecting assets in the digital world is fully accepted, the data owner must assess the risk associated with the data being protected.

Assessing Risk

In order to provide proper and reasonable protection of the data in question, the data owner must first figure out exactly what he is trying to protect. Archived files, personnel information, customer information, and proprietary processes all need to be protected. Of course, depending upon the type of organization you are in, you may be charged with protecting different types of assets. Deciding exactly what will be protected, and how, involves creating a list of assets, identifying the risks posed against those assets, and deciding how best to deal with those risks. See the chapter on risk management for more details on this process.

Crafting Security Policies

Once the assets and risks are documented, policies designed to protect organizational assets must be created and put into action. Successful policies cannot be arrived at quickly and with little thought. The policies must be thorough, but not so mired in minutiae as to create an environment so burdened with details that the "real work" of the organization cannot occur. When designing security policies, be sure to make every reasonable effort to make the policies easy to apply and practical. Remember to craft your security with the appropriate attention paid to each level of security. For instance, don't try to reproduce the security of Fort Knox if you are in charge of a small company and want to protect a certain manufacturing process from your competition. It cannot be stressed enough that policies should flow with the workflow, not bring it to a screeching halt in the name of security. Instead, make sure the policies complement the existing procedures. If policies are forced upon employees and don't feel like a natural part of their daily processes, they will be far less likely to adopt them into their normal operations. More on creating security policy can be found in the chapter about crafting a security policy.

Training at All Levels

Once policies are created, employees at every level of the organization must be trained on the policies. A thorough training program will educate employees on the reasons why certain policies are being put into place. By trusting employees with the full picture, they will not only feel valued, but they will have a deeper understanding of how best to protect the assets they are charged with in their daily operations.

It is important not to forget that everyone in the organization must be trained on the policies of their departments and individual roles in the organization. Everyone from the CEO to the customer service representative must be properly trained on how his or her individual position in the company affects the bottom line in terms of security. If one person fails to perform the steps necessary to secure the assets with which he works, a hole in the organization's security will open, and a successful attack upon the organization's data will be far more likely. For this reason, seniority and position within an organization should never be allowed to override the security measures put into place. A good training program will take this into account and will provide an organization with a solid framework of security throughout the corporation.

Creating Benchmarks for Success

Before an organization can determine if policies are actually working, benchmarks to measure against must be put into place. These metrics and benchmarks can be used later during audits to determine successful policies as well as problem areas needing further attention and improvement. It is critical for organizations to quantify success in an accurate and meaningful way. Otherwise, the efforts your information security team are making may not be making an impact where it is most needed. See the chapters on metrics and auditing for more information.

Security Audits

Like water, people like to follow the path of least resistance. Over time, if a policy is not enforced, it may or may not be followed depending upon how easily and naturally it fits into daily operations. Using benchmarks created in the preceding step, audits can be performed, which will build a good picture of the state of security within an organization. After this picture is formed, areas for improvement can be clearly seen and appropriate measures may be taken to remedy any problems affecting security. See the chapter on security audits for more details.

Encouraging Secure Operations

It is important to create an environment where employees feel both empowered and encouraged to implement security measures. Individuals will respond far better to rewards and recognition for success rather than being scared into compliance with the threat of losing their jobs. Be sure managers acknowledge employees who are keeping the organization safe and saving money by successfully implementing security policies.

Building a Security Team

A security team should be made up of representatives from all portions of the company who are properly trained in information technology and information security (IS) in general. These don't necessarily have to be IT or IS professionals, but may be people from anywhere in the organization who have a passion and talent for keeping data safe. See the chapter on security teams for more details.

Planning for Disaster

No matter how thorough policies are and no matter what steps are taken to mitigate risk and train employees, organizations should be ready for disaster to strike. Disaster may come in the form of a successful software virus that takes down a main server, or it may be a natural disaster that strikes the campus of the organization. All sorts of events might qualify as disasters, and all reasonable steps should be taken to plan for such events. See the chapter about disaster planning for more details.

Remaining Dynamic

One of the main factors pertaining to the creation of a successful culture of security awareness is the ability of an organization to remain dynamic in the face of changing industries and technologies. An organization should not simply put policies into place and put the issue of security to rest. Instead, a continual review of policies and their effectiveness should be instituted. If a policy isn't working, or if a piece of technology is not providing the operations your organization requires, change it! This goes for functionality as well as security.

Security is worthless if it prohibits employees from performing their job functions. An extreme example is an unplugged computer without wireless access. Sure, the computer would be secure from attacks over the Internet, but it would not allow the user to actually use the computer in any meaningful way. In an effort to stay dynamic and improve productivity while maintaining the best possible security, be sure to listen to employees on the "front lines." The end user, or the person who is actually using the computer, knows what security policy does to productivity. You may have created Fort Knox in the server room, but if you cannot service any computers because of all the physical security, you have lost the fight and the cyber criminals have won. Whether you are a service-related nonprofit or a for-profit business, make sure that whatever policies are put into place, they do not hurt your organization's bottom line. Staying dynamic in your approach will allow your organization to adapt to security needs while protecting that bottom line.

2

OVERVIEW OF SECURITY AWARENESS CATEGORIES

Better be despised for too anxious apprehensions, than ruined by too confident security.

Edmund Burke

Before diving into the process of building or altering your organization's security awareness culture, let's take a look at the different areas in which security awareness is an absolute necessity (see Figure 2.1). Because every organization is a unique entity, it would be an impossible task to provide an all-inclusive list of the areas of concern for your specific company. Instead, this chapter provides some overviews of the more common categories of security awareness. These categories don't necessarily cover specific policies and the process of implementing security guidelines, but instead these are areas of security awareness that should act as a general guide for consideration of such issues. Generally speaking, the security awareness categories for almost any organization or department will include the following.

1. Industry standards
2. Privacy concerns
3. Password management
4. Customer file management
5. Health file management (HIPAA)
6. Credit card compliance (PCI)
7. General file management
8. File access control
9. Physical access control

Nine Realms of Security Awareness

1. Industry Standards
2. Privacy Concerns
3. Password Management
4. Customer File Management
5. Health Record Management
6. Credit Card Compliance
7. General File Management
8. File Access Control
9. Physical Access Control

Figure 2.1   Security Awareness Realms

Industry Standards

Perhaps some of the most essential sources for improving security within an organization will be the industry standards for your organization's particular industry. These standards may come in the form of governmental requirements, they may be required for obtaining industry certifications, or they might be found within accepted modes of operation within the industry. For instance, dozens of laws, regulations, and industry standards exist in the banking industry. Any lending institution will, by necessity of compliance with these laws, regulations, and operating standards, provide a thorough and secure environment for the data it manages. The same is true for hospitals and the healthcare industry in general. The strict requirements for dealing with any health-related data will affect all manner of individuals and corporations, including every entity from an ambulance driver to a human resources worker dealing with an on-the-job injury form. The sensitive nature of both financial information for banks and health records for patients in the healthcare industry obviously require diligent protection of records. However, it should be noted that even smaller companies whose general business doesn't revolve around such sensitive data are required to follow proper management of credit card data, customer data, and employee records.

Many of the requirements for private and governmental security measures will overlap, so make sure your organization is implementing the strongest denominator-overlapping requirements. For complex pieces of legislation and certification, it helps to create a spreadsheet to see where the two overlap. For example, if a piece of government legislation requires files to be stored in a locked cabinet, and a private certification such as an ISO rating requires the files to be locked in a fire-protected cabinet with double locks, make sure the files follow the ISO requirements, inasmuch as it meets both the ISO and the governmental requirements. Wherever the standards affecting your particular organization may be derived from, make sure your organization has taken them all into account when creating security policies. Implementing policies, procedures, and protective measures can be a costly process, and it would be a terrible financial waste to have all of the efforts and finances spent to accomplish the security, just to find out one of the myriad requirements wasn't met, and as a result disaster struck.

Privacy Concerns

Regardless of what service or product your organization provides to its clients, privacy will be a security issue. In fact, at the heart of information security is the act of keeping data private. Most of the requirements for how best to handle privacy issues will likely be outlined in the standards of your organization's particular industry, but make certain to think through some of the less obvious security issues surrounding privacy that are sometimes forgotten. For instance, not only will private records need to be kept under lock and key in a secure environment, but be certain to consider the areas in which conversations about such information may be held. Sometimes, upon entering your facility, clients will need to inform a receptionist of what they need from your organization. Services and products are often paid for in the same area. This is why you should be sure to keep in mind visual and auditory privacy safeguards when considering your reception area. If physical blockades are impossible or just impractical to install, and your industry standards don't call for separate rooms for discussing client needs, be sure to post signage indicating that client privacy cannot be guaranteed in that area. You will often see such signage in hospital waiting rooms informing patients of the potential privacy risks when discussing needs with the intake nurse or receptionist.

To help you locate otherwise overlooked areas of privacy concern, it is a good idea to do a "walkthrough" of your organization. Start by going through the motions as though you were a customer of your organization. Walk through the door an average customer would use and speak with the receptionist or whoever is in charge of greeting your organization's customers. Go through a mock purchase, or a discussion of the services offered by your organization.

During the walkthrough of your organization, be sure to pay special attention to areas of visual, auditory, and digital data privacy.

Visual Data Privacy Protection

Areas in which visual data privacy protection should be considered include any area wherein an unauthorized individual might see a process or document that should otherwise be private. For instance, customer service centers usually have several employees on the telephone sitting in front of computers and speaking with customers. Are the computers visually unprotected, or are they situated in such a manner as to ensure a passerby could not easily look over the shoulder of a customer service agent to see personal information of a customer? If you are protecting a manufacturing environment, are there any special methods or procedures that are considered proprietary? Are these processes visually hidden from all but authorized personnel?

When performing the walkthrough, it is important to keep a critical eye. Although it is safe to assume the usual customer will not be interested in any information sitting on top of a desktop, it is not the casual customer about whom you should be worried. Instead, it is the person who is snooping for malicious reasons. Whether this "snooper" is looking for credit card numbers, the latest designs from your engineering department, or just the personal prize and satisfaction of gaining some sensitive information in their walk through of the building, he is an unauthorized viewer, and his prying eyes should be considered when setting up office space, computer locations, and monitor positions. It may seem like overkill to perform a physical walkthrough of the facility, but it is usually a very surprising and enlightening experience to walk through an organization with this purpose in mind.

Auditory Privacy Protection

Perhaps one of the hardest areas of privacy to protect is that of auditory privacy. Health care facilities have an especially difficult task trying to keep everything spoken within their walls private. Any time a patient walks through the doors, a health care professional will invariably ask very sensitive and personal questions regarding why the patient is visiting. This is one of the reasons HIPAA compliance focuses so heavily on auditory privacy. Health care professionals are not the only people who need to be concerned with auditory privacy. Any customer service representative of an organization who is discussing financial or any other personal information with customers, such as social security numbers, addresses, and contact information, should be careful to avoid speaking so loudly that everyone in the room can hear the discussion.

If the physical layout of the office area in which customers and customer service representatives hold discussions is such that it prohibits complete auditory privacy, consider erecting small desktop barriers or half-walls between customer service representatives. If these barriers are either impractical to build, or simply not enough to accomplish the intent of providing auditory privacy, be sure your customers are aware that any discussion they hold in your office may be overheard by someone else in the office.

Digital Data Privacy

There are too many digital data privacy issues to even overview in just one chapter. The majority of the rest of this book deals with policies, procedures, and concepts regarding keeping digital data private and well protected. Be sure to read the relevant chapters for whichever data types and devices you are trying to protect.

Health Information Concerns

As mentioned above, healthcare information is a huge concern in regard to security awareness. This is why there are myriad and complex requirements surrounding the handling of medical records. Not surprisingly, these requirements are not limited to the scope of a hospital, but in fact apply to any health-related data regardless of industry.

The Health Insurance Portability and Accountability Act of 1996 (HIPAA) provides all of the governmental requirements regarding how an organization must deal with any health information. Some organizations are fortunate to be able to afford offering their employees healthcare benefits. The proper handling of these data is dealt with by HIPAA. Even if your company doesn't offer health benefits to employees, there may be on-the-job injuries or leaves of absence that are health related. Because these issues deal directly with the health records of your organization's employees, they will need to be in compliance with HIPAA. In other words, HIPAA requirements should be of paramount concern for any organization, and should play a large role in determining how best to handle the private health records of your organization. See the chapter on HIPAA compliance for more details.

Client Records

Not only must your organization protect the privacy of employee records, but client records must also be kept safe and private. If you are in the health industry, virtually every transaction between the organization and its clients will fall under the requirements of HIPAA. If your organization is a financial institution, there are several federal and bank-specific laws and regulations that must be followed. Any government office will fall under a whole new set of regulations in regard to keeping taxpayer information protected. Client records also include credit card payment information, which require organizations to follow specific card handling procedures. Regardless of the services or products your company offers, or even which industry your organization serves, be sure to know the standards, regulations and laws pertaining to the ways in which you store and manage client records.

Password Management

Something as basic as mishandling passwords could bring your organization to its knees. This is one of the simplest and cheapest areas where most organizations can improve security, and yet, because of the habitual mishandling of passwords most of us engage in, it can be one of the most elusive and difficult areas in which to see improvement. See Chapter 5 concerning password management for more details on how your organization can properly handle passwords to keep data safe, and strategies for getting employees on board with changes.

Credit Card Compliance (PCI)

Regardless of the industry within which your organization operates, it is likely that your organization will accept payment in the form of credit cards. Very specific requirements are laid out for different types and sizes of organizations. Be sure your organization is in compliance before taking credit card payments from clients. For more details, see Chapter 5.

General File Management

Much practical application of information security boils down to file management practices. The manner in which your company must deal with each file will depend on the size, format, and security level of each file. For more information, see Chapter 5.

File Access Control

File access control is central to data security. Whereas file management is primarily concerned with how and where data are stored, proper file access control will dictate who has access to particular files and when those files can be accessed. In addition, file access control will decide the level of access each user has. For instance, some users may be able to simply read files, some may be able to move files around within directories, and others may be able to alter, delete, and create files depending on their level of clearance. In Chapter 18 detailing file access control, different methods of controlling access are shown, depending upon the type and size of your organization, as well as how secure your data must be kept. Every organization from the military to banks to schools must determine how best to control access to files.

Physical Access Control

In addition to controlling the digital aspects of file control, organizations must also consider how best to protect files from physical harm. Not only are physical invoices, proprietary documents, client records, health forms, and other sensitive documents necessary to protect, but even the digital data must reside in a physical location, such as in a server room. Don't forget that physical security extends far beyond the criminal realm, and protective measures should include consideration of accidental damage and natural disasters. For more information, see Chapter 10 on physical access control.

Examples of Security Regulations and Laws

In an effort to better understand how the various realms of information security apply to different secure environments, it is helpful to review briefly some of the more common regulations and laws regarding data storage and security, and which industries they affect. This is not to be considered a complete list of regulations on the subject of security, nor will the overviews contained herein be sufficient to assist in any meaningful way in regard to building a security policy for any organization. Instead, this list is included to illustrate some of the many industries in which security has taken a front seat, and how these industries are dealing with them. Some of these laws or entities are covered in greater detail at later points within this book.

Financial Institutions

The ability of a financial institution to protect its client data is paramount to success. Some institutions, such as banks and credit unions, must provide physical security for large amounts of cash. All financial institutions must also provide protection for digital information such as account balances, transaction data, and personal information such as client social security numbers (SSNs), contact information, and credit information. Depending on which area of the financial industry a bank serves, the organization will be forced to comply with many different legal requirements. These requirements stem primarily from various pieces of legislation, but may also come directly from the authority of different governmental organizations. A list of some of the main entities and regulations affecting information security decisions follows.

FDIC   Created by the Glass–Steagall Act of 1933, the FDIC is a corporation owned and operated by the U.S. government. The FDIC is a consumer protection corporation, and oversees operations of banks and financial institutions across the United States. As stated in the *FDIC Compliance Examination Manual*:

> The Federal Deposit Insurance Corporation (FDIC) promotes compliance with federal consumer protection laws, fair lending statutes and regulations, and the Community Reinvestment Act through supervisory and outreach programs. The FDIC conducts three types of supervisory activities to review an institution's compliance posture—compliance examinations, visitations, and investigations.

In other words, the FDIC is a governmental entity that ensures banks are following a standard set of rules and laws that protect the interests of consumers. The FDIC also provides insurance for individuals and corporations who deposit money with a bank. If a bank goes under, the FDIC will insure deposits up to $250,000 per depositor, per bank.

The Securities Exchange Commision (SEC) and Financial Industry Regulatory Authority (FINRA)   The rules set forth by the SEC and FINRA are essentially in place to protect the public from financial institutions engaging in fraudulent activities. Some of the main regulations coming from the SEC and FINRA require certain procedures be followed for record keeping and data storage. These procedures ensure records are not deleted prematurely in case fraud is suspected and an investigation needs to occur. In addition, the regulations call for third-party auditing to make certain no conflicts of interest occur. Many of these regulations are in place to mitigate market volatility by keeping a rein on Wall Street.

The Office of Thrift Supervision (OTS)   The OTS is a supervisory entity that oversees and regulates the daily operations of financial institutions across the United States. The OTS provides thrift institutions, such as savings and loans, a charter within which to operate. This charter allows branches located in different states, as well as subsidiary companies of a larger financial institution, to all operate under one supervisory authority. This single point of authority is an efficient framework within which financial institutions can operate without having to worry about satisfying regulations and rules from various authorities.

Electronic Fund Transfer (EFT) Act   The EFT Act was passed by Congress in 1978, and provides rules for individuals and organizations participating in the use and acceptance of ATM cards, wire transfers, and other forms of electronic monetary transfers. Although this act is primarily concerned with which party is liable for monetary losses during such transactions, the act does require institutions to keep records of transactions for certain periods of time, which is directly related to data security.

Gramm–Leach–Bliley Act (GLBA)   Passed by Congress in 1999, the Gramm–Leach–Bliley Act is also known as the Financial Services Modernization Act of 1999. At the core of this act was the repealing of the Glass–Steagall Act of 1933. When the Glass–Steagall Act was repealed, it allowed investment firms, securities firms, insurance companies, and banks to merge into larger conglomerations. Although at first blush this may appear to have nothing to do with data security, there is a portion of the act called the Financial Privacy Rule, which deals directly with requirements of the aforementioned financial institutions to adequately protect the financial data of customers.

Not only does this act require protection of the financial information of clients, it goes even further, requiring at least one employee be dedicated to safeguarding the information. In addition to requiring the design and implementation of data security measures for each department within each financial institution, the act also mandates frequent review of the implemented measures and requires the measures to be altered if and when they are found to be lacking.

Sarbanes–Oxley Act of 2002   When reviewing the many pieces of legislation, as well as the multiple agencies and corporations whose functions include protecting consumer data, it is interesting to recognize the origins of the entities. The Sarbanes–Oxley Act, or SOX, applies only to publicly held corporations, and was created in reaction to the many financial scandals immediately preceding the bill's passage. The intentions of the act are to make it very difficult for publicly traded organizations to commit financial fraud, thus inflating the price of their stock and creating a volatile market. Because fraud is at the center of this piece of legislation, the majority of security measures deal directly with audit control. Even the IT requirements of this legislation are designed to ensure auditing can be easily and efficiently performed. Regardless of the intention, this act is considered an essential piece of legislation in the information security world.

Children's Internet Protection Act (CIPA) CIPA is a federal act, and was passed in 2001 by Congress. The main concern of CIPA was the appropriate filtering of offensive content in schools and libraries. CIPA requires certain schools to implement and enforce policies that monitor online activities of minors. In addition, these schools and libraries must maintain an Internet safety policy that not only attempts to protect minors from viewing inappropriate matter on the Internet, but also seeks to protect minors from disclosing personal information via e-mail, online forms, in chat sessions, or any other form of online communication.

It is interesting to note that CIPA does not in fact apply to all schools, but only those receiving money from the federal E-Rate program, which provides qualifying schools and libraries with federal funding for access to the Internet.

Industry-Specific Regulations

Of course, there are many more laws and regulations that directly and indirectly affect how organizations may provide data security, but the above text contains many of the main examples of laws and regulations affecting some of the more security-centric industries today. If you are unsure of which laws and regulations apply to your specific organization and industry, it would be a wise idea to consult a good business lawyer who is familiar with your industry.

Also, when determining your level of compliance, be sure not to get so caught up in meeting the requirements of a particular piece of legislation that you forget to fulfill the requirements of another. When crafting a security policy for your organization, take every requirement into account, and determine where they overlap so that the organization is not duplicating efforts and being ineffective in its approach. Security should be complete, but not bog down your productivity and cause your organization to fail at its mission. Remember, the point of these certifications and pieces of legislation is to assist your company in keeping your records safe while still offering great products and service to your customer.

3

WHO IS AN IS PROFESSIONAL?

Act like a man of thought—think like a man of action.

Thomas Mann

Once information security (IS) has been accepted as an essential part of an organization's mission, the task of actually implementing IS policies must be assigned to authorized employees. But with whom shall the responsibility for information security rest? Within your particular organization, who is an information security professional? Who has been trained and authorized to be tasked with the implementation of IS policy? This chapter looks at all tiers of a standard organization and evaluates what role each position should play in the structure of IS implementation (see Figure 3.1). We look at why every level needs to be concerned about IS, how proper and improper implementation can affect jobs, what resources each position can bring to the table, and what resources need to be acquired from other portions of the organization.

Empowering Security Professionals

In many successful manufacturing facilities, efforts have been made to empower each and every employee to feel responsible for quality. For example, Japanese auto manufacturers became famous for what they called *kaizen*, which is essentially recognizing that within an organization there can never be perfection, and so continual improvement and refinement is necessary to stay on the path to the best quality. With kaizen, each employee is encouraged to share his or her ideas for improving quality control with management. If any employee sees a product that is subpar rolling along a production line, they can stop the line until the product is fixed, and the source of the problem is

**Top Down Approach of
Security Measures**

1. Security measures originate with C-level managers.

2. Security measures are adopted by directors and departmental managers.

3. Trainers modify programs to incorporate new systems, procedures, and policies into curriculum and training structures.

4. Supervisors reinforce training in real world applications.

5. End users apply concepts and measures in daily operations.

6. Any necessary changes to the policies must be reviewed, and will need to start at the top of the sequence for maximum success.

Figure 3.   Top-Down Approach

remedied. By empowering employees and giving them responsibility for ensuring only the best products are delivered to customers, the idea of kaizen infuses the manufacturing process with a culture of quality control. If it doesn't meet the highest standards of production, it doesn't ship. Period.

Similarly, a key component of building security awareness within an organization is creating an environment wherein everybody is responsible for, and encouraged to participate in, security. Although there should be groups or departments charged with the actual creation and enforcement of security policy within the organization, individual employees must feel empowered and encouraged to participate in the continual process of ensuring security throughout the organization. Naturally, depending on where an employee serves within an organization will largely determine her role in security. Each position will require a different approach, including the unique tools and skillsets needed to accomplish various security-related tasks.

Every role within an organization brings with it a unique perspective of how information security issues affect daily operations. An employee at the shipping and receiving dock will have a much different perspective than someone who works in marketing. The security at the shipping and receiving dock will be primarily physical in nature, whereas the Marketing Department will work with Engineering to promote the newest and greatest features of upcoming products while still protecting as-yet unreleased designs. Different regulations, physical and financial limitations, and industry requirements will affect each department of the organization.

Top-Down Approach

In order for any policy to successfully take hold throughout an organization, it must originate and be implemented from the very top of the organization. Security is no different. Beginning with the C-level executives in the boardroom, this chapter briefly discusses the different roles each station within an organization will play in regard to successful organization-wide security.

C-Level Managers

We begin our evaluation with the individuals tasked with running the organization, C-level managers, or CEOs, CFOs, CIOs, and the like, are the policy drivers and vision casters of any major organization. Their role in the security world is best summed up as corporate accountability. They are entrusted with making sure the direction of the company is held accountable to the mission statement; the decisions affecting profits are accountable to the shareholders (if the organization is incorporated); the policies created and implemented from the top are accountable to any governmental and industrial regulations; the company is accountable to a certain standard of ethics and morality; and the people who work within the company are accountable to the standards and policies derived from all of the above. If an action taken by an employee of the organization adversely affects the organization, and that action was allowed due to an incomplete or nonexistent policy or procedure, then the C-level manager is ultimately to blame for the resulting adverse effect.

The Chief Executive Officer (CEO), Chief Financial Officer (CFO), Chief Operations Officer (COO), and Chief Information Systems Officer (CISO) are all examples of C-level players within an organization. The C-level managers are at the very top of their particular spheres within the organization, which means they call all of the shots with regard to policy creation, funding, and implementation.

Policy Creation   One of the biggest reasons for needing C-level professionals involved with information security is because they provide the leadership and necessary oversight to create and implement thorough policies. The macro-level view of the C-level leader allows him or her to monitor the operations of each department within the organization, and how they interact. Understanding how each department depends upon and affects all of the other departments allows the C-level professional to observe how each new policy will affect the organization as a whole. In addition to the unique oversight provided by the C-level position, the obvious authority to change policy and get things accomplished without having to go through several more layers of the organization makes the C-level manager a necessary player in creating crucial and organization-wide policies having to do with security issues.

Funding   No matter how thorough and attractive a plan or policy may be, it must be appropriately funded in order to have any discernable effect on the culture of an organization. Because security policy needs to be infused throughout all facets of the company, complete and proper implementation is costly. Although some organizations may decide to handle security issues differently among the various departments, the initial funding should originate from the top. Among the many facets of information security, money must be allocated for security research, training of personnel, up-to-date equipment, and auditing of policies and procedures.

Implementation   When a C-level leader goes out of her way to create or change policy, everyone in the organization listens. The authority behind any decision or policy implementation directed by a C-level leader within an organization brings with it more weight than had the policy been directed by a lower-level person within the organization. The critical nature of information security policy creation demands such authority. Without it, the policies will be sure to eventually fail at some point within the organization.

Compromised Data = Loss of Capital C-level managers understand compromised data mean loss of capital. If IS policies are not properly crafted or enforced and fail, the organization is in great danger of having critical data compromised. This loss of capital includes money, labor, goodwill, and efficiency. All of these are of paramount concern to C-level management.

Direct Loss of Money and Labor Any time an event successfully removes a computer from the network, infects a server, compromises sensitive data, or otherwise creates an unfavorable security outcome for the owners of the data, money is lost for an organization. This loss of money is perhaps the largest concern of the C-level manger, in terms of security. The loss of money is directly related to the cost of labor and resources to remedy the compromised data. IT personnel will need to be diverted from their daily operations to "clean up" the issue, which is a diversion of primary organizational labor. In other words, the primary task of an IT person under normal circumstances is to keep the networks, hardware, and software running smoothly. Normal circumstances do not include the breaching of network systems by malicious software or cyber criminals. By reallocating labor from the primary purpose of their function to deal with the essential task of fixing a problem, the continuous flow of daily operations is interrupted, and inefficiency rears its ugly head.

Loss of Goodwill Perhaps a less tangible, but just as serious and negative outcome of a successful digital crime, is that of loss of goodwill. Goodwill is essentially the positive reputation and trust capital of an organization. If customer credit cards are jeopardized by a successful attack on an organization's network, customers will not feel as good about the organization and the goodwill will suffer. This is not simply a "feel good" issue, but actually translates into sales and profit. If a customer has to choose between Company A and Company B, and all features between the offered products are equal, than the customer will likely ask his colleagues or friends with which company it is better to work. How long the company has been doing business, how well they handle customer service issues, and how long you have to wait on hold to get to a live person on the phone are all factors of an organization's goodwill. Whether a customer's credit card information is going to be handled safely is a major consideration of goodwill, and it wouldn't take many failures of security to turn customers from an organization's doors for this reason.

All of these issues indicate why it is absolutely imperative that C-level managers take an integral part in the creation and implementation of the organization's IS policies. Without their approval and involvement, any policy will be doomed to fail right out of the gate. Although a lot can and should be learned from end users, information should never be approached as a grassroots endeavor; it must be driven from the top down in order to succeed. Without direct involvement from a C-level professional, the IS policy may suffer from a lack of funding and organization-wide authority, causing it to be ineffective.

Upper Management

Company directors and division managers are among the upper management of an organization. These people bridge the gap between mid-level management and the C-level executives. Having this unique position allows them a full overview of the internal operations of the department within which they serve. They don't just make policy, but have a direct hand in the implementation of the policies. This combined pairing of organizational overview coupled with the weight of the position they hold within an organization gives the individuals in upper management the ability to both craft security policy and directly see how it affects all levels of operations.

IS Concerns of Upper Management Upper management will have many of the same concerns as C-level managers regarding costs associated with the lack of proper security measures. Costs and loss of goodwill due to improperly executed or incomplete IS policies definitely rank among these concerns. Because these professionals are more focused on the operations of their particular department, they will have a much more accurate handle on which regulations affect their realm. Accountants will be up on the latest requirements for handling finances, HR professionals will know how to properly handle employee healthcare information, and production personnel will know how to protect proprietary procedures and methods used in the building of product in a manufacturing environment.

Depending on the department run by the individual, each member of upper management will be concerned with different aspects of information security.

Costs Costs associated with poorly implemented and incomplete security policy solutions will be detrimental to departmental budgets. This loss of revenue will be realized due to misallocated manpower during responses and upgrades to systems. Projects and plans may need to be temporarily set aside until fires are put out and systems are put into place to prevent similar incidents from occurring in the future. Of course, the same loss of goodwill affecting the CEOs will have an impact on the bottom line for the departments too. Fewer customers means everybody suffers.

Morale Issues In addition, the morale of the managers working under a high-level manager will suffer due to their closer proximity to the issue. This means upper management will need to be prepared to deal with managers as they scramble to put out fires, order the upgrading of systems, and deal with the fallout of an attack. Upper management will still need to focus on running the department, but must also make it clear to the managers dealing more directly with the problem that whatever resource is needed will be provided. It is the upper manager's job to make sure the managers below them are given the tools necessary to accomplish the requirements of their particular job.

Industry Regulations In addition, the individuals in charge of each department will necessarily be more aware of industry standards for their particular domain. The responsibility for staying on top of industry requirements and regulations rests solely on the shoulders of these managers. A lower-level manager does not have the time, nor in many cases the expertise to determine what requirements need to be met. This responsibility therefore rests solely with upper management.

Mid-Level Managers

The next tier on the chain of command is the mid-level manager. The mid-level manager is usually charged with managing a department of roughly 20 to 50 people, and is much more concerned about the functions of the specific department, or sub-department. These managers usually have a good feel for what is occurring on the workstations of their employees. They are generally in a good position to see if policies are being executed, and also have the authority to make on-the-fly changes to frontline security measures (within reason) to ensure proper and complete adherence to company security policies. These managers are close enough to the end user to see firsthand what is occurring at a client level, yet they also have the ear of upper management, making them good conduits for quick and practical changes throughout an organization.

Low-Level Managers

These professionals are frontline leaders, the lieutenants of the cyber war. If a response is required to a successful cyber attack, the low-level manager will likely be the one putting out fires and helping the incident response team with investigative tasks. This tier of management includes positions commonly referred to as Supervisor Team Leads. To a large extent, these employees are in direct contact with the public and end user. Because these supervisors are constantly training incoming users and are often the people handling escalated issues within a data system, these employees are often some of the most skilled users of any organization's data storage application. Because of this expertise and high awareness of the system, these are often the professionals who will first sound an alarm if anything goes awry within a system. Organizations would serve themselves well to recognize these professionals as the front line of the fight on cyber crime, and should invest in them accordingly with proper awareness training.

Putting Out Fires   When an incident occurs, it is up to these managers to rally their employees to respond. This means the manager will be making on-the-spot decisions regarding how best to respond. If a system is down and employees cannot input information into a database, the manager must determine how employees must proceed. Do the employees manually write information onto prebuilt forms and input the data at a later date? If so, how will those data be protected in the meantime? Will they be stored in a predetermined place, or will the manager clear out a section in a lockable file for later retrieval? These types of ad hoc decisions during an incident response are almost always handled by low- to mid-level managers.

Investigating When an incident occurs, the incident response team (IRT) will need to involve management in the process of investigating. Managers will provide login histories of employees, employee records, and whatever else the IRT needs to successfully finish the investigation. Part of this process is properly allocating labor during the investigation. If several employees are being interviewed, or are suspended during the tenure of an investigation, the manager must determine how best to fill those vacancies. Sometimes, this means hiring new employees. Other times, managers may be required to fill vacancies themselves while waiting for the investigation to end.

Processing New Employees Perhaps the biggest step a company can take toward the goal of effective security is the proper vetting of incoming employees, or end users. Most of the time, these end users constitute the biggest hole in the security of an organization's otherwise secure environment. This is not to say every end user is out to get the organization. In fact, many security issues are simply due to a lack of knowledge or training. Not only should managers be looking for the most qualified person, they need to take proper steps to ensure the new employees will be good stewards of the information entrusted to them by the organization.

Training Once employees are selected, they need to be trained. Managers should be an integral part of the training process from the beginning. In addition to making sure the employee is properly trained on how best to do his job, the manager must take the time to properly equip each incoming employee with a thorough understanding of the security issues directly related to his role in the organization. Because the manager is often the first person with whom an incoming employee interacts, it is critical that the manager accept the role of being a sort of ambassador of security to newcomers during training.

End Users

Perhaps the most critical tier in the structure of an organization is that of the end user. The end users are the people who are on the front lines of the information security world, collecting, analyzing, and inputting sensitive data into databases. It is the end user who takes customer information over the phone and through e-mails. It doesn't matter how many technical measures are put into place to protect the data; all it takes is a single end user to compromise the integrity of the entire network, whether intentionally or by accident.

Accidental Compromise   Although most information security measures are designed to protect against malicious attacks launched by remote cyber criminals, the biggest threat organizations should concern themselves with is that of the accidental compromise of security. This could come in the form of someone spilling a drink on his console, or creating an opportunity for a malicious attack to occur by not locking her station when she takes a break. Most of these accidental threats can be planned for and mitigated with policies and minimal technological applications. Policies can be put into place and enforced that do not allow people to drink or eat food at their workstations or while in the server room. If leaving workstations unlocked is a concern, simply set the auto-lock feature to lock the station after a reasonably short time, such as one to two minutes. In addition, make sure these settings are locked so the end users cannot simply change them to whatever they prefer.

Intentional Compromise   This issue is far less common than an occasional accidental compromise of security, however, it is an issue that must be addressed. One method of decreasing the chances of such an attack is by properly vetting each new employee who comes through the doors. This process includes thorough background checks, and a complete check of at least three to five different references for anyone whose job will require him to work with sensitive data such as customer financial records or employee healthcare records. Although it may sound like a common sense process, vetting a new employee does not come naturally to most managers. Instead, some managers rely upon interviews to determine if someone is trustworthy. It can be an admirable part of human nature to trust someone based on an initial meeting and discussion, but it makes for bad management. Do not let your first impression of a new employee allow her to bypass the necessary vetting processes of your organization, no matter how charming or trustworthy she appears to be during an interview process.

Proper Training In addition to the occasional accident and the rare (although quite possible) malicious, intentional attack, people are sometimes simply trained incorrectly. Proper training is the backbone of a thorough and complete solution to preventing data from being compromised. As a part of this continuous process, improper training should be identified and corrected. Improper training can occur in many forms, including internal and external sources of information.

Internal Sources of Training Internal sources of bad training can include poor trainers, incorrect or outdated information, or ad hoc training and unauthorized training. Poor trainers are among the worst issues any organization can face, security-related or not. Poor trainers may not understand the material being presented, they may be disorganized and unable to communicate to others well, or they simply might not have the time to communicate the entirety of the information to their audience.

Incorrect or outdated information or procedures can be a huge problem, especially if the information was passed down from employee to employee over the years. Make sure any important document includes a revision number and date. Whenever the document is changed, make sure there is only one master from which all copies are derived, and that the master document is the only document ever changed. A list of who should have that document should be kept on file, and whenever the document is changed, those people should be notified of the change and given a new copy, with an explanation of what changed and why. Training sessions may be necessary. Follow this simple approach, and there should be no issues with outdated information or procedures. Whatever the issue, find it and get rid of it.

Ad Hoc Training No matter how thorough or up to date a trainer is in her material, there will occasionally be end users who will run into problems not covered in their training. In these circumstances, many people will come up with their own best guesses at the problem, or might seek the help of other employees to come up with ad hoc answers to their problems. If a user has a problem with logging into his account, he may be tempted to try using a colleague's login credentials, or he might write down customer information onto a tablet and input it later. Of course, there are huge potential problems associated with logging into a system with someone else's login, and writing down customer information on a tablet creates the possibility of the information being thrown out into the trash without being properly shredded. There should be clear and decisive policies in place that prohibit users from guessing at how to proceed in such situations.

A Workforce of Security Professionals

It is clear to see that each employee directly affects the bottom line of security within each organization. Everyone from the executives in the boardroom to the trainer who prepares incoming employees is responsible for his or her piece of the security pie. Policies and training need to be put into place to help create an environment throughout the organization that promotes security awareness. Creating an environment wherein everybody is aware of his or her role and responsibility regarding security is key to building the culture of security awareness that is required for a successful, continuous, and robust security solution. The goodwill of the company, as well as the efficiency of the network and the end users who rely upon that network, depend upon the success of that awareness.

4

DIPLOMACY

Diplomacy is the art of letting someone have your way.

Daniel Vare

Security specialists cannot afford to stay in their offices and simply study network topology diagrams and the current penetration testing techniques. They must get out and interact with the people they serve in order to most effectively protect their work and precious data from being lost or compromised. They must also not look at the situation as though they were somehow like Prometheus, bringing some sacred and hitherto unknown knowledge to the masses. By getting to know the people they serve, security specialists will not only be imparting critical security training to the end users who need assured access to their data; end users will have the opportunity to learn firsthand how they can do a better job to help with security solutions. It is only through cultivating relationships and channels of effective and daily communication that the security specialists will fully begin to understand how to best protect and serve the organization's networks.

The "People" Portion of Information Security

Far too often, the personal aspect of information security is overlooked. This is not to say the topic of social engineering and the criminal mind have been neglected. Indeed, entire books have been written about the minds of cyber criminals, and how best to combat them psychologically. This book also has a chapter dedicated to social engineering attacks and how to protect against them. The point of the current chapter is not to go over social engineering attacks, but instead to evaluate how a lack of communication between people within an organization can have a direct and negative effect on how secure the data on the network are.

A Breakdown in Trust = A Breakdown in Security

If there is a fundamental breakdown of understanding and trust between end users and the people charged with taking care of the data (information security specialists), policies may not be understood or not be followed, and as a result, security suffers. In this chapter the information security (IS) specialist and the unique requirements, stress factors, and ever-changing landscape of her highly technical job will be taken into consideration. Diplomacy, and how it can be used as a part of the IS specialist's collection of tools, is discussed. Finally, the end users and their needs, and the diplomatic requirements of their jobs are also investigated. The hope is that a mutual understanding and respect of one another's role and responsibility within the security paradigm of the organization will result in increased efficiency and success with regard to network security.

The IS Specialist

Although this book was born from the philosophy that every person within an organization is an IS professional regardless of his job description, within each organization there are obviously some employees whose sole job function is providing security for data. These people are IS professionals in every sense of the word, and they have usually completed extensive, formal training and years of IT, networking, and programming experience to earn their current position within a company. Many of them hold computer networking and security certifications and degrees. For the sake of this chapter, anytime the term "IS specialist" is used, these are the employees being discussed.

Furthermore, it must be said that the author has had the opportunity to work with engineers, programmers, database designers, script hackers, network administrators, and almost every other type of IT professional and computer expert under the sun. Most of these people are some of the nicest people you would ever have the opportunity to meet, and they are true experts in their profession. It has been the author's experience that most of these security specialists, who are able to program in C, understand the Cisco CLI, and know how to perform extensive security hacks on a Linux Shell, also know how to get along very well with their coworkers. Most of these skilled veterans of the IT world would take hours of their time to explain any detail of their highly technical craft, and would be thankful for your interest, if asked.

An Issue of Communication

The point of this chapter is not to single out and deride these IS specialists; it was written to point out some very real and common differences in language, technical expertise, and network security-related stress levels that exist within any organization. If true efficiency and security are to be realized, these differences must be first recognized, if they in fact exist. Beyond simply illustrating these differences, this chapter attempts to offer suggestions on how best to deal with them so they don't turn into security problems. It is not uncommon for IS specialists to get frustrated at end users for contributing to network security issues, and for end users to get frustrated at IS specialists because they see them as the people responsible for locking out portions of their computers, changing their passwords, or otherwise prohibiting them from accessing some area of their computers. This frustration can lead to hurt feelings, and the result can sometimes be incomplete or incorrect security solutions.

Two Different Worlds

The goal is to get beyond these hurt feelings, and so end users and IS specialists must attempt to understand each other. They both exist in different professional worlds, and this chapter illustrates how their personalities are generally different as well. We all have different personalities, so this may at first all seem inconsequential. Far from it, this difference in personalities is often the main source for some common issues with which the IS specialist must contend. This chapter illustrates some of these very general differences between the IS specialists and the end users they serve. By recognizing these differences, we can start to bridge a gap that all too often exists between IS specialists and the rest of the organizations within which they operate.

We begin with a look at the IS specialists. At the very core of an IS specialist's world is the computer. Some of these professionals are so focused on their world of computer security they can literally think in computer code. This tunnel vision focus on all things computer-related doesn't usually stop when the IS specialist leaves work. Most people's idea of vacation has nothing to do with whatever concerns them during an average workday. This is usually not the case with many IS specialists. Many of them will set up entire networks within their home to play with, sometimes performing penetration tests and playing war games with their other IS specialist friends. Such constant interaction and manipulation of computers means that a good IS specialist knows most operating systems inside and out.

This kind of focus and passion for networks and coding gives many IS specialists the experience and knowledge necessary to accomplish the highest levels of security within their organizations. This highly technical, focused expertise of the IS specialist, coupled with most end users' comparatively low level of ability to use a computer creates a verbal divide between the two professionals. The IS specialist lives in a world full of exotic and ever-changing vernacular. Phrases such as session hijacking, shoulder surfing, data diddling, man-in-the-middle attack, maximum transmission unit, buffer overflow, SQL injection, and more are all a part of the lexicon of any IS specialist. The list could fill a book, and each one offers different technical threats and responses.

In addition to the technical jargon known and used by the IS specialist, there is usually a different method of operation for getting things accomplished in the computer world. I've heard it referred to as a "shotgun approach" in the troubleshooting world. If something doesn't work, remove it and replace it with something that does work. If elegant solutions are failing, use a brute force attack to get to an acceptable solution. Shotgun it. A shotgun approach is only successful if coupled with highly technical know-how of the system being shotgunned. This ability to quickly deal with technical issues is a mandatory tool in the IS toolbox.

There are very few comparisons that can be drawn in the rest of the professional world, but an ER room doctor is probably one of the best analogies to a good IS specialist. An ER doctor has a tunnel-vision focus, which centers solely on the survival of the patient: if something isn't working to increase the vital signs of the patient, try something different. Niceties are secondary to the message, "Save the patient."

Like the IS specialist, the job requires a highly technical and ever-changing skillset. If they fall behind in their expertise of a job-related technology, they may be unsuccessful in their tasks. The cost of failure is very high, and could result in massive lawsuits. Doctors also must be familiar with an exotic, ever-changing vernacular, just as the IS specialist. Among those in the medical profession, ER doctors are generally on the front lines of their particular brand of medicine, and are often faced with myriad different challenges, which often require immediate and unique decisions that other medical professionals are not generally required to handle. The same is true when considering the IS specialist's position within the IT community. ER doctors are often on call, and must leave family obligations, fun, and vacation plans when responding to issues for which only they are qualified. So too must IS specialists be on call for problems only they can handle.

If you put aside the fact that ER doctors are literally dealing with life and death decisions, and IS specialists are dealing with data, you have two professions that are arguably analogous in terms of the current discussion. Although it might be nice for either profession to take some extra time to spread cheer, it is not a benchmark for their success. ER doctors should not be hired on their ability to make their coworkers feel warm and fuzzy, but instead on their ability to save lives when patients have the misfortune to show up in their ER. Likewise, the success of an IS specialist is not generally based on his skill at working well with other departments, but instead is measured by his success in keeping data secure, responding to cyber incidents whenever they occur, and keeping the networks safe in general.

In short, the requirements of an IS specialist do not include the ability to work well with others. The ability of an IS specialist to secure the network is of such paramount importance, virtually nothing else matters. Diplomacy skills don't enter into the job interview process, and many would argue they shouldn't. But should they?

Diplomacy—The IS Professional's Best Friend

Diplomacy should be considered an essential skill of any information security professional. Yet all too often diplomacy is discarded by IS specialists in favor of pushing mandates and wielding borrowed power. As discussed, this usually has far less to do with the disposition of the IS specialist and more to do with the importance of the information being shared with other people within an organization. The IS specialist is concerned with securing the network, getting the data secure, and "saving the patient." Because the IS specialist is acutely aware of the entire picture of network security—what is at risk, how it is threatened, the time constraints placed on resolving any threats, and the potential loss if those threats are realized—a feeling of urgency sometimes overtakes the message being imparted to coworkers.

The result is that sometimes the IS professional is so concerned with taking care of security or perhaps some other network issue that taking care of their coworker takes a back seat to the process. This can cause both hurt feelings and incomplete solutions. Hurt feelings will occur if an end user is unintentionally made to feel stupid, or feel as though they are a problem instead of a person needing the assistance of an IS specialist. Incomplete solutions will result if end users don't share the whole picture with the IS specialist, or if policy is not followed because an end user doesn't understand or care about what is required of him. Although many CEOs would even argue that getting the job done is far more important than taking care of somebody's feelings, the point being made here is that taking care of a coworker's feelings is central to the success of getting the job done in the first place. If IS specialists are being faced with end users who don't follow policies, or who seem not to understand what is required of them, perhaps a change in diplomatic strategy is in order (see Figure 4.1).

Softening the Security Message

Whether new IS rules are required by governmental regulations or are handed down from the CEO and are not the idea of the IS specialist in charge of implementation, it is important that the IS specialist present such regulations in the best light possible. Instead of being aggressive, arrogant, or pushy, an effective IS specialist will present a well-thought-out presentation of how the new rules benefit not only the organization as a whole, but also the individual departments, departmental managers, and the users who will be implementing them on a daily basis.

The IS Professional and Empowering the End User

Be Nice

It sounds simple, but by treating people with respect, they will likely reciprocate the favor. IS professionals will reap the security benefits of softening a technical message by winning over end users. End users will realize benefits by making friends with the caretakers of the tool they utilize most during their day; their computer.

Empower Super Users

Many organizations are lucky enough to employ technically adept end users. Reward them for their knowledge, and encourage them to take an active role in the organization's ongoing security efforts. Consider creating an official category of end user called a Techspert.

Offer Formal Opportunities for Education

To really encourage participation, consider offering formal certification classes to Techsperts. Not only will this make your end users feel highly valued, it will do wonders for increasing security awareness to have such technically able users embedded throughout the workforce.

Figure 4.1   Empowering the End User

For instance, a policy requiring user passwords to be changed on a regular basis protects not only the organization overall, but also helps build an environment in which the end users' work is also protected. Changing computer settings so that workstations automatically lock after a short period of inactivity protects the end users' work and promotes an environment of privacy. This policy will likely seem like an obvious security measure to most IS specialists, but may also prove to be a source of dissent among end users. This will be especially true if the policy is being implemented after a long period during which end users were not required to lock their stations or change passwords on a regular basis. By taking the time discussed above to thoroughly explain the policy, how it will improve security, and how failing to adopt such measures could adversely affect the organization as a whole and the individual end user in particular end users will have a better understanding of the policy, and will also feel more respected. These two seemingly irrelevant results can have tremendous impacts on the actual follow-through of any security policy.

If the end users completely understand the policy change and have an opportunity to discuss the issues surrounding the policy, they will be able to fully grasp the weight of the requirement. It is one thing to be told what to do by someone who "knows better," and quite another to possess the knowledge and know-how yourself. In addition, by being actively involved in the process by having a genuine concern shown for their work, the IS specialists will feel respected; as though they were part of a team. Instead of having end users who are subservient to a necessary policy change, by involving the end users in the process, the IS specialist will start winning allies to the cause of security.

The IS Servant

One helpful way to look at the function of a good IS professional is as a servant to those who have the task of using the computer. The organization does not exist to service the IS professional, but instead the IS professional was hired to serve the organization. Taking it a step farther, although the IS professional's job is critical to the success of any organization, his job does not directly affect the bottom line of most organizations. Computers are there to facilitate the job of the end user, and the IT and IS professionals are there to facilitate the smooth operation of the networks upon which the users operate. It is always surprising to overhear or witness an IT professional speaking down to a user, or complaining about somebody's lack of computer savvy, as though the end user were somehow interfering with an otherwise good day at work. They forget that they are at their job to serve the end user.

A Caretaker's Approach

If the thought of serving the user is too difficult a pill to swallow for an IS professional, at the very least she should consider herself a caretaker of the network and data contained on it. If she is to properly care for the data and protect the physical and digital aspects of the infrastructure, it is not just a good idea to get along with the people using the computers, but absolutely critical. By approaching the end user as an ally instead of an irritant with which they must cope as part of their jobs, IS and IT professionals will build bridges of communication that will serve them well in regard to determining exactly where and when issues arise in the network.

End Users Are Great Network Monitors

In addition to getting along with their coworkers, IS and IT professionals will learn a lot more about the network when they have the support and cooperation of the end users. Without a good rapport with those users, how is an IS professional to know what problems plague a system? Although it is true that network sniffers, computer monitoring software, and router logs can all paint a picture of what is happening in the network, it is a lot more effective to have a relationship with the users wherein they will communicate any time there is an issue.

For instance, let's say an HR professional is backing up some large databases as part of the scheduled weekly backup. Instead of having to search on a network to determine why network speeds are bottlenecking on the HR Department's network, if an IS professional has a good rapport with the users, those users in HR will know to inform him before they begin backing up the company comp list or transferring employee files to an offsite server. Better yet, the IS specialist will put automatic backup systems in place, which will provide a service to the HR Department, protect the backed-up data from loss, and will allow the IS specialist to be in charge of the scheduled backup. This way, everyone involved is taken care of, including the data.

Super-Users

Taking the idea of empowering the end user even further, the IS specialist may decide to offer training to end users. Every department within the organization has end users who are a bit more computer savvy than their counterparts. In IT circles, these users are often referred to as "super-users." These so-called super-users are the ones to whom all other users go when anything goes wrong with an application or computer. If a computer crashes, or an error message appears on the screen of another user, a super-user is usually consulted before calling an IT or IS specialist. If a printer jams, the first person end users seek out is the departmental super-user. Virtually any computer issue that is not immediately solved by the end user is escalated first to a super-user.

Super-users are some of the best untapped potential for protecting networks. Unfortunately, some IT Departments and IS specialists officially forbid super-users assisting their technically challenged coworkers. In some organizations, employees are even written up for helping other coworkers. Of course, the obvious reason for this reaction to the assistance of super-users is the real possibility these super-users could change an important program setting, misplace a file, make the initial problem worse, or somehow just "mess something up" in general. These are all valid fears, but these fears should not be allowed to dictate policy.

Forbidding super-users assisting their coworkers creates two main problems. The first problem is that the super-users are made to feel less than competent and are being told what to do by IS specialists. This ties back to the original issue of unintentionally creating a gap between end users and IS specialists. Super-users, if told what to do in a negative manner, will be alienated from even wanting to assist in implementing the security solutions of the organization. Remember, the goal is to create allies in the security fight, not adversaries.

The second issue is the fact that the super-users will, in all likelihood, help their coworkers regardless of what policy dictates. It doesn't matter how many times these users have been told not to get into program settings or update system drivers. They will help when and where needed. This is not because of a distaste for authority, but instead, the super-users sincerely want to help. Most people, if seen as the only source of immediate help, will not turn down friends in the workplace, but will gladly offer their services, even if they've been told not to. After all, who else is going to do it?

Empowering the Super-User   In order to encourage a full, more robust culture of security throughout the organization, IS specialists will need to win over the super-users and empower them to make decisions. Instead of shackling super-users with mandates to ignore computer issues, give them a framework within which to assist other users. These super-users should be rewarded for taking the initiative to learn more than the fundamentals of computer usage, and should be thanked for their willingness to help. A suggestion of how best to encourage these super-users is to certify them as end user technology experts, or techsperts.

IT and IS specialists could offer lunchtime, off-hour, or paid classes to employees who desire to learn more about computers. A tiered training program could be created, wherein a techspert could be certified in basic printer troubleshooting, basic application trouble-shooting, network connection troubleshooting, and so on. By giving the super-users an official title and framework to work within, the organization will benefit in several ways. First of all, the techspert will be given formal training according to best practices. Depending on the depth of training, the techspert could learn how to work with networks, computers, peripherals, and software. This training will not only outline what authority the techspert has to perform such tasks, but will also go over what the techspert is not qualified to work on. In this manner, the techsperts can feel encouraged by their certification and recognition of work while still protecting the networks from unqualified personnel.

A good training program will eventually end up in realized savings and improved efficiency. For example, even if your organization is large enough to have a tech support desk, the techs are generally higher-paid technicians, who are certified by a neutral vendor. This is not bad, although it can become very costly. It might be a good idea to have the IT Department create an internal training program for users who desire to become techsperts. Consider the fact that many local PC repair stations will charge at least $100 to $200 per visit, and the cost per computer problem will quickly begin to outweigh the costs of educating an existing employee in the basics of computer mainte-nance. If the techspert excels at providing tech support, he would be a natural candidate for receiving further training. As your organization grows, the techspert may even grow into the IT tech position.

Make sure the techspert training is incentivized by either providing free or paid training. In addition, recognize the trainees as an integral part of the IT and IS solution within the organization. If money for bonuses or even techspert lunches is available, give every techspert something extra when appropriate. Techspert T-shirts, mugs, and the like might all be ideas to let these super-users know they are a part of a larger information security team.

Make Sure the Training Counts   If your organization decides to create a program such as the techspert training above, make sure to hold your training program accountable to some industry standards. Of course, you will want the techsperts to be familiar with whatever proprietary software and equipment your organization uses, but it may also be a good idea for the training to help them achieve a formal, third-party certification. For example, the A+ certification is a widely accepted computer technician certification, and the benchmarks for that certification could be very useful when creating what might become a formal techspert training program.

The End User's Diplomatic Responsibility

Up to this point, we've discussed the diplomatic role of IT professionals, IS specialists, and techsperts. Indeed, these individuals are the keepers of the network, and will bear the largest burden in terms of making sure everything runs smoothly, including the communication channels necessary to build bridges and create allies within the other departments.

Obviously, the responsibility for diplomatic relationships does not solely fall on the shoulders of IS specialists. The end user must also put her best foot forward when communicating. End users should not expect an IT professional, IS specialist, or techspert to drop everything and come running to the rescue, but should instead be patient and understanding when waiting for their computers to return to service.

It should come as no surprise that again, the whole of information security is most successful when everyone works together. End users must be understanding of the pressure under which IT and IS specialists operate, and the specialists must be understanding of the frustration of having a downed computer. Both groups should keep a clear line of communication to encourage more secure operations. End users will benefit from smoother computer operations by communicating network issues, error messages, and any other issue that may help IS specialists pinpoint and fix potential network issues. IS specialists will benefit by the knowledge gained from having educated and respected end users who feel empowered to participate in the information security battle.

5
PRIVACY CONCERNS

Relying on the government to protect your privacy is like asking a peeping tom to install your window blinds.

John Perry Barlow

What Is Privacy?

When most people think of privacy, they think of fences, houses, private rooms, or other barriers that allow people to live without the possibility of others seeing or overhearing them. These are all good examples of physical privacy, but what about digital privacy? Every day, organizations are entrusted with their customers' and employees' personal information. Having this information is a critical portion of most organizations' daily operations. Without knowing where customers are located, organizations cannot ship them material. If organizations didn't take credit card information from customers it would make selling products and services very difficult. If health information wasn't kept, providing health benefits to employees would be nearly impossible. By necessity, organizations must have this information in order to survive.

Even though organizations may "need" this information, they should consider having access to this information a privilege. Customers are obviously not mandated to purchase products from specific companies, and employees don't necessarily have to work for their present employer.

Why Does Privacy Matter?

Being trusted with important data from customers and employees is a privilege. With each privilege, there is an associated duty, or responsibility. This has been the case since the beginning of law. It is no different today, when discussing the privilege of utilizing computers for improved productivity and efficiency in the workplace. Although massive amounts of data can be stored, sorted, and retrieved with a few keystrokes, there exists a necessity to protect those data from falling into criminal hands. Without proper digital controls and thorough network protection, important files can be lost or damaged. It is the legal responsibility of data owners to keep the data they hold safe from prying unauthorized eyes.

There are many forms of corporate privacy issues, including proper collection, storage, and protection of private data. Anybody who has worked with human resources and medical reimbursements at an organization is familiar with the requirements of HIPAA. HIPAA covers a broad spectrum of workplace issues, all having to do with privacy concerning medical records and history. The Gramm–Leach–Bliley Act (GLB) is concerned with the collection and preservation of financial information from customers of financial institutions. The presence of children online presents a slew of other issues having to do with the safety and privacy rights of children, so Congress passed the Children's Online Privacy Protection Act. This act speaks directly to the issue of the collection of personal information from children online.

Before discussing developing a privacy policy, it would be wise to familiarize yourself with the laws that particularly apply to your industry and organization. Be sure to know all of the regulations required for your organization, including federal, state, city, and county legislation. If there are any industry requirements or certifications, be sure to keep them in mind when considering privacy issues. Keep in mind that if two requirements don't seem to be in harmony with each other, in almost all cases the stricter of the two laws supersedes the other. At the end of this chapter is a brief introduction and discussion of various pieces of privacy-related legislation. Be aware that this is not an all inclusive, in-depth look into the regulations. Consult an appropriate lawyer or specialist to ensure you are aware of and implementing everything required of your organization.

Types of Private Information

PROPRIETARY INFORMATION

Proprietary information is usually comprised of hard-learned lessons in regards to standard operations. This is especially true for some manufacturing companies, whose highly specialized procedures and processes allow them to compete.

CUSTOMER RECORDS

Customer records include everything from contact information to credit card information.

EMPLOYEE RECORDS

Employee records include tax information, employee performance history, payroll information, social security numbers, and any contact information.

HEALTH INFORMATION

Any health-related document, including those regarding on-the-job injuries and health benefits is included under this category.

INDUSTRY/MARKET RESEARCH

Industry and market research are necessary for expanding into new markets and growing existing ones. This information is critical to the survival of many companies, and should be accordingly protected.

Figure 5.1   Private Data

Types of Private Data

Of course, not every iota of information must be kept under lock and key. However, as discussed in previous chapters, there are certain types of files that should always be protected from prying eyes. These types of data include proprietary information, customer records, employee records, health-related information, and industry research. Let's take a brief look at these types of data, and why they must be protected (see Figure 5.1).

Proprietary Information

In fact, most of the other categories of private data could be considered proprietary. Companies do not give out customer lists or employee information, and they would be foolish to publish their unique industry research. Any piece of data obtained by an organization that is unique to that organization could conceivably be considered proprietary. True though this may be, for the sake of clarity, this chapter considers proprietary information to include technical procedures, corporate processes, and other "earned knowledge" that the organization in question has obtained during its tenure in business.

Technical procedures are a specific set of steps, to be followed in order, toward the end of accomplishing a goal. For instance, a document listing all of the steps, in order, for building a particular circuit board in an electronics manufacturing plant would be considered a set of procedures. Because of the unique tools used, the proprietary fixtures needed to accomplish tasks, and the knowledge of parts required to be successful, manufacturing procedures may not be immediately understood by somebody outside the industry. However, a competitor might be able to derive proprietary secrets from such documents. These documents are especially valuable for older companies, because these companies have spent years, sometimes decades refining their techniques and procedures. If a newer company had access to these documents, they would gain many years of knowledge without putting in the same resources of time, money, and labor required by the owner of the data.

Customer Records

For most organizations, customers are the sole source of income. As a result, most organizations hold their customer list among the most valuable of their assets. It can take several years for even the most successful organizations to build a solid customer base. An established customer base is essentially a pre-existing market through which an organization can advertise new products and services, with little effort and expenditures. Not only does a customer provide a built-in source of revenue for organizations, but the loss of such data could create massive peripheral financial losses for the organization in charge of the data. For instance, imagine an organization didn't do a good enough job of protecting customer data and as a result a malicious hacker broke into the network and stole customer addresses. The customers whose information was stolen would have a good case for a lawsuit. The lawsuit would mean both huge financial losses in the form of damages awarded, plus the considerable loss of goodwill within the industry. In other words, not only would the organization lose existing customers, but in all likelihood, a substantial number of potential future customers would also be lost.

Employment Records

Personnel records are among the most sensitive data a company has the privilege to protect. There is an assumed level of trust between the employee and employer. For tax reasons, employers are required by law to obtain social security numbers, addresses, and general contact information for any employee. The employee reasonably assumes that the information will only be used for verification and legal purposes, and it will not be viewable by unauthorized persons. This goes for both personal information as well as work performance records. Make certain your organization is doing a thorough job of protecting employee data from leaking into unauthorized hands. Losing the trust of a prospective customer is a small matter when compared to losing the trust of an existing employee.

Health-Related Information

HIPAA regulations are not just for hospitals. In addition to other privacy requirements, employers are required to keep employee health-related information secure and viewable only by certain people. Employee A should not find out from a supervisor that Employee B is having surgery and won't be in on Friday. Showing concern is one thing, but making sure everyone is aware of the situation is going too far. If Employee B wants Employee A to know about the surgery, that's fine, but it is not management's job to spread the word.

Health information should also be kept completely separate from any work-related records of the employee. In larger companies, employees in HR are most commonly the individuals authorized to view, file, and protect healthcare-related employee files. The reason for this is twofold. First of all, the primary function of Human Resources is to handle personnel issues such as healthcare. The HR Department will be trained to appropriately handle all files in accordance to HIPAA regulations. Second, by keeping healthcare files separate from performance records, employment decisions (including promotions, hiring, firing, training, etc.) cannot be based upon healthcare knowledge. For instance, if an employee is receiving medical treatments every week that have no direct impact on his performance, then, during a review, the treatments cannot be taken into account when deciding whether the employee gets a raise.

Industry Research

Industry research is a very broad category for information, but it essentially includes any knowledge "earned" by an organization through investment of time, labor, and other resources. Usually, market analysis is what comes to mind when discussing industry research. This could include how large the market is in terms of individuals and money spent, what methods of delivering goods exist in the industry, what current market trends are forecast, what the competition looks like, advertising opportunities, and potential products. Most of the investment in obtaining research information is simply the labor required for gathering available data for analysis. For instance, any information legally obtained about a competitor's operations is considered industry research.

Keeping Files Private

So what methods are available for keeping data private and secure? There are essentially three types of data that need to be protected; digital, physical, and verbal. Each will require a different set of policies and controls to ensure proper security. Although this chapter briefly discusses all three, a more in-depth discussion for each can be found in further chapters.

Digital Data

Digital data are the actual data contained on the computers and throughout the networks of an organization. These data could reside on a particular server or computer, or could be contained on a data storage device. The topic of "protecting digital data" is so immense that it could fill several volumes, each larger than this book. In addition, each network will require different measures for protecting data, depending on the topology, geography, scope, and size.

Regardless of the network and data being protected, some basic measures must be present on any network on which sensitive data are stored. To begin with, firewalls are essential data "gatekeepers" that should exist for both directions of traffic. That is to say, firewalls protect the network from unauthorized files entering the network, and from sensitive files leaving the network without proper authorization. At their most basic level, firewalls are simply routers set up to block and allow certain IP addresses. For incoming traffic, particular IP addresses can be prohibited from gaining access to internal databases, or particular IP addresses can be allowed and all others prohibited.

In addition to IP routing capabilities, firewalls can either be used in tandem with, or include some, intrusion detection system (IDS) capabilities. An IDS provides file behavior and signature analysis on the fly, and makes access decisions based on that analyzed behavior. For instance, many viruses have a signature that is detectable by an IDS or antivirus program. Certain ones and zeroes in a row are suspicious to the IDS, and it will block and flag the file. Another mode of detecting malicious software is analyzing the file's "intent," or behavior. If there are instructions within a file that would allow it to access registry files or other unauthorized operating system settings, the IDS would flag it and prohibit it from entering the network.

Beyond the firewall, network analyzers are a key tool in protecting sensitive data. Network analyzers essentially capture packets of data traveling through the network and analyze them for the same types of behaviors and signatures that an IDS does. If a packet is suspicious, the network administrator is sometimes alerted, or the packet is dropped and flagged. Network analyzers are also sometimes referred to as packet sniffers or network sniffers.

Even with packets being analyzed on the fly, it is still possible to have a virus successfully implant itself in a network. This is where antimalware comes into play. Essentially, antimalware is any software dedicated to the detection and removal of malicious software. When networks began, virus detection was often difficult and met with mixed results. Nowadays, most commercial-off-the-shelf (COTS) antivirus programs offer robust solutions to ridding computers and networks of malware, including key-loggers, worms, Trojan horses, spyware, and any other virus.

In addition to the software solutions available for protecting digital data, don't forget the need to physically protect the equipment housing such information. Server rooms need to be appropriately protected with strong doors, key locks, and possibly video surveillance equipment. Computers need to be protected from the environment, including adequate cooling and air conditioning. See the physical security section of this book to learn more about protecting the physical incarnation of your organization's digital data.

Physical Data

Not all files will be solely stored on computers. Many companies still keep hard copies of invoices and other company transactions. Depending on the scope and importance of the data contained in the files, the security requirements will vary. Client purchase records may require reasonably locked and secure filing cabinets, but corporate records such as articles of incorporation and company stocks may need to be kept in a fireproof safe or in an offsite safe deposit box. Customer credit card information should be kept in appropriately safe and lockable cabinets, with limited physical access and authorization. For large enough organizations, a filing clerk could be assigned to keep the credit card information secure, and the cabinets could be kept in a lockable room. In the end, many of the requirements for protecting physical files will be congruous with those required for proper securing of digital files stored on physical media.

Management Notes

An often forgotten file type is that of the management note. Some managers keep copious notes about employees, meetings, products, and market research; notes could be on any facet of the organization. Although these notes may not seem like a critical portion of the information security puzzle, in some states, these casual notes can be subpoenaed in trials. If you are a manager who needs to keep notes in order to keep thoughts straight, it may not be a bad idea to convert the usable notes into office documents and destroy the rest. For instance, you may keep notes that are written on your employees that include employee strengths and weaknesses in regard to their position at work. The notes may include attendance issues, ability and willingness to learn new skills, past performance issues, and how well they get along with other people on their team, insofar as it affects their job performance. These are all fine reasons for keeping notes on employees, but just be sure you don't document your personal opinion of the employee.

For example, if an employee is frequently late, doesn't finish his production build schedule on time, and wears strange clothing to work, you might casually write something like the following.

> Employee A must be a very lazy person, because they obviously can't drag themselves to work on time, and then they are either too dumb or too lazy to finish their production work. I wish they would quit, and soon, because I don't know if I can take another day of their ugly purple sweaters and green boots!

Although all of this may be true, it may come back to bite whomever wrote it if Employee A is ever fired. The notes don't simply stop at stating facts, but go beyond into the realm of a clouded negative view of Employee A. If an employee ever felt she was wrongfully terminated, she might have a case, considering the apparently strong negative feelings the manager has for the employee.

If a manager feels the need to document his experience with the employee, he may do better by writing something along the lines of the following.

> **ISSUE 1:** Employee A is frequently late to work and has been more than 15 minutes late on [Date1], [Date2], [Date3], and [Date4]. After Employee A arrived late on [Date3], I advised Employee A he would be written up if he continued to arrive late. I explained how his failure to show up on time has negatively affected his production team. After arriving late again on [Date4], I wrote up Employee A and advised him if he continued to fail to arrive to work on time, further disciplinary action would be taken, including and up to termination. Ever since he was written up, Employee A has arrived to work on time.
>
> **ISSUE 2:** In addition to arriving late, Employee A has had difficulty completing his build schedule. Overall, Employee A has ceased producing at standard times. In an effort to determine the cause for the slowed times

in production, a lead production team member has been sitting with the employee to ascertain what could be done to improve the build times of Employee A. Employee A was spoken to regarding the necessity to meet standard build times. If Employee A's build times don't substantially improve, or if they continue to fall, the next action to be taken will be discussing retraining and possible probation.

In the casually written example, the prevailing feeling of the notes was a negative attitude about the employee. The second, issue-oriented example has a more concrete feel of facts, actions taken, and provisionary plans if Employee A fails to improve. Notice that nowhere in the second example is a mention of Employee A's fashion, as it doesn't have anything to do with job performance. In addition, the notes clearly document a history of the employee's failure to perform and the incremental chances given to him to improve, as well as the tools (provisional training) provided to improve. Nowhere in those notes is a negative overtone clouding the judgment of a manager.

Regardless of whether you are a manager who makes casual notes on notepads for later retrieval, or one who clearly and objectively documents everything in a Word file for later review, be careful of what you write. Know that whatever you write about an employee could be potentially used as evidence in a wrongful termination suit against your organization.

Verbal Data

One of the most difficult things to secure is an employee's willingness and ability to discuss otherwise private matters. Policies should be in place that explicitly outline the expectations of employees privileged with such information, and what the consequences are for failing to keep data safe. Consequences should include those suffered by the employee as well as the organization. For instance, failure to comply with SEC requirements for protecting customer credit card-related information could result in governmental fines and industry-related losses, including loss of both existing and future customers. Due to the serious consequences associated with a failure in compliance with these regulations, disciplinary actions against the offending employee, up to and including termination may be taken at the discretion of management.

Privacy-Related Regulations and Laws

There are many industry-specific regulations and congressional acts that address privacy concerns. Below is a list of a handful of these laws, along with a brief summary of their requirements.

Gramm–Leach–Bliley (GLB) Financial Modernization Act of 1999—Year Enacted: 1999

Overview of Legislation One of the major pieces of legislation affecting corporations today, in regard to protecting consumer data, is the Gramm–Leach–Bliley Act, or GLB. GLB is primarily concerned with protecting nonpublic personal information being held by financial institutions. For instance, social security number, date of birth, credit records, income data, and so forth are all considered "nonpublic" in nature. The act makes provisions for protecting data in regard to the three areas of administrative, technical, and physical safeguards.

Administrative Safeguards This entire book is mainly concerned with administrative safeguards in regard to providing proper and thorough protection of critical data. All other provisions of safeguarding data, including technical and physical safeguards, must necessarily flow from properly written and implemented administrative measures. Without a solid administrative approach to protecting data, all attempts to protect data would undoubtedly fail. Administrative safeguards include any administrative action, policy, or procedure implemented in the organization. For instance, an administrative action might be the development of a business continuity plan. Associated administrative policies might be included in that plan, and putting the plan into action and training individuals on proper methods of responding to situations wherein the plan would be put into action is directly associated with administrative procedures. Although this example is limited in scope, it serves to illustrate the various facets of a total administrative approach to one security related issue.

The GLB Act is divided into three main sections, or rules, known as the Financial Privacy Rule, the Safeguards Rule, and Pretexting.

Financial Privacy Rule   The Financial Privacy Rule of the GLB Act essentially mandates that financial institutions must communicate with their customers regarding the collection and sharing of customer information. Customers must also be given an option to limit some of the use and dissemination of their data to other institutions. For instance, banks offering loans may require certain financial information from their customers during the loan approval process. These institutions must be forthright in how that information may be shared with the affiliates of the financial institution. If they plan on selling customer information to other institutions or organizations, the customer has a right to know and should be given a chance to opt out of sharing that information.

It is also important to note that there is a distinction made within the act concerning *Consumers* versus *Customers*. A *Consumer* is an individual who simply uses a one-time service of the bank. For example, a consumer may use a coin-counting machine at a local bank branch, but simply because they used the coin machine doesn't automatically make them a customer. A customer is an individual with a longstanding ongoing relationship with a financial institution. This person could have a loan through the institution, a checking account, or could be paying the institution for ongoing credit counseling services.

The reason it is important to note these differences is that a customer is required to be automatically notified if the financial institution is planning on sharing his or her information with an affiliated organization. Consumers, on the other hand, do not need to be notified, unless the financial institution shares their information with another organization with which it is not affiliated. The notification can be delivered in person or by mail, but must be conspicuous and clearly worded.

Safeguards Rule   The GLB Act outlines specific requirements for financial institutions to have a documented security plan that protects both the confidentiality and integrity of personal information. You may remember confidentiality and integrity are part of the CIA triad of information security. Confidentiality is concerned, not surprisingly, with keeping the information confidential, except to those who have proper authority to access the information. The security plan must thoroughly cover network security measures, cryptographic measures, departmental policies, and access control methods used to ensure the confidentiality of the personal information of their customers. In brief, the integrity of the data is the assurance that the data have not been tampered with by unauthorized users. Again, the security plan must outline all of the measures implemented in the effort to protect and ensure the integrity of the personal customer data being stored on the organization's networks.

Pretexting   The portion of the act forbidding what is known as "pretexting" is directed at people and organizations other than authorized financial institutions. Pretexting is the illegal act of attempting to trick individuals into giving personal details under false pretenses. For instance, a criminal may call you claiming to be your financial institution, and ask for your social security number and date of birth. They could then use that information, along with information gathered from simple public record searches on the Internet, to obtain credit in your name. Or, if they don't personally want to open a credit card or buy a car in your name, they will often sell your information to another criminal who collects such fraudulently obtained information and resells it to even more criminals. Ultimately, the chances are high that if you've been "pretexted," or tricked under false pretenses into giving your information to a criminal, your information will eventually be used for illegal purchases.

Where Rules Apply   GLB applies distinctly to "financial institutions," as listed in Section 6805(a) of the Act. Basically, financial institutions are those organizations that provide financial services, such as banks, securities firms, and insurance companies. Other organizations that provide loan servicing, filing of individual tax returns, financial advice, and debt collection are also among those financial institutions affected by the legislation. There are some provisions that include subsidiaries and exclude others, but the main idea is that the Act was written specifically to address the concerns of keeping customer financial data secure.

Enforcement of Act   The authority to enforce the rules listed in the GLB Act is divided among eight federal agencies and the individual states.

Where to Learn More   More information can be found on the GLB Act online at the Federal Trade Commision's website, http://www. ftc.gov/privacy/privacyinitiatives/glbact.html.

Health Insurance Portability and Accountability Act (HIPAA)—Year Enacted: 2003 (Final Ruling)

Overview of Legislation   HIPAA puts into place a nationwide federal set of rules for protecting individuals' health information. The standards set forth in HIPAA are concerned primarily with the privacy of health information, and provisions regarding how organizations with access to this information can use and disclose it are outlined. The information protected by HIPAA rules includes medical records, health insurance claims, medical billing records, medical research files, Medicare prescription drug card sponsors, and tissue bank samples. In addition to the use and disclosure of such information, organizations must also take measures to protect the data from being compromised.

Like the GLB Act, HIPAA delineates requirements into separate safeguards, but also includes some requirements and security standards. These include security standards and general rules, administrative safeguards, physical safeguards, technical safeguards, organizational requirements, policies and procedures, and documents requirements.

Security Standards and General Rules   This portion of HIPAA is basically an overview of how an entity is allowed to meet the criteria listed for adherence to HIPAA standards. Standards and implementation methods are outlined, as well as how flexible an organization is allowed to be in its approach to fulfilling these standards and requirements. Also listed are the standards of maintenance and security measures that must be taken to protect the data. In essence, it must be shown that an organization is meeting all HIPAA requirements, and that a plan is in place to maintain the proper and required levels of security for all HIPAA-covered documents and data.

Administrative Safeguards   Just as with the GLB Act, this portion of HIPAA speaks directly to the actions being taken by the administration of the organization in question in regard to the efforts being taken to establish a secure environment for health-related records. All policies, procedures, and methods employed by the company to achieve and maintain satisfactory levels of security are considered administrative safeguards.

Employment Records Employment records include W-4s, employee hire date, work reviews, internal organization certifications, resumes, work history, process certifications, miscellaneous employee information, and so on. In most cases, these files are consulted to determine how qualified certain individuals are in particular jobs. Because healthcare information has zero bearing on someone's qualification within a position, the employment records should never mix with the medical files.

Medical Records Proper and separate storage of medical and employment records cannot be stressed enough. If medical records are kept with employment records, liability issues arise. For instance, if an employee is up for a promotion, but does not receive the promotion due to a substantiated poor employment record, the issue is pretty cut and dried. But if the same employee also had a disability claim due to back issues, a successful argument might be made against the organization regarding discrimination based on medical reasons. For this reason, it is important that whoever handles your organization's medical records not have authority to decide employment advancement or termination. Usually, the answer to this separation is assigning responsibility for keeping these files to the HR Department.

Technical Safeguards Technical safeguards are usually more concerned with protecting data and systems through the use of software. Firewalls, antivirus programs, cryptography, e-mail filtering, proxy routers, and data logging are all technical measures that can be employed as a part of an organization's technical arsenal. Not only does this portion of HIPAA pertain to the actual technical measures implemented, but it also discusses the policies and procedures directing the use of those technical measures. In essence, any measure and policy intended to control access to protected data through the implementation of technical measures falls into the category of technical safeguards.

Organizational Requirements   This portion of HIPAA mainly outlines requirements for group health plans, although it also includes some rules pertaining to contracts between business associates and entities covered by health insurance plans.

Policies, Procedures, and Documentation Requirements   This portion of HIPAA sets forth the rules to comply with the requirements for proper handling of data protected by HIPAA regulations. Notice that not only must files be appropriately protected and secured, but documentation to that effect must also be created. Keep in mind, different HIPAA requirements exist for different corporations and employee files. Be sure your organization is meeting all of the specific requirements for your industry.

Where It Applies   HIPAA rules essentially apply to any organization that has authorized access to a patient's medical information. These organizations include health insurance plans, health care providers, health insurance billing agents or clearinghouses, Human Resources departments, and any other entity that is privy to a patient's health record.

HIPAA not only affects the storage of medical records, but applies to all aspects of medical privacy. For instance, firefighters and paramedics must also undergo special HIPAA training to ensure privacy of patients when responding on the scene, and doctors and medical staff must be trained on appropriate protection of patient privacy while in the care of medical facilities and staff. In addition, if your organization reimburses medical expenses or otherwise handles any issues regarding health insurance claims, you will be subject to different laws and regulations.

In other words, this book doesn't even begin to cover all of the various areas that HIPAA regulates. This book simply offers a reminder to be aware that HIPAA exists, and your organization should be making certain it is within the boundaries of the act. Be sure to have a clear understanding of when, where, and how your organization is affected by the HIPAA rules. It may be wise to seek legal counsel to determine how your organization can best achieve compliance, considering the multitude of facets presented by the legislation.

Enforcement   HIPAA is overseen by the Department of Health and Human Services.

Where to Learn More   A good overview of HIPAA, in regard to the security rule, is located online at: http://csrc.nist.gov/publications/nistpubs/800-66-Rev1/SP-800-66-Revision1.pdf.

Children's Online Privacy Protection Act—Year Enacted: 1998

Overview of Legislation   The Children's Online Privacy Protection Act is concerned with disclosing to parents when personal information is being collected from their children. The purpose is to both avoid inappropriate marketing of minors, and to protect minors from obvious safety concerns associated with openly sharing information over the Internet.

Operators who administer websites that are directed at gathering information from children, or whose websites are known to gather information from children, must inform the parents of the children when information is being gathered. Websites could include everything from online gaming communities and social networking sites to educational sites used at schools. Furthermore, the act forbids the same operators to give prizes or otherwise entice children into providing more personal information. If, at any time, the notified parents request a copy of the information being gathered about their children, the operators must provide such information. Parents can also prohibit these operators from gathering information from their children.

In addition to the provisions in the act regarding parents and children, and the gathering of personal information, there are rules requiring operators to protect the personal data that have been collected through the establishment and maintenance of information security measures.

Included in the act are provisions for when parental consent is not required to obtain personal information from the child. These provisions include asking for information in order to gain parental consent, and gathering information from a child for a one-time response to a request. If a child's response is used for a one-time request, the operator cannot use that child's information to contact the child beyond the scope of the request. In addition to the requirements of the act, it goes on to list proper methods of compliance, who enforces the law, and how to appeal if wrongfully accused of breaching the law's guidelines.

Where It Applies   Any administrator of a website whose site has direct contact with children and attempts to obtain personal information from them is subject to the requirements of this Act. If your company is engaged in actively reaching children through the corporate website, and you are collecting any personal information from them, your organization must adhere to this piece of legislation.

Enforcement of Act   The Federal Trade Commission enforces this act.

Where to Learn More   http://www.ftc.gov/ogc/coppa1.htm

Privacy Policies

Privacy policies are official documents that list what your organization requires in regard to privacy, and how you plan on achieving it. This policy can be included as a subset of your overall security policy, or it can be a stand-alone document. Regardless, your organization should have one on file. Just as with your security policy, your privacy policy should not be an arcane document that is written once and then stored in a drawer somewhere, only to be forgotten to antiquity. The document, just like your security policy, needs to be considered a living document, in constant review. Anytime a law is enacted, or an industry regulation is put into place that could affect the methods your organization uses to conduct business, make sure your organization's privacy policy includes any changes that would affect the way you protect your customer's privacy.

Once you are familiar with every applicable law that affects your organization, write a summary of what is required to adhere to those laws. If a law requires a specific router configuration for protecting customer data, document it and include it in the policy. It's a good idea to have a checklist of the requirements affecting your network security, to ensure proper adherence to the policy. Be sure to include dates of when the last audit was performed, who performed it, what was found, and how any issues were remedied, if applicable. The audit doesn't necessarily need to accompany each copy of the privacy policy, however, each audit should have a copy of the privacy policy.

6

INTERDEPARTMENTAL SECURITY

No employer today is independent of those about him. He cannot succeed alone, no matter how great his ability or capital. Business today is more than ever a question of cooperation.

Orison Swett Marden

Interdepartmental Security

Every department within an organization has a role to play in creating a security-aware environment (see Figure 6.1). This chapter illustrates these roles using a manufacturing company model. Arguably, a manufacturing-based organization includes every category of department, including accounting, human resources, manufacturing, engineering and administrative personnel, and others. Collectively, the departments within an organization work to provide greater contributions to an organization's security than they do alone. This chapter gives a brief overview of each department, and how each depends on another to achieve security.

Administrative Personnel

In earlier chapters, we discussed the need for a top-down approach to the creation and implementation of security-related policies and procedures. The top-down approach requires C-level executives at the top of the organization to be an integral part of the organization's security solution. These executives have the entire "big picture" of the organization, and understand how all of the various facets of each department work with and depend on one another. This overview of the organization sometimes allows administrative personnel to see

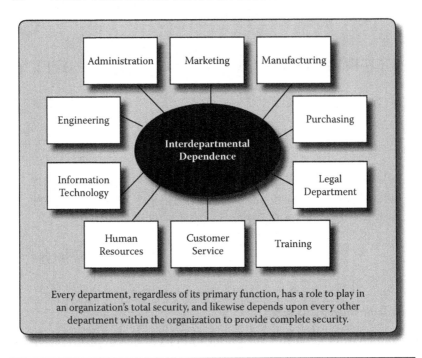

Figure 6.1   Interdepartmental Dependence

more clearly how other departments are interdependent. In addition to their high-level view of the organization, administrators bring with them the backing of authority and financial follow-through that other departments may lack. Without the authority and financial backing of the administrative personnel, company-wide policies are sure to fail.

Interdependency of Administrative Personnel   The main role of the administrative personnel is to initiate the security policy creation process. Other departments are dependent upon the administrative personnel for follow-through by helping with organization-wide implementation of the policy. Administrative personnel are dependent upon other organizations to follow through with created security policies and procedures.

Human Resources Department

It is the Human Resources Department's job to make sure the organization is following proper legal methods for the hiring, firing, and managing of personnel. It is usually the first department with whom an incoming employee interviews, and the last department with whom a terminated, transferred, retiring, or otherwise exiting employee will speak during the exit interview. As the keeper of all things personnel related, HR is also charged with keeping all employee records private. Everything from employee complaints and on-the-job injury forms to healthcare records may be kept by HR, and these must be kept secure and private from unauthorized viewers.

Perhaps more than any other department, the Human Resources Department will also need to be knowledgeable about HIPAA requirements. If an employee injures herself on the job, an HR representative must file the appropriate claim, and follow up with the employee as appropriate. HR is also the most likely source for any healthcare-related questions an employee may have, such as coverage, copay, and costs. If an employee misses work due to a healthcare-related issue, he will need to interface with HR. Some larger companies have HR handle employee counseling, mediation, and conduct training. If an employee is written up or disciplined, managers will often have an HR person present during the discussion with the employee being disciplined, both as a witness and to ensure proper guidelines are being followed.

In other words, HR professionals are privy to most of the behind-the-scenes issues occurring within an organization, as far as personnel are concerned. Because it is wise to keep employee performance records separate from healthcare material (to avoid a wrongful termination suit), HR personnel are usually the sole keepers of healthcare information and records. Because they are given such unprecedented accesses to private information, HR professionals have a special burden to be sure the guidelines they are following are up to date, and the data they are protecting are secure.

Interdependency of Human Resources   As the keepers of some of the most private data in the organization, the HR Department is relied upon by all of the other departments to ensure the personal data of employees are properly protected. Human resources relies upon other departments to convey personnel data such as reviews, raises, hiring, and termination of employment.

In addition to securely communicating personnel issues, HR will handle the vetting process of incoming employees. This means HR personnel will be required to call past references and will be in charge of ensuring proper background checks have been performed for key personnel. Anybody whose job could possibly allow them to handle cash, view credit card information (company, customer, or otherwise), or handle valuable inventory or any sensitive information should have a complete background check performed prior to his first day on the job. It is HR's responsibility to provide this service to all other departments.

Not only does HR vet incoming employees, they will be in charge of processing exiting employees. When employment is terminated, HR will need to do the following.

1. Retrieve any company property from the exiting employee, such as tools, computer equipment, telephone headsets, and so on. Of paramount security importance will be getting back any key or ID fob that allows employees access into otherwise restricted areas.
2. Alert accounting of the terminated employment. Accounting will need to make sure the terminated employee is no longer in the payroll system, except for tax reasons.
3. Let security know the person is no longer employed with the organization, to ensure she is not allowed to physically access restricted areas.
4. Let the IT Department know the person is no longer employed, so appropriate passwords and access codes can be changed.
5. Perform an exit interview with the exiting employee. Exiting interviews are a great way to learn more about why the employee is leaving (if he is choosing to leave), and even perhaps what the organization can improve on to help morale. These interviews also allow HR personnel to find out if the leaving employee is unduly upset and poses a threat to the organization. Employees who are being unwillingly let go will be understandably upset, even if they messed up. They may even raise their voice in an exit interview or curse when explaining why their being let go is not fair. Tears may be

shed, and other people may be blamed. HR personnel need to keep in mind that losing one's job is a traumatic experience, and people will react with the same confusion, denial, seemingly inappropriate humor, and sometimes anger that accompanies traumatic losses. If the exiting employee is not posing a threat, give him as much time as he needs to console himself in private before asking him to leave the premises. If someone is simply uncontrollably filled with rage and poses a serious threat to people and property, try to contain her in a private room until security can deal with her. Of course, rage-filled persons are very rare cases and most employment terminations, though not pleasant, are at least amicable.

Accounting Department

The Accounting Department keeps track of all things financial related to the company, including profit and loss statements, account reconciling, taxes, and petty cash records. If it has to do with money, it all falls under the domain of Accounting. Although some organizations have HR perform payroll functions, many have chosen to keep payroll as a separate function within the Accounting Department. Regardless of which department handles payroll, Accounting still has oversight of the process, inasmuch as they can see what is being paid each employee.

In addition to the obvious privacy issues related to having access to personnel data such as employee compensation, Accounting must also have access to the organization's credit cards and bank accounts. In fact, as the keepers of an organization's accounts payable, they are largely responsible for and in charge of the organization's accounts. In addition to being charged with handling the corporation's accounts and (possibly) doling out checks to employees on payday, Accounting usually has access to customer accounts as well. As part of accounts receivable, Accounting will process checks, and sometimes customer credit cards to obtain payment for outstanding debts owed to the organization.

Interdependency of Accounting As the bankers of the organization, Accounting personnel must follow the strictest of security measures to ensure the data entrusted to them are secure. They must work with all other departments to ensure other departments are following proper handling of financial information of the organization, and of customers. In addition to ensuring proper handling of company, employee, and customer financials, Accounting relies upon the Human Resources Department to know when a worker's employment has been terminated, so payroll checks can be stopped.

Legal Department

Although many smaller organizations have the Administrative and HR Departments split much of the responsibility of handling legal affairs, some organizations have entire departments dedicated to providing legal counsel and research. This department will likely have the last word on many topics, including methods used to research competitors, advertisement claims, product liability, and so forth. The Legal Department will be at the forefront of many otherwise private organizational operations. If the organization is involved in a lawsuit, the Legal Department will be working in the background to handle it. If the organization is either searching out acquisitions or is in the process of being acquired, the Legal Department will be heavily involved in the negotiations. The main security issue related to the Legal Department is similar, but not the same as, that of the HR Department. The Legal Department is the keeper of private information, and must make certain the data it protects are secure.

Interdependency of the Legal Department   The Legal Department is considered a service department. Therefore, the primary interdependency of this department is in the form of other departments relying on it for counsel. As far as security-related issues are concerned, the Legal Department will need to make sure all other departments are following any legal regulations for keeping data secure and private.

Information Technology (IT) Department

For the sake of this chapter, information technology (IT) will include anything related to computers including networking, software, network administration, hardware, programming, database management, and information security (IS). The IT Department is the keeper of the network and all data contained therein. Naturally, this department will carry much of the weight in terms of providing security to the other departments. This security will be achieved through the application of hardware, software, and procedural solutions.

Hardware Solutions Security-related hardware solutions are a major component of the information security puzzle. In addition to the computers, routers, cabling, and network peripherals that make up a physical network, there are many other hardware components that directly relate to network security. These generally fall into the categories of traffic routing, access control, and continued service.

Traffic routing includes the routers and intrusion detection systems (IDS) that protect networks by monitoring and providing secure routing for all incoming and outgoing network traffic. These devices usually provide this monitoring service at the packet level, and look for either suspicious packet characteristics or IP addresses. The IT Department helps provide this protection by ensuring software patches for the routers, as well as virus definitions, are up to date. Traffic routing is essential to protecting files, however, it doesn't stop malicious users from gaining physical access to computers and files. This is where the access control portion of hardware security comes into play.

Access control refers to measures put into place in an effort to allow only those users who are authorized access to particular systems and files. Access control is generally discussed as a software-related topic, however, there are several physical, or hardware-related, methods that can be put into place to prevent unauthorized access to files. One of the most basic and effective measures for physically controlling access to a computer is the removal of certain drives. The IT Department may lock or remove CD-ROM drives, ensuring nobody can install harmful software via that drive. The same can be done for USB ports, and in some cases with older computers, floppy drives as well. Once access control and traffic routing have been addressed, the IT Department will put measures into place to ensure the computers and networks don't fail, and if failure is unavoidable, backup measures are in place to ensure continued service.

Continued service is a critical component to the success of any network. The IT Department needs to install network hardware with this in mind. For instance, uninterruptible power supplies (UPS) should be installed for any computer whose function requires it to be constantly running. Hot-swappable drives should be used in server rooms where possible, so if one hard drive needs to be serviced, it can be removed and replaced with minimal disruption to network processes.

Software Solutions   Software solutions are paramount to keeping network systems running. Network monitoring packages, antivirus programs, and firewalling suites are all part of a robust software solution. In addition to these antimalware solutions, the IT Department will need to provide backup solutions for the files of other departments. Backing up important data could be considered a physical, or hardware, solution, inasmuch as the media upon which the data will be stored will ultimately always be physically stored somewhere. Although this is true, the software portion of backing up data is far more critical to the process. Anybody who is somewhat familiar with computers knows how to back up data onto a disk, but an IT technician should be able to provide an elegant solution to backing up data that provides automatic backing up of data with minimal disruptions to data flow.

Procedural Solutions   The IT Department will likely be the main source for how end users are permitted to interact with the computers and networks of an organization. For instance, the IT Department will likely be in charge of setting up permission levels of users, password management policies, workstation automatic lockout times, data storage procedures, and helpdesk technical requests, to name a few.

Interdependency of the IT Department   The IT Department relies heavily on the other departments to communicate with them regarding network issues, computer problems, and any other issue relating to an organization's network. If problems are occurring and other departments are not communicating with the IT Department about them, the IT Department will be hamstrung.

Every other department within an organization relies upon the IT Department for guidance regarding how best to implement network security measures. Customer data, employee records, company financials, and vendor information will all need to be stored in secure encrypted databases with easy retrieval. The Legal and HR Departments, especially, will turn to the IT Department to ensure proper measures are being taken to ensure legal and regulatory compliance issues are being met. Likewise, Accounting will require secure access to all things financial. Customer Service, Shipping & Receiving, and the Sales Departments will depend on the personnel in IT to provide continuous service and availability of the networks and systems necessary to perform their jobs.

Purchasing

In a manufacturing environment, Purchasing is in charge of managing a database of approved parts and vendors. Although this information may not seem confidential, many organizations hold their parts list and approved vendor list as one of the most valuable assets they have in their possession. It takes many months, sometimes years, of testing and negotiating to locate and approve parts and vendors for the manufacturing process.

Interdependency of Purchasing   The Purchasing Department needs a secure database within which records of these approved vendors and parts will be stored. The creation and maintenance of this database will likely be the responsibility of the IT Department.

Sales and Customer Service

Both Sales and Customer Service work directly with customers, and are often required to handle customer credit cards. The IT Department will need to provide secure and accessible databases for this account information. Sometimes, Customer Service personnel will have an insider's perspective in regard to product failures and other issues they may have to deal with on the phones or in e-mails with customers. This is to say, if a bad component or faulty part is affecting the performance of a product, Customer Service will need to know about it before it becomes a major issue to contend with on the phone. Because such product issues are not public knowledge, they fall under the proprietary information category and should be handled with the due care and sensitivity. If a product recall is in order, Customer Service personnel will need to know what to tell customers calling in to complain or inquire about the failed product. Usually, the procedures associated with such delicate matters are best left up to Customer Service Management and the organization's Legal counsel. Failure to handle these issues properly could bring a company to its knees, so it is absolutely critical to act as fast as possible to protect the company and the affected public from any further damage, inasmuch as is possible.

Interdependency of Customer Service   Customer Service will require secure accessible databases for storing customer information. The HR Department will need to vet the incoming Customer Service representatives to ensure they meet the background requirements for handling customer credit cards, and the Legal Department will need to ensure they are following proper and legal methods of handling customer information.

Marketing Department

Market research is heavily used when deciding what markets to go into and how to advertise products to individuals within those markets. This information is not easily won, and companies guard their own market research fiercely. Pricing details, product features, expected market share, competitor information, and target market are all considered a part of market research. Advertising, which arguably falls under the heading of marketing, will include making claims about an organization's products as well as the competition's.

Interdependency of Marketing   The hard-earned marketing information will require secure accessible databases. In addition, the Legal Department will need to be involved to review advertising claims to make sure they are legally accurate and not too far-reaching. Engineering will likewise work with Marketing to allow for marketing campaigns to be completed and in place simultaneously with upcoming product release dates, but no sooner. This coordination of timed releasing of sensitive product data to the public makes the relationship between Engineering and Marketing unique.

Manufacturing

Manufacturing has two major concerns when dealing with data. First of all, the employees in a manufacturing environment are often the firsthand keepers of trade secrets and company knowledge. They know how each product is built, and what special processes are used to accomplish each step. If given time and material, many workers could duplicate those same processes in another manufacturing environment. There are four main ways to protect the intellectual property of experienced manufacturing employees.

Increase Morale, Decrease Security Concerns   To begin with, do what you can to keep your most knowledgeable employees working for you, and not your competition. This can be accomplished by taking the time to recognize how important these keepers of trade secrets are to your company. Oftentimes, manufacturing companies do not treat their producing employees with the respect and care owed every employee, regardless of station. Take the time to acknowledge how much these people are respected and admired for their hard work and industry knowledge, and you will have employees who want to come to work. Increase morale, and decrease security concerns. Besides, treating people kindly is, and always will be, the right way to run a business and live life.

Craft an Intellectual Property Policy   The second way to protect your trade secrets from getting to your competition is to make sure employees know just how important these processes are. By crafting thorough and clear policies regarding how to handle the manufacturing secrets of your organization, employees will realize the seriousness and weight of the information they carry. This will go further toward giving the people in the Manufacturing Department a picture of just how critical they truly are to the organization.

A policy should be created to ensure these secrets are kept within the walls of your organization. A well-crafted document regarding this intellectual process will both inform the worker of her importance, and explain the consequences of such information leaving the organization. The document should describe how hard your organization has worked to obtain the information, what it allows the company to do, and what the severe fallout would be if a competitor gained the knowledge through carelessness.

Integrity of Information   A third concern with documented manufacturing processes has to do with the integrity of the documentation. Sometimes the Engineering Department will change a part to a product, or a fixture will change, which forces processes to change too. Any time a fixture is changed, a part altered, or a product's build process is otherwise made different, be sure any documentation is appropriately updated. For each process, there should be a "process owner" who is in charge of the process. Processes should not be officially changed without the signoff of these owners. In turn, the process owners will be expected to keep the documentation of the processes up to date.

File Storage and Security   The fourth and final method of protecting the intellectual property within a Manufacturing Department is through conventional digital and physical means. Whether the processes and trade secret data are kept in a database on the network or in a filing cabinet, make sure appropriate measures are taken to protect them.

Facilities Crew

In no way is this book trying to suggest that one department is more or less trustworthy than the next. The overwhelming majority of people pose no threat at all to an organization. The point of the following discussion is to be sure consistent security policies and vetting processes are in place for all employees, regardless of their position within the company.

It has always been surprising to see the dichotomy of security occurring in some of the most seemingly secure environments when it comes to maintenance and facilities crews. For all intents and purposes, these employees are given the same, and in some cases more, physical access than the rest of the company, to the organization's campus. Yet, many companies fail to perform any meaningful forms of background checks on the people cleaning the floors and emptying trash bins throughout the organization. In many cases, keys and pass codes to buildings are simply handed over to unvetted maintenance personnel, when a similar level of trust would not be extended to any other employee on her first day.

In addition to the total physical access often given to facilities crews, the hours they work usually do not coincide with the rest of the organization. Most facilities crew members arrive when the lights are off and it is dark. If someone wanted to steal anything from an organization, this would be the perfect time to do so. There are a few measures an organization can and should take when hiring facilities crew members.

Background Checks Because facilities crew members will likely be walking through every office and area from Shipping & Receiving to a CEO's office, they will almost certainly see or learn something that would otherwise be considered sensitive or confidential. For any other employee, background checks would be required, so be sure these workers are completely vetted and checked out before having them show up for their first day.

Day Shift Some companies simply choose to have their facilities crew work during the same shift as everyone else, which is usually in the day. The presence of other employees is usually enough to dissuade all but the most brazen of criminals and snoopers. In addition, many companies will save a few dollars by not having to pay shift differentials for swing and graveyard shifts.

Cameras Very few work environments exist wherein having facilities workers operate would be disruptive. However, if your organization decides it cannot have the facilities crew working with the rest of the employees, consider installing security cameras for off-hours operations. In addition to keeping an eye on late-working employees, having visible security cameras is usually a good deterrent.

Interdependency of Facilities Crew   The facilities crew has unprecedented access to the physical campus of an organization. The main dependency falls upon HR, which will be responsible for thoroughly vetting incoming facilities crew members.

Shipping & Receiving Department

The primary concerns of information security in the Shipping & Receiving Department have to do with data integrity. Customer information, shipment tracking numbers, delivery dates, and pricing are all the domain of the shipper. This information needs to be readily available when Customer Service asks for it on behalf of a customer.

In addition to integrity of shipment data, Shipping & Receiving will likely also handle credit card numbers and bank accounts as part of invoices. Appropriate background checks and follow-up with references should be done. Of course, proper vetting of employees is necessary, but perhaps just as important is the digitally secure storage of the credit cards.

Interdependency of Shipping & Receiving   In adddition to the standard HR and Accounting tie-ins (for background checks and payroll), Shipping & Receiving will require secure databases and logins for shipping and invoice data. If physical invoices are stored, physical security and appropriate policies will likewise need to be provided.

Interdepartmental IS Committee

The main point to remember, regardless of the department being discussed, is that information security must be a team effort, extending across the borders of departments. Departments do not exist in a vacuum, and each department offers something different to the bigger security picture of an organization. Because this is a concept sometimes missed, ignored, or otherwise forgotten in the shuffle of daily operations, some organizations may benefit from the creation of an IS Committee.

This group of five to ten security-minded individuals would offer security-centric observations from different corners of the organization to top-level policy makers. An interdepartmental IS Committee would not be just an advisory committee, but would also be a vehicle for promoting security awareness throughout the different departments. Similar to Safety Committees, the IS Committee should be comprised of employees from all portions and levels within the organization who are interested in bettering security.

7

RISK MANAGEMENT

It is the risk element which ensures security. Risk brings out the ingenuity and resourcefulness which ensure success.

Robert Rawls

Risk Management and Asset Protection

The main function of information assurance is to protect the informational assets of a company from being accessed, manipulated, or deleted by unauthorized users. A company is comprised of assets and liabilities. Liabilities include debt, depreciation, a bad reputation, and any other thing costing the organization capital expenditures. Of course, assets include buildings, real estate, product lines, personnel, and any other item that may give value to the organization. Not all assets are tangible, though. Data should also be considered assets. For instance, a proprietary design of an innovative new product is an essential asset that, in the wrong hands, could bring a company to its knees. A new method of manufacturing widgets, or an otherwise unknown process that puts an organization at a distinct advantage over the competition is an asset as well. These ideas are considered *intellectual property*, because although they are owned by the organization that created them, they reside in the minds of people, and are ideas rather than physical items.

Even though these pieces of intellectual property are ideas and not physical assets, they do have tangible value. Time, manpower, and resources saved due to these ideas and concepts all add up to money in the bank. A company should spend an appropriate amount of time to determine, as closely as possible, how much an idea is worth in dollars and cents. This is naturally easier said than done of course, but it is an imperative step to the end goal of providing proper and complete asset protection for your company. After all, protecting assets costs money, so it is ideal to know how much a particular idea is worth to your company.

One of the best ways of estimating the value of an idea is to determine how much the idea would cost if your organization lost control over it. For instance, if you are a design and manufacturing business, how much money did your company put into engineering for the idea? How much does your Marketing Department estimate your company will profit from the new idea or product? What is the market share you expect to take due to the ownership of this process or idea? How will the idea or process benefit your company's image? How do these concepts translate into profits? These are all ideas that are sometimes difficult to ascertain precisely, but if you are able to get a handle on them, they will go a long way in determining the exact value of intellectual property.

Another intangible source of data is customer and employee data. These data are pieces of information that are generally related to the cost of loss as opposed to profit as a result of ownership. Essentially, having this information doesn't intrinsically benefit your company, but the loss of such data could be potentially devastating, financially speaking. The lawsuits and loss of customer goodwill could put some companies out of business. If credit card numbers, social security numbers, phone numbers, addresses, and other customer and employee information fell into the wrong hands, fraudulent purchases and identity theft would only be the beginning of the bad news to follow. If the company is big enough, or if the damages caused by the compromised data are catastrophic enough, the media will undoubtedly grab the story and run with it, which will at the very least seriously damage the goodwill of your organization, and at the worst could bring the organization to the brink of bankruptcy.

Data Loss

Before a discussion of how to properly protect an asset is undertaken, we must first determine what threats exist to the asset in question. Just as with structures, equipment, and other physical assets owned by a company, there are several ways in which data can be compromised. The main categories of data loss can be broken down into the categories of accidental user actions, criminal actions, disasters, and system failures.

Accidental User Actions The user can cause data loss through accidental actions. Unlike malicious actions, which are criminal in nature and are taken by a user with the intent of harming information in a direct and meaningful manner (such as uploading a virus from a workstation or giving an unauthorized user access to a system), accidental actions are ones unintentionally made by users that, nevertheless, could cause damage to the network and its subsystems.

Such actions may be software related (e.g., a user accessing a portion of an application or database that he or she was not intended to interface with and deleting or moving files, subsequently causing damage or otherwise causing the system to be unavailable in its intended entirety). Frequently, however, these actions are physical in nature (e.g., accidentally spilling food or beverages onto workstations or knocking entire systems off a cart or desk, causing damage to hardware). Another type of physical "accident" can occur when someone forgets to lock a door or close a window, potentially allowing an unauthorized user or natural elements to enter and attack or damage the system.

Such accidental damage can be protected against with the employment and follow-through of proper policies. For instance, software "gates" in applications, which would require user verification and authorization before allowing access to critical portions of a database or other important functions, is a good measure towards preventing unintended software accidents. To protect against spills, a policy banning users from eating or drinking at their desks, or one mandating that all drinks be in spill-proof containers and that certain types of food (such as those requiring utensils, with sauces, that leave crumbs, etc.) are not allowed at workstations, are options. Guarding against unlocked doors and open windows could involve a high-tech option (e.g., installing sensors that force such openings to be shut when the work shift is over) or a low-tech approach (e.g., checklists for the start and end of each shift). As with all policies, however, common sense should prevail so be sure to emphasize ease of implementation when writing them. If someone has to go completely out of his or her way to implement of follow a new policy, there may very well be a simpler, and perhaps better, way to provide a similar solution.

Criminal Actions   Unfortunately, failures caused by people don't only include accidents. Some individuals, including both malicious internal users and external cyber criminals, are intent on inflicting damage upon systems. These individuals are interested in compromising the security of an organization's data by hacking into a network and maliciously manipulating the data found therein. Their actions could be as benign as viewing files they are not authorized to access, or they could be as harmful as downloading a worm onto the network with the intent of causing a network-wide shutdown. These categories can be broken into several other categories, including unauthorized viewing of files, data manipulation, deleting critical files, uploading spyware, and uploading viruses and worms. Each of these attacks on the system presents its own unique challenges and issues to consider.

The cyber criminal who decides to simply view files he is otherwise not authorized to view can potentially be just as dangerous as the more seemingly dangerous criminal who uploads malware onto the network. Whereas a network administrator has the chance of detecting and eliminating the malware, a skilled cyber criminal has the ability to gain access to the system, view important files, and log off the system without leaving a trace. Why does it matter if somebody simply views files on the network without authorization? The issue becomes very apparent when one thinks of all the proprietary information contained on various storage devices connected to the network. If the wrong person gains access to these company secrets, not only will competitive advantages be lost, but liability issues also arise. Competitive advantage will be lost due to obvious reasons, but liability issues arise once personal information of employees or customers is lost. One only needs to look at current events to realize how important it is to keep such files out of the wrong hands through the implementation of a robust security policy. Lawsuits can ensue if people's social security numbers, medical records, addresses, and other personal information is lost. Once a cyber criminal has these key pieces of personal information, it is as though he has a key to unlock a person's life in order to wreak havoc and steal as much money as the stolen identity will yield.

In order to stop unauthorized people from viewing files, it is critical to maintain several layers of defense. For starters, authorized users should only have access to the files they need to successfully perform the functions of their job. For instance, somebody in Manufacturing does not need to view customer files in a customer service database, although they may need specific customer information to build product to specifications called out by particular customer orders. As discussed before, internal users are not the only threat to the system. Outside cyber criminals will also try to breach the perimeter of the network. To protect against such attacks, key ports should be closed, and open ports should be properly monitored, filtered, and logged to assist in the prevention of outside attackers.

Usually, attackers are not simply interested in viewing information. Most likely, they will want to manipulate the data in some manner. For instance, some attackers like to hack into websites and change words on the website to reflect the fact that they've been hacked. This way, they can brag to all of their criminal buddies that they too have broken several laws in order to change some words on a screen for their own entertainment. Some of the most "successful" cyber criminals have decided to break into computer systems illegally for the sheer "fun" of it, and for nothing else.

Other hackers want to vandalize files in other ways, including uploading viruses. Basically, any unauthorized piece of software that is installed on a system that makes the system perform harmful actions is a virus. Viruses have a wide range of types, and vary depending on the intent of the cyber criminal. For instance, there are keyloggers, Trojan horses, worms, spyware, adware, and denial-of-service (DoS) attacks, just to name a few. A catchall name for all of these types of illegal software is malware, which is short for "malicious software."

Disasters

Floods, fires, earthquakes, massive storms, and even volcanoes can bring unplanned havoc to any system. Disasters can mean the downfall of even the most robust networks and "secure" infrastructures. During or directly following a disaster is NOT the time to begin

> ### Options for Managing Risk
>
> **MITIGATE THE RISK**
> Decrease the risk associated with a particular asset.
>
> **TRANSFER THE RISK**
> Usually accomplished through purchasing insurance, pay a third party entity to manage the risk associated with a particular asset.
>
> **ACCEPT THE RISK**
> Realize the costs associated with managing the risk are too great, and simply accept the risk.
>
> **AVOID THE RISK**
> Put controls in place that don't allow certain behaviors associated with the risk to occur.

Figure 7.1   Risk Management

planning. Because proper planning requires thoughtful and thorough discussion and evaluation of various scenarios, it is best to plan often and with many different minds at the table. The key to weathering an attack by Mother Nature is to plan thoroughly, with redundancy in mind. Although it's impossible to account for every possible disaster scenario, there are fundamentals in planning and response that are true for any disaster, and all of them must be taken into consideration.

First of all, planning for disasters should focus first on the aspect of safety, and then on the aspect of recovery. Once all associated personnel have been safely evacuated from any dangerous areas, and risks to personal health and property are not a factor, recovery of systems can begin. Recovery assumes that major systems have been hit hard, and data will likely be compromised or lost after the event.

Keeping safety in mind, and assuming systems will be hit by any major disaster, redundancy of important systems is of very high importance. If your organization cannot function without access to particular database, consider mirroring the entire database (with frequent backups) offsite. Consider the feasibility and necessity of having another workforce trained and in place in case of an emergency.

If lives or safety depends on the continued function of your network (as in the case with a 9-1-1 dispatch center or a hospital) you may need to have a secondary location set up, with hot-swappable hard drives and systems, in the event that a move is required.

The bottom line when dealing with disasters is to identify BEFORE A DISASTER STRIKES which systems are critical and what level of criticality those systems fall under, backing them up accordingly.

More information on incident response and planning can be found in Chapter 9.

System Failures   Data lost due to system failures comprise a very low percentage of lost information. System failures include such things as power outages, connection losses, voltage spikes, hard drive motor failures, and any other failure that is internal to a system that contributes to the loss or corruption of a file. Power outages can be prevented by redundant, uninterruptable power supplies (UPSs). A good UPS will continue supplying power to computer equipment even when the main power is gone. Every critical computer in the network infrastructure should have a proper UPS. UPSs are rated by how much power they can provide and for how long, much like automotive batteries. Be sure to consider these stats when purchasing backup power supplies. If you cannot afford to have a system go offline at all, make sure you provide it with plenty of backup power in the case of main power loss.

Component failures include bad RAM sticks, hard drive motor failures, motherboard failures, and so on. Most of the components inside a PC are relatively cheap to replace, in regard to actual cost and the labor involved. This is why many IT Departments have field replaceable units (FRUs), or replacement components, available on hand. There are a couple of methods to use in order to cut the overall cost of FRUs even further. For instance, keep in mind when purchasing motherboards the compatibility of on-hand FRUs. Remember that some motherboards require different power supplies or accept different central processing units (CPUs) for their onboard sockets. It would be a waste of money to have several different power supplies, RAM sticks, and CPUs on hand simply to accommodate the fact that your organization has several different types of motherboards. This cannot always be avoided, as technology changes, although it is wise to try to standardize as much as possible.

Risk Management

Risk management considers assets, the possibility of various types of damage occurring to those assets, and the costs associated with the occurrence of those damages (see Figure 7.1). Notice it is called "risk management," instead of "risk elimination." The fact is, it is impossible to create a situation wherein information is perfectly protected from external and internal threats. This is because every organization and individual therein has only a limited number of resources and labor hours to dedicate toward the end of protecting data, whereas there are unlimited numbers of vulnerabilities within the network being served. The best we can do is put policies and controls in place that serve to protect the data to the best of our ability while not breaking the bank of the organization we are seeking to protect. In order to achieve success, it is absolutely critical that top management be committed to the risk management of information. Without top-level management's direct involvement, asset allocation required to assess and protect the network infrastructure will not occur.

Risk Analysis

In order to determine how best to protect the data on your organization's network, a detailed risk analysis must first be performed. A risk analysis, if done properly and thoroughly, will inform management about those assets needing protection and the costs involved. A thorough risk analysis will include a list of assets and associated asset values, potential costs associated with asset failure or damage, an analysis of threats posed against protected assets, an estimate of potential annual losses for each asset, and methods and procedures for mitigating the risk posed against the listed assets.

Build a List of Assets   A list of assets is exactly what it sounds like. This list should include the hardware, software, labor, files, and all other equipment and property otherwise necessary to protect data on the organization's servers and networks.

Determine Asset Value (AV) Once a list of assets is completed, it is important to assess the value of each asset. When determining asset values, it is important to consider how much the data or asset is worth to the organization to which it belongs. Although it is impossible to simply place an accurate value on every asset, it can help to consider the following questions when seeking to determine asset values:

- *How Much Would the Asset Be Worth to a Competitor?* Don't forget that proprietary information about competitors is hugely valuable to most organizations. There are two main reasons for this, and both of them are strategic in nature. First of all, if a competitor knows about a specific product or technology your organization is developing, they may decide to double their own efforts to beat your company to the punch in order to gain a first foothold in the market. This could put your company in a poor light, making it appear as though you are playing catch-up when in reality your organization provided the leg up for your competitor. Another issue to consider regarding new product development is the customer. If a customer is planning on purchasing a product from your organization, but hears that you may be coming out with a better product, they may wait to buy that better product instead of purchasing from your current product line. This "wait to buy" syndrome can quickly kill companies, and it is one of the best reasons to keep a lid on your product development plans.
- *What Is the Operational Cost of the Asset?* Be sure to estimate and include labor, equipment, and software required to maintain the assets in question. Product upgrades, patch downloads, and training should also be included in the assessment of operational costs. Don't make the wrong assumption that a resource or asset is "free" after the initial purchase cost.
- *What Is the Replacement Cost of the Asset?* If the asset is a piece of hardware, make sure you keep in mind the speedy pace of technology. In other words, you may be able to get an equivalent or better product than the one currently being used. CPU speeds, RAM, and hard drive sizes are constantly increasing, so don't feel the need to always buy the latest and greatest. Instead, buy what your company needs, plus enough to handle

a year or more of expanded capacity. Keeping the needs of your company in mind, as opposed to always getting the best equipment money can buy, will save your organization many thousands of dollars a year.

- *What Was the Original Cost to Purchase and Implement the Asset?* This original dollar cost is a good number to keep in mind, inasmuch as it will likely cost about the same to replace the asset to its current level of performance. As mentioned above, you will likely be able to get your hands on something that performs better for less money, but it is a wise idea to plan for the worst instead of counting on getting a "good deal" and being disappointed.
- *Does the Asset Produce Any Profit for the Organization, and If So, How Much Does It Help Produce Annually?* The types of assets that generate money for a company are generally associated with engineering. For instance, proprietary information regarding a new product design, a new method, or a custom product line would constitute data that help sustain a revenue stream for an organization.
- *What Sort of Liability Would the Organization Need to Deal with if the Asset Were Lost, Damaged, or Stolen?* These liabilities include legal fees, customer goodwill, public opinion, and so forth. For instance, if customer or employee data were stolen and the public found out about it, how would such an occurrence affect your marketing and sales? Would it create a problem with employee morale and indirectly affect productivity?

Determine the Exposure Factor (EF)   The purpose of determining the EF of an asset is to try to build a realistic, monetary-based estimate of asset exposure to loss. For instance, if we consider a building in a location where tornadoes frequently occur, it may be likely that the building would suffer damage; however, it is not likely that the building would be completely destroyed. For example, if it is determined that wind damage will cause $200,000 of damage to a building that costs $1,000,000, the exposure factor, or EF, is 20%. The EF of an asset plays into the single loss expectancy (SLE) of that asset. Other questions and issues to consider when determining EF are:

- What types of damages can occur to the asset, and what costs are associated with each occurrence of damage?
- What would the effect be on productivity, in regard to cost and efficiency?
- Consider proprietary information and the value that could be jeopardized if such information were lost or compromised.
- What are the costs associated with recovery from each threat posed against particular assets?

Determine the Single Loss Expectancy (SLE)

Once the issues surrounding asset losses and their associated costs are considered, the single loss expectancy will be able to be calculated. Calculating the SLE of assets is a standard method used in information security for considering what it would cost every time a risk happens against an organization's asset. The basic equation for determining single loss expectancy of an asset is as follows.

$$\text{Single Loss Expectancy (SLE)} =$$
$$\text{Asset Value (AV)} * \text{Exposure Factor (EF)}$$

Complete a Threat Analysis

Okay, so we've got a list of basic assets, the value of each asset, and an estimated cost to replace each of the assets. This is only part of the equation, though. To complete the analysis of threats posed against the network assets, you will need to perform some basic research and calculations regarding the loss statistics of your organization. First of all, locate any security records and computer logs that would indicate historical records for your network. These will point to past failures. If your organization is too new to keep such records, search the Internet and talk with colleagues and employees in an attempt to determine how often each type of system experiences failures, and what types of failures occur most often. For each asset, assign an annual rate of occurrence (ARO) for failure. This ARO is simply a calculated number of times a failure is likely to occur in a 12-month period.

Calculate Annual Loss Expectancy (ALE)

The ALE is the expected annual loss associated with each asset. To calculate this number, simply multiply single loss expectancy by the annual rate of occurrence. For instance, let's take the $1,000,000 building discussed above. We already know the SLE is $200,000 but what is the ARO? Let's say we looked at average wind speeds per year, and the rate of occurrence for such damage to occur ($200,000) in the area happened about once every 25 years. This annual rate of occurrence means that there is a 4% chance of the occurrence happening annually. This means that the ALE for this threat would be = $200,000 × .04, or $8,000.

Manage the Risk

Once the risk posed against each asset is derived from the process of determining the ALE, we must address how we want to manage the risk. There are only a few options available in regard to risk. These options include risk mitigation, risk transference, risk acceptance, and risk avoidance. For some assets, only specific types of risk management options are feasible. When reviewing the specific options for each asset in your organization, consider the cost effectiveness of each option, and consider the criticality of the resource you are trying to protect.

Sometimes it is not simply a matter of financial loss or gain. There will likely be varying degrees of importance for maintaining each asset. Some assets may cost a lot of money to replace, but they add little value to the main processes or production value of your company. Others may cost little to replace but they add a ton of value to your organization. If the main function of your organization will be completely halted due to the loss of particular resource, be sure to keep that in mind when considering your options.

Risk Mitigation   Risk mitigation focuses on trying to decrease the risk involved with an asset. The methods associated with risk mitigation usually use a combination of security controls, firewalls, new procedures, and environmental changes. For instance, if unauthorized software is being frequently downloaded onto the network, there is a good chance that malware will eventually make its way onto the computers being served. To mitigate the chances of this occurring, firewalls could be tweaked to prevent software other than those programs approved to be downloaded, and network traffic "sniffers" could be installed to monitor which users are responsible for downloading the software.

Risk Transference   Risk transference places the risk upon another entity. This is most commonly done through the purchase of a good insurance policy. Many insurance policies will cost much less than the annual loss expectancy for the assets protected. Umbrella policies allow for a large monetary coverage of many different asset failures and losses. For instance, some insurance policies may cover damage and losses occurring against a physical asset such as the building the organization is housed in, as well as liability insurance associated with products and advertising.

Risk Acceptance   Sometimes it is simply too costly to mitigate or manage a risk effectively enough to ensure the asset being protected will be properly protected. If insurance is not an option due to cost, or an asset cannot be insured, and the exposure is so small that paying the amount of money it would cost to protect would be cost prohibitive, then your organization may simply decide to accept the risk as part of doing business. Risk acceptance is when an organization accepts the risks associated with threats to the asset and spends no money toward its protection. Simply accepting risk is not the ideal method for protecting assets, although sometimes it's the only affordable one. Be sure your organization can survive with the loss of an asset before deciding to accept the threat posed against it.

Risk Avoidance   Risk avoidance simply puts controls and procedures in place to prevent or discontinue certain behaviors and actions. For instance, the IT manager may place controls on user computers to prevent them from downloading unauthorized software in order to avoid the risk associated with unknown authors of such programs. Risk avoidance is usually the easiest and least costly method of risk management to implement, however, the activity that is bringing risk to the network may be impossible to avoid. For instance, logging onto the Internet puts the network in jeopardy of being attacked by viruses and other criminal malicious software. The fact of the matter is that virtually no organization can exist without connecting to the Internet, so avoiding the activity is not a viable solution. Therefore, risk mitigation in the form of antivirus and good Internet usage policies and enforcement would be the most likely answer.

Choosing Your Response   For each risk, you'll need to decide which is best: mitigate, avoid, transfer, or accept the risk. The answer to this arrives only after more analysis of the risk. Many organizations, when faced with deciding what to do regarding risks, will simply calculate the ALE and then find out how much it would cost to protect against that risk. If the cost outweighs the ALE, management frequently decides it's too expensive to protect against. This is a shortsighted and incomplete method of approaching risk management. Managers should consider the peripheral risks involved with the primary risk being considered. If one risk is left unchecked, it may lead to several other risks being exposed, should a threat be realized. For example, let's again take the $200,000 damage to the building. If the ALE is $8,000 and the insurance to protect it is $12,000 a year, management may decide that the cost/benefit ratio is not profitable and will therefore not support it. There are peripheral considerations that must be made, though. If management decides against purchasing the insurance necessary to protect the building, then if disaster strikes and the building suffers, the money required to repair the physical structure may be too heavy a burden to financially cope with, and the organization may be forced to close the doors.

Another example might be in regard to credit card storage procedures. An organization may be well within its rights and industry requirements not to encrypt credit card numbers in their customer database due to the small number of accounts they process annually, but would that be wise? Imagine if someone broke into the organization's database and customer cards were compromised. Even though it would have still been possible for a cyber criminal to decrypt a group of encrypted credit cards, customers would probably be more enraged to find out their information wasn't even protected at a minimal level. The fallout caused by poor customer opinion could have a massively negative effect on sales and profit, which in turn could force an organization to go out of business.

8

SOCIAL ENGINEERING

Trickery and treachery are the practices of fools that have not
the wits enough to be honest.

Benjamin Franklin

What Is Social Engineering?

Most security solutions directed at protecting data contained within
the confines of an organization's network are generally software cen-
tric. IT and IS professionals will labor for hours configuring firewalls,
filtering traffic, and monitoring data packets to ensure proper network
security. These same professionals will travel across the continent
to attend security seminars in order to hone their technical prowess. Volume upon volume of books exist decrying the importance of
a good technical defense, although only recently has the largest gap
in the security profile begun to close. Within the past few years, the
issue of social engineering has started to make an appearance in information security literature.

Social engineering is essentially a low-tech or no-tech approach to
hacking. The primary goal of social engineering is to gain access to
systems and physical locations without having to physically or digitally break into any systems. Serious cyber criminals will seek to find
as much information about the organization they are planning on
attacking in order to make their planned attack easier. Often times,
they will pose as someone legitimate within the organization they
plan on attacking. Other times, the criminals will simply gather as
much information as possible by rummaging through an organization's trash. Once enough information is gathered to form a thorough

picture of an organization's network, the cyber criminal can plan his or her attack with confidence.

The steps required to build a complete picture of a network through the skillful implementation of social engineering is much easier than one might think, as the examples below explain. It is important to first understand the different types of social engineering, in order to understand how a social engineering criminal thinks. Just like protecting against a computer virus, once the "signature" or behavior of the attacker is understood, a proper and complete defense can be mounted, and successful protection of data can be accomplished. Therefore, it should be part of a system administrator's job to understand the psychology of social engineering, and the associated tricks of their trade.

Psychology of Social Engineering

It is interesting to note the duplicity of skills required in order for a social engineering attack to be successful. When most people think of cyber criminals, they usually envision an incredibly intelligent, technically minded individual with little to no social skills. Although this is sometimes the case with some cyber criminals, a good social engineering attack relies heavily on understanding people and being able to interact, influence, and manipulate people into giving the criminals whatever information they need to successfully attack a system. A good social engineer understands that people will, in general, consistently react to certain situations. This is based on a series of assumptions about human psychology. In brief, the rules are essentially as follows.

1. Recognition of and respect for authority
2. Politeness, professional customs, and courtesy
3. Conformity in the workforce

Recognition of and Respect for Authority

If a social engineering cyber criminal poses as someone in authority and is believed to be legitimate, people are far more likely to obey directions and assist the cyber criminal. For instance, one of the common social engineering attacks involves pretending to be a company officer requesting assistance with a login. The first step requires discovering the name and location of a company executive. Most social engineers will select somebody who will appear in a company directory as an executive, but who is unlikely to be personally known by a helpdesk technician. For instance, a criminal may choose to pose as a Vice President or Director of Accounting, the Legal Department, or some other department that is generally behind closed doors and is obscured from a company-wide presence. The cyber criminal would then locate the number for the company helpdesk and call, pretending to be the selected company officer or manager in need of assistance.

An added step in this type of attack is working around the officer or manager's schedule. For instance, it doesn't take much snooping to find out when a higher-up in an organization is on vacation. A cyber criminal might wait until the individual they plan on posing as is out of the office to call the helpdesk. Waiting for such a time provides the criminal with two advantages. The first advantage is that there is a very good chance that whomever the criminal is posing as will not be logged into his account, due to the fact he is not in the office. This allows the criminal to have free access (once obtained), without being hindered by having the actual person he is posing as interfere with his illegal activities.

The second advantage is that there is a ready excuse if the helpdesk technician offers to physically visit or send a technician to reset or provide maintenance to the person's computer. If a helpdesk technician offers such service, the criminal simply reminds them that they are "on vacation" or otherwise away from the office. The schedule, if checked, will show that the executive is in fact on vacation.

Not only will a check of the schedule reinforce the claim of the cyber criminal, but most helpdesk technicians will feel even more eager to help resolve the issue of not being able to login remotely to the organization's server. If a user is physically present at the organization, the helpdesk technician may be more prone to make the poser wait for help until security issues can be properly cleared. If the helpdesk technician feels he is inconveniencing the executive who is "on vacation," he will be far more likely to help the poser on the other end of the phone, and will probably be less likely to stop and ask deeper questions to vet the caller.

Possible Defenses   Within organizations, hierarchies exist to maintain order and a flow of authority and associated responsibilities. Without a clear distinction of command and delineation of responsibilities, projects would generally not get accomplished in a timely and efficient manner. When somebody in authority needs to get onto her computer, therefore, she should not have to go through miles of red tape in order to gain access to her account. Nor should she be penalized if she forgets her password or login credentials.

So what is the helpdesk technician to do? The easiest and most effective measure for protecting the organization's networks from an imposter requesting secured access is to require the caller to provide information unique to the user. Many banks require such information when calling to get information about a personal account. This information could be as standard as a mother's maiden name, or it can be the user's favorite pet's name, or whatever your organization decides upon. The bottom line is that if somebody calls asking for help accessing the network, the helpdesk technician assisting that person should have some other method of verifying the user than the user's assertion that she is in fact who she says she is. Considering the fact that company officers have a lot to lose if the data on the organization's network are compromised, they should be the first to sign off on and endorse such a policy.

Politeness, Professional Customs, and Courtesy

Without politeness, going to work and serving people wouldn't be nearly as enjoyable as it usually is. Being polite helps build unity and develops continuity throughout an organization. It is the "grease" that helps the cogs of an organization move, and it is indispensable. At least in professional society, people are generally polite by nature. People will usually hold elevator doors open for each other, help each other carry large pieces of equipment from one place to another, and even walk each other to the parking lot for mutual protection at night. This is definitely the best and most common way to do business with customers, including the "customers" we all serve in the various departments of our respective organizations. However, as with many other conventions of human society, being polite is not only a wonderful way to do business with each other, but it introduces its own set of challenges with regard to security.

For instance, let us discuss the example of assisting a fellow worker with the transportation of a piece of large equipment. It is a natural assumption that if somebody is removing computer equipment from an area, they are not only authorized to do so, but they probably have a really good reason to do it. This is not a ridiculous assumption, and in fact is most likely true the vast majority of the time. It is not, however, true all of the time. Criminals relying on the psychology of social engineering count on this assumption, and could use it to walk into an area they are not authorized to be in, pick up a computer, disk, file, or other storage device and simply walk out of the office without anybody suspecting them of doing anything wrong or illicit. It has been done before and will be done again.

Because of the rules of politeness, it would actually be perceived as rude and awkward to walk up to somebody and say, "Excuse me, but do you have prior authorization to remove that equipment? Could I see your credentials?" or, "Wait here while I call security, because I think you're stealing that computer." Because people don't stop to consider how best to approach somebody they think is suspicious or up to no good, they will generally not question any activity that seems unusual.

Possible Defense The short answer to how to deal with this type of social engineering attack is simple: engage the person whom you find suspicious. Notice the word used here is "engage," and not "confront." Many people think the only way to approach a suspicious person is to immediately start barraging them with questions. An appropriate response to a suspicious individual is simply to approach them and introduce yourself as you would a stranger at a party, and engage them in simple conversation.

For instance, imagine Albert is working at his desk and in walks a man who proceeds to rummage through his coworker Maryann's desk. Albert has worked in this department for five years, and has never seen this man before, and his coworker, Maryann, hasn't mentioned to Albert that a man is supposed to stop by to pick something up from her desk. Albert could approach the man and engage him in conversation.

"Hello, I don't think we've met. My name is Albert." Albert smiles his friendliest smile as he extends his hand to the unknown man.

"Hello, Albert, my name is Ron." Ron smiles back and extends his hand. The two shake amiably as Ron continues to scan Maryann's desk.

"Welcome to Widgets Unlimited, Ron. Maryann should be back any moment. Is there anything I can help you with in the meantime?"

Ron continues to smile, and says, "I'm from Engineering, and I need to get a copy of the In Stock Components List. Is that something you might have?"

"Of course. I'll e-mail it to you as a PDF attachment." Albert smiles, temporarily assured that Ron is an engineer, which is further evidenced by Ron's messy hair and undone tie. Albert finds Ron's e-mail on the Engineering e-mail list and sends over a copy of the vendor list with a note indicating he is sending it, "per your request."

Albert was not only friendly in his dealing with Ron, but also inquired the nature of his visit to Maryann's desk without being awkward or rude. In fact, it would have been somewhat rude to simply sit there and watch Ron as he attempted to locate something without assistance. Furthermore, by e-mailing the attachment to Ron, Albert gave Ron an updated copy of the needed document for Ron to save on his hard drive, while also maintaining an additional level of security by e-mailing the document to an approved recipient. This way, even if "Ron" happened to be a thoughtfully disguised criminal, the worst thing that would happen is the real Ron would get the copy of the vendor list and wonder why Albert had sent it. If Ron didn't actually request the vendor list, he would likely follow up with an e-mail stating he never requested it, in which case Albert and Ron could launch a search for the imposter. As a follow-up, Albert could mention the incident to Maryann, who might have told Albert she knew Ron and had told him to grab a copy of the In Stock Components List from her desk.

The point of this illustration is to highlight the importance and incorporation of politeness in the security process. When used correctly, politeness can enhance security, instead of hinder it, by turning the tables on the would-be attacker. For instance, an imposter would likely be at a loss to come up with a good reason why Albert shouldn't e-mail a PDF file, because the vast majority of people prefer having a digital copy on record.

Taking the PDF example a step further, for truly secure documents, it may be a wise policy to not allow an employee to print a document for another employee. In the example above, even if Ron had insisted Albert print a copy for him to take back to Engineering, Albert could have declined (politely) by stating a copy had been e-mailed, and company policy would not allow him to print a copy for Ron. Ron would have been forced to return to his work area and log into his own computer to print a copy. Considering the amount of proprietary data contained on most organization's approved component list, this is not an unreasonable policy to enforce.

Conformity in the Workplace

Regardless of what policies exist in your organization, the workplace environment will dictate the actions somebody actually takes when confronted with the decision to follow or break company protocol. Just because an organization's policy mandates that everybody e-mail PDFs to each other instead of printing them out, will your employees actually follow that rule?

Consider how easy it is to e-mail or print out documents for the employees affected by the policy, and you will have your answer. Don't place an undue burden on your employees by requiring unrealistic goals or expectations. For instance, don't create a policy that requires people to go through a security checkpoint to get into and out of the lunchroom or bathroom. If somebody must pass through several checkpoints to get from Point A to Point B, your employees are far likelier to lend each other security passes and generally ignore security, because it will become a hindrance instead of an enhancement to their job. In other words, try to minimize the levels of physical security that an employee must pass through, in order to facilitate a smoother workflow without having an employee feel like they work in a prison. Think through the policies your organization is planning on implementing, and be sure to consider how they might be modified to better encourage a security-minded workforce, without encouraging breaking the rules.

Possible Defense   The goal is to create an ever-present blanket of security awareness without interfering with daily operations. This is why it is essential to think through policies before implementing them. Consider how feasible the goals of the policy are, and how best to implement those goals. If the policy will require too much of an employee, or if it will stop an employee from performing his job with a maximum amount of efficiency, rethink the approach of the policy and how best to implement the intent of the policy. In addition to how the policy will affect the employee's efficiency, consider whether the policy is easy to remember and execute.

For instance, a physical security checkpoint is not a bad idea to maintain an extremely high level of security. On the other hand, if a checkpoint is implemented to protect the supply room instead of high-level corporate secrets, the employees in charge of checking people through the checkpoint may not administer the security requirements in accordance with the policy.

Social Engineering Information Gathering Methods

There are many different methods employed by social engineering criminals to illegally gather information. Regardless of the method being used, most seek to build a more complete picture of the organization being attacked. Some methods avoid interaction with people, but simply count on human nature. Others are heavily focused on dealing directly with people, and use people's natural trust of each other to leverage and manipulate other people into providing otherwise secure information. Both types of social engineering attacks have straightforward defenses that can be easily implemented with minor cost, and with little disruption to the daily flow of your organization.

Dumpster Diving

One of the most commonly known and discussed social engineering attacks, which avoids any contact with people, is known as dumpster diving. Dumpster diving is a method of social engineering wherein the would-be cyber criminal rummages through the trash of an organization in an attempt to gain valuable information. What could possibly be in the trash that would allow somebody to gain access to an organization's network? There have been documented cases in which individuals have located all manner of important documents, including vendor lists, tax records, product designs, and more. Perhaps the mother lode find for a dumpster diver is an organization's phone directory. Phone directories, although generally useless to workers at an organization, hold great value and power in the hands of a criminal. For instance, phone directories usually not only contain phone numbers, but also the names and positions of people associated with them. This allows a criminal to pose as an internal user from a remote location, as mentioned in the helpdesk scenario at the beginning of this chapter.

Locating a phone directory is just one possibility with dumpster diving. Old hard drives, company financial information, employee compensation lists, credit card information, customer data, and more can all be unknowingly thrown out with the trash. Any of these things will aid a cyber criminal in obtaining the information they are after, or could be the very information they want. If your organization uses a publically accessible trash source, consider anything that goes into that source as public. In other words, don't throw account numbers, customer information, or any other sensitive data in the trash. In some cases even if it's been shredded, don't throw it in the trash. Shredders do a good job of making it difficult for people to determine what was printed on the shredded paper, although it still isn't impossible. Even cross-shredded paper can be reassembled with enough skill and patience. Consider hiring an offsite, bonded shredding company to perform the shredding of your organization's most secure documents.

Possible Defense   There are a few methods of protecting your trash from rummaging social engineering attacks. The first is to destroy any piece of "trash" that contains information that could possibly assist somebody in attacking your network. Remember there are two types of information to consider: physical and digital.

Destroying Physical Information   For most companies, cross-shredded paper is probably fine, although it would be wise to get a certified shredder to come in and take away your already shredded paper. Taking this step is for peace of mind and for liability. Having a weekly, biweekly, or monthly shredder pickup date would not only ensure all sensitive material is properly destroyed, it will add to the culture of security awareness you are trying to build.

Destroying Digital Information Destroying digital information is both easier and more difficult than the process of physical data destruction. On one hand it is a simple "point and click" operation. The user only needs to delete the information for it to be gone from most prying eyes. Emptying the recycle bin on your desktop adds another small layer of protection from unwanted retrieval, although someone with enough time and the proper tools could possibly still retrieve any data you delete.

The problem is that "deleting" a file doesn't actually "erase" it. When a file is created, there is a pointer that points to the remnants of the deleted file. During normal operations (before the file has been deleted), whenever the pointer is accessed the file can be found and opened. Generally, when a file is deleted, only the pointer is removed from the hard drive. This means the original file, the one you wanted to get rid of, is still lurking on your hard drive. The operating system doesn't see the file, but it can still be accessed with the right tools. If somebody is looking for a "deleted" file on your hard drive, all he would need to do is download one of multiple free software recovery programs to locate and open the file. Most of these programs are very easy to use, and don't even require the user to be tech savvy.

If you have deleted data on your hard drive and want to make absolutely certain it is gone for good, make sure to download or purchase a program that is actually going to "erase" the file. Erasing files is the only way to ensure the file is not on the hard drive, and cannot be found. An online search for "Digital Shredders" will provide a massive number of available tools.

Sometimes data owners don't want to delete a file, but simply want to make it unavailable to all but authorized users. The best way to keep a file on your hard drive while guaranteeing it will not be located is through the use of cryptography. Because there are myriad cryptographic algorithms available, be sure to select one that is secure enough to protect your data, but not too cumbersome to implement.

Tailgating

The author used to work at a bank call center with over 500 other call representatives. In order to gain access to the call center floor, there was a main door through which every worker had to pass. The door had a keypad on it, on which employees were required to enter in a six-digit code. This was a weak approach to security at best. The main issue with this implementation of security was that it allowed for people to tailgate, or "piggyback" behind somebody who had entered the correct code. First off, because there were over 500 employees, there was a constant stream of employees walking in and out the door. Secondly, because the call center needed to maintain staffing levels, there were always fresh faces coming and going through that door. This made it even easier for somebody to pose as a new employee. Even though the bank changed the key code monthly, all somebody would have to do is ask somebody just coming out of the door, "What is this month's code?"

I had been privy to dozens of people asking what the code was, and every time somebody would tell them. I even caught myself giving out the code to new employees I had never seen before. Looking back, I would have felt incredibly terrible if one of the people I'd given the code to had caused damage to the bank in some manner.

The story of the bank and the security illustrates how easily somebody can gain access to an environment that is otherwise very secure. Before I was allowed to work at the bank, I had to go through eight full-time weeks of training and pass a background check. At the time, I thought the call center was so secure because of these strict requirements. In fact, many people I knew who had quit working at the bank did piggyback behind friends to come in and "visit" with old colleagues. This is especially alarming in retrospect, considering the fact that former employees, especially those spurned by former supervisors or company policies, are some of the most likely to attempt to sabotage the system. It didn't strike me how insecure the call center was until I began studying security.

A coded door lock is generally a good idea for a secure closet or room that has very little foot traffic, making it next to impossible to piggyback without getting noticed. A coded door is useless for a location that has such heavy foot traffic as a bank call center. People just don't want to be rude to somebody who clearly needs to get into a main room. Of course, the proper thing to do is escort a person attempting to piggyback to the security desk, but really, who is going to do that?

Possible Defense   One of the surest methods for protecting an otherwise secure doorway from unauthorized access is posting an employee at the doorway. This employee doesn't necessarily need to be part of the organization's security personnel, but she must have a clear line of sight to the door, and vice versa. If you want to protect that doorway, put a reception desk next to it, to ensure the people coming in see the receptionist, and the receptionist sees them.

By relying on human nature and the goodwill of most people, social engineers will often try to slip past receptionists and into unauthorized areas with a simple smile or greeting. The receptionist needs realize he or she is not just there to perfunctorily greet people, but actually serves as another security gateway in a layered structure of gateways through which individuals must pass before gaining further access into an organization. The receptionist should not only greet people as they walk in, he or she should also feel empowered to ask where they intend to go within the organization and who they are meeting. A person trying to get past the receptionist had better have a name of a specific employee within the organization, or they should not be granted access beyond the reception desk. Furthermore, the receptionist should not allow the visitor to pass without an employee to escort them into the organization (preferably the employee who the visitor has come to see, although this is not always possible—common sense should prevail).

Shoulder Surfing

Shoulder surfing occurs when a cyber criminal stands in such a manner as to view otherwise inaccessible information being displayed on a computer being used by an authorized user. Often, the cyber criminal will peer over the shoulder of the authorized user in order to view PINs, passwords, and other information that would otherwise be confidential.

Possible Defense   The best defense against a casual observer shoulder surfing is awareness. If the employees at your organization are aware of the issue, they will be far more likely to notice when somebody is checking their screen out from across the way. If they spot somebody peering over someone else's shoulder in an attempt to steal information, a simple, "Hello. May I help you?" will go a long way in halting the activity. If social engineers even think somebody is onto them, they will likely slip out the back door and not return. Having security-aware personnel is key to this defense.

Another option available for stopping people from viewing unauthorized data on employee screens is the installation of blinders on key monitors throughout your organization's office. The blinders act to provide clear viewing of a screen when viewed directly, but if viewed from even a slightly different angle, the data being displayed on the screen are completely unreadable. Although these screens are often priced over a hundred dollars, it may be a wise decision to at least make sure they are installed on the most vulnerable monitors. For instance, any monitor that is open to the public should be protected with a screen. A receptionist's computer should be considered open to the public, as should any computer viewable through a window. Even in many high-rise buildings, some computers can be easily viewed through a window with the use of a telescopic device. For a focused criminal, it would not be a big deal to take up residence in a room across the street from such an office and begin surveillance.

If your organization cannot afford the blinding screens for the monitors, another practical option is placing monitors in less viewable locations. For instance, employees with critical, company-sensitive data on their computers may want to have their computer monitors facing inward from any doorway to their workstation. If anybody were to walk into their office, only the back of their computer monitor would be visible. If employees are in cubicles and not offices, there are some steps that can be taken to mitigate the possibility of unauthorized viewers. First of all, many companies cordon off areas of an office to facilitate the grouping of similarly employed workers. For instance, all HR personnel may be located in one corner of the office, the advertising personnel in another, the legal personnel in another, and so on. In this manner, if any one of the employees were to see the data on another's monitor, there would be no cause for concern, inasmuch as they all work with the same data. Manager's computers can always be placed such that their screen faces into a corner, so their computer is not viewable except by actually walking to that corner.

In addition to grouping employees with similar work functions together, placing items in direct line of sight from the monitor is also an option. Although placing computers in the middle of a cubicle workstation's desk is often the most efficient use of the desktop space, placing the computer monitor to one side or the other is usually the most secure option. This is because it enables the monitor to be placed in such a manner as to prohibit a casual passerby from simply looking into the cubicle and viewing the contents being displayed.

Another step that can be taken to prohibit unauthorized eyes from viewing sensitive data is simply keeping unauthorized personnel from entering an area in which data can be viewed. Many companies allow family and friends to visit workers during break, or even after hours. The author even worked at one corporation as a customer service representative where people were managing bank information, and family members were allowed to walk freely onto the "floor" and talk with their spouses. Not only was this a bad idea for productivity, it was horrible for security.

Posing as an Employee

If a social engineer wants information, she needs to convince somebody to give it to her. This is essentially the core concept behind all social engineering attacks. The social engineer is not allowed on the target organization's campus. In order to get around this issue the social engineer simply poses as somebody with authority. This can be done in person, over the phone, or on the computer.

In Person—Not Wearing Badges   Some policies designed to protect people and data actually provide easy access to criminals. For instance, many organizations require badges for all visitors, and none for workers and staff. This policy, although well intentioned, couldn't make it easier for a criminal wishing to remain anonymous. All they have to do to blend in with the full-time crew is simply not wear a badge! Consider large corporate and academic campuses, where thousands of people mill about the buildings and grounds, and anonymity is all but assured. This is especially alarming considering the fact that many elementary schools use this method for physically authenticating visitors.

Possible Defense   If an organization such as a school wants to implement the security badge philosophy with any amount of success, they need to make all staff, regardless of rank or office wear a badge. This way, the people without badges will stand out. CEOs, vice presidents, and directors don't get to graduate to a level wherein badges are no longer needed. Indeed, the strongest message to employees in regard to the importance of wearing a security badge is the strict adherence to the policy by the management who crafted that policy in the first place. If the policy is actually followed, it can be a good method for immediately spotting people who don't belong on an organization's campus.

Forging Badges   Although access badges are not a bad idea for organizations, there are some issues that need to be taken into consideration. Anybody with access to a color printer and laminating machine can make at least a reasonable facsimile of any badge they can take a picture of from a distance. All somebody has to do is snap a digital photo of somebody wearing a badge from the organization they want to infiltrate, copy the design of the badge, and then make one with their own picture on it. A cursory inspection of the badge will likely grant him access to any building on the organization's campus.

Possible Defense   If your organization decides to implement a security plan that includes security badges for all employees, make certain of a couple things. If at all possible, make sure there is some marking or item on the badge that upon closer inspection will reveal if the badge is legitimate. For instance, a watermark or holographic picture located on the badge will probably not be seen in a photograph taken by a potential forger, and will also likely miss the attention of all but the most attentive forgers.

Keep in mind that most criminals don't expect people to look closely at their identity badge, because quite honestly, most people don't. The best protection against forged badges is a keen eye. If you hire a person to serve as part of a security checkpoint to look at badges for validity, be sure they are actually checking them! Test them by creating some fake badges and having employees wear them to security checkpoints. Give rewards if the posing employees are caught.

Another detail that should be included on any badge is some sort of barcode or digital strip that can be easily swiped or scanned to identify the person's identity digitally. If the legitimacy of an employee's credentials is called into question, simply scan the ID to see if she is who she claims to be. This barcode or magnetic strip should be located on the back of the card so that a person attempting to create a forged ID will not see it when he is taking reconnaissance photographs. This may seem paranoid to most people, but the fact is, criminals consider breaking into places as their job. They will do whatever is necessary to gain access; snapping a few photos to get an accurate representation of an ID is not out of the ordinary for them.

Radio Frequency Identification (RFID) Badges   RFID has been implemented by retail stores, car manufacturers, and as of late, even the United States government is looking into the possibility of having U.S. passports issued with embedded RFID tags. These issues are fodder for a whole other book, but suffice it to say, RFID is here to stay. Among the many different applications of RFID, some organizations use it as part of their badge and access systems. In these systems, the RFID badges are worn by authorized users and provide them with a key to gain access to otherwise locked doorways on an organization's campus. These badges have circuitry embedded inside them, including a small transmitter that outputs a unique ID. The system works as follows.

1. The RFID Badge has a small chip, battery, and transmitter embedded inside it.
2. A reader is mounted next to a secure entrance. The reader is constantly transmitting a signal that will activate the RFID card.
3. Once an RFID card receives the signal from the reader, it responds by transmitting its own unique ID.
4. The reader receives the RFID signal and opens the door to which it is connected.

The Problem   The RFID security solution for keeping unauthorized users from passing through certain doors sounds like a wonderful security idea. Indeed, RFID offers a massive step upward in security from a keypad system or traditional lock. It does not, however, get rid of piggybacking. People will still likely hold the door open for somebody wanting to gain entrance into the building. This can be combated with the steps mentioned above for piggybacking.

An additional problem is that tech-savvy criminals could potentially copy the RFID cards. This may sound like a farfetched impossibility. It is not. There are many professionals who are very capable of copying RFID cards on the fly. There are even circuit designs available on the Internet that explain in detail how to accomplish this feat. Nowadays, most designs are small enough to fit into your pocket, and many designs are placed into decoys such as gutted out MP3 players. After copying an RFID card, all the social engineer has to do is walk up to the reader and transmit his copied card.

Possible Defense An RFID approach to security should be thoroughly thought out prior to implementation. Clearly, if your organization has implemented an RFID solution for doorways, you are likely protecting data and assets of great value. This is why it is important not to implement a solution simply because it sounds as though it might work. You must ensure it will work by playing out all of the possible scenarios. There are a couple of implementations that will act to enhance the already strong security offered by an RFID system.

To begin with, we should understand how most RFID systems work, in theory. This will help facilitate closing the loopholes. Some RFID systems are usually constantly transmitting a signal. Once an RFID is activated by this signal and responds, the reader receives the RFID and unlocks the associated door. This essentially means a reader is constantly looking for a signal to respond. If a criminal presents a forged RFID card to the reader, the reader will not know the difference.

The problem is that all a criminal needs to do is stand next to somebody with an RFID card, activate his own forged "reader," and then duplicate the card. The best method for protecting the cards from this forgery is strong encryption keys. As an example of how weak some supposedly powerful RFID technology really can be, consider the RFID chips used in many newer cars. The owners of these cars only need to have a key on their person in order to unlock the car and start it. These cars don't require a key to actually operate the vehicle.

Some manufacturers designed their keys with excellent encryption schemes, however, others were not so diligent. There was a particular vehicle manufacturer whose keys were easily broken in an investigation performed by students at top American universities. The RFIDs were stolen and hacked within hours, making it possible for students to duplicate the RFID and start the associated cars during the time an average person would be inside working.

The point being made regarding RFID passkeys is that they are not failsafe. Do not place all of your trust in one portion of security. If that one layer breaks, your company will be devastated. Instead, build a strong layered approach to security, wherein multiple levels of security must be overcome including digital, physical, and personal. Social engineering criminals don't simply go after the technical attacks, but instead focus a ton of energy toward gaining as much information as possible from people prior to making their attack.

Keeping the multitiered approach to security in mind, the best "backup" to an RFID system is a vigilant receptionist, and a globally enforced badge system. The three of these implementations will create an environment wherein social engineers will have a very difficult time gaining access to properly protected systems.

9
INCIDENT DETECTION
AND RESPONSE

An emergency is not the time to plan; it's the time to react, so be informed.

Tom Ridge

What Is an Incident?

In regard to computers, an incident is the occurrence of any unwanted or unauthorized network event. These events could be the result of malicious intent or accident, but the end result always causes damage or disruption to network operations.

Incident Detection

Although firewalls are an excellent and necessary means of preventing malicious digital data packets from entering a network, firewalls are not foolproof and all firewalls will eventually allow in some "bad" traffic. Because firewalls are only gatekeepers located at the perimeter of a network, they have no capability to detect, prevent, or otherwise prohibit malicious digital activity within the network. A requirement for any robust security solution is therefore the ability to detect network incidents occurring on the network and respond to them in real-time. One of the best methods for achieving this requirement is the implementation of a good intrusion detection system (IDS). Because of their inherent prevention measures, some systems are referred to as intrusion detection and prevention systems (IDPS; see Figure 9.1).

An IDS monitors events occurring on the network and analyzes them in real-time to determine whether intrusions are occurring. If

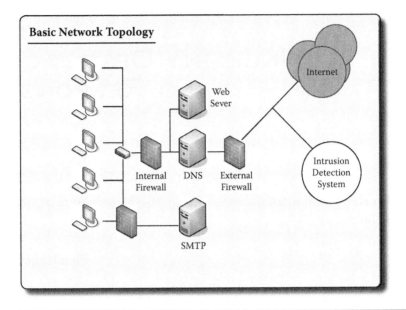

Figure 9.1   Basic Network Topology

the IDS sees malicious traffic occurring, it is recorded and sent to a system administrator. Many IDSs are also vulnerability assessment systems (VASs). A VAS has a baseline of stored variables, which are key indicators of a system's vulnerability. For instance, particular variables of specific firewalls might be checked at intervals, such as traffic patterns and throughput variables. The stored baseline variables are compared against the current state of the variables, and the VAS makes a determination in regard to the system vulnerability; the system reports the state of vulnerability to system administrators.

Types of Intrusion Detection System Installations

When installing an IDS, there are four common installation configurations available to system administrators. These installations include the following.

Signature-Based   Certain worms, viruses, and other malware have a signature of ones and zeros unique only to them. Signature-based

IDSs constantly monitor network activity and look for any file signature that is commonly associated with known malware.

Host-Based   A host-based intrusion detection system (HIDS) is a collection of installations of IDS software installed on several different hosts throughout the network. The IDS software can detect and report upon transfers of data to and from each host. In addition to the data transfer information, HIDS installations can record and report changes occurring on the specific hosts, such as CPU allocation, operating system registry file changes, and so on.

Network-Based   A network-based IDS (often referred to as NIDS) is usually a group of packet analyzers, set up at strategic points in the network. The locations of these analyzers are at specific places where traffic enters or leaves the network. These packet analyzers work together to form a picture of activity throughout the network; they then determine if any of the packet traffic is malicious, and report back to a system administrator.

Anomaly-Based   For any given network traffic, there is a "normal" flow of digital traffic. Sessions are started and terminated, applications are accessed, databases are written to, and files are retrieved, edited, stored, and deleted. Every normal activity has an associated digital pattern. A virus, worm, rootkit, denial-of-service attack, and virtually every other manifestation of malware has an associated pattern as well. These malware patterns appear as anomalies when compared to the normal network traffic. Of course, an IDS doesn't just "know" what is abnormal, but the settings must be programmed by an administrator. In addition, frequent patch updates need to be performed to make sure up-to-date malware definitions are installed.

Process of Intrusion Detection Systems

An IDS is constantly monitoring network activity for any malicious behavior. This process can be broken into the following three distinct stages: event generators, data analysis, and response.

Event Generators   Event generators are the source data being monitored by the IDS. An IDS could be set to monitor activity on the network, on a specific host, or generated by specific applications. Regardless of what source is being monitored by an IDS, whenever suspicious activity is detected, it is further analyzed, recorded, and reported to management.

At this point in the process, a point of distinction may be drawn between an intrusion detection system and an intrusion detection and prevention system. An IDS is considered a passive system, and an IDPS is considered an active system. When an IDS detects what it suspects is malicious activity occurring on the network, it logs it and sends an alert file to the system administrator for further action. An IDPS is active, and may set a firewall to block malicious traffic from the source IP, and then attempt to reestablish the session.

Data Analysis   If the system is strictly an IDS and has no direct response capabilities, then the data are analyzed. Source information analysis may illuminate further security issues, such as an open firewall which has been reset to factory defaults, or unauthorized access to an otherwise secure database. The analysis will provide administrators with the pertinent details of the attack, such as the source IP, destination IP, type of traffic, time of day, files affected, and duration of attack. These pieces of information can be used to very quickly determine the nature of the attack, and what measures should be taken next.

Response   At this point, either the IDS will automatically respond, or an administrator will get involved. Even if the IDS is active and has automatically taken care of the problem, the administrator will still need to follow up on the incident. If a firewall has been reset, for instance, an investigation into how it was reset would need to occur. Questions such as where the firewall is located, who has access to the firewall, whether anybody has logged into the firewall recently, and all recent traffic would need to be considered.

After the initial response takes place, a longer-term response will need to occur. Controls will need to be put into place to prevent similar incidents from occurring, including IDS settings, firewall settings, policy changes, and whatever else is required to protect the network.

Much of the long-term response is covered below in the discussion of computer security incident response teams.

IDS Considerations

As with any security implementation, a system administrator should consider the benefits, drawbacks, and potential pitfalls associated with an IDS. Only through thoughtful consideration of each piece of the security puzzle will the network be protected.

IDS Benefits

- As with most network devices, IDSs can be updated with patches to protect against the ever-changing threats facing the network.
- Because technical workers will not be forced to monitor networks constantly for malicious occurrences, implementing an IDS will save large amounts of technical labor.
- Even nontechnical users are able to work with an IDS to determine the state of the network, and whether the network is especially vulnerable or secure based on current parameters.
- IDSs can be easily used to determine the vulnerability of systems after major changes have occurred to the network, such as the addition of new nodes, replacement and resetting of firewalls, upgrading of operating systems, changing of system hardware components, and so forth.

IDS Drawbacks and Weaknesses

- Because the IDS contains a wealth of information about a particular network's state of security and potential vulnerabilities, having one installed presents another security issue: the need to physically protect the IDS. The IDS, if used for protecting the network, can be an effective and powerful tool. Used in the hands of a digital criminal, the IDS can likewise be an effective and powerful tool for causing harm to an organization.

- Some administrators rely too heavily upon the security provided by IDSs, and as a result have a false sense of security.
IDSs are not meant to be installed and then forgotten. These
systems are not a complete system, and must be used in tandem with solid firewalling, up-to-date antivirus measures,
secure access controls, and good security policy.
- Although these systems point out security failures, vulnerabilities, and attacks occurring on the network, they do not
provide measures for fixing these attacks. Administrators will
still need to respond to attacks.
- If administrators fail to keep the current IDS patches up to
date, vulnerabilities will fail to be recognized. Administrators
and users may fail to see gaping growing holes in security due
to out-of-date firmware.

Incident Response

Eventually, malicious traffic will make it past the perimeter firewalls
of your organization. When this happens, and your IDS alerts network administrators, what is the next step? Depending on the scope
and size of the incident, the associated follow-up for an incident may
not be major. A router may need to have a patch updated, or a operating system may need to be reset to an earlier saved restore point.

Sometimes incidents occur and the results are technically disastrous. Such incidents can be physical or digital in nature. Incidents
could include anything from a natural disaster to a successful attack
and compromise of a customer database. Follow-up for such events is
usually extremely costly and time consuming, and causes damage to
an organization's goodwill. In these cases, the scope of the required
response is so far outside the range of normal operations that a special
team of professionals needs to respond.

Computer Security Incident Response Teams

Through proper and continued maintenance of network equipment
and software, many problems associated with your organization's network infrastructure can be prevented or at least diminished. The fact
remains, though, no matter how prepared an organization is, disaster

cannot be held at bay forever. When issues too large to be fixed by a system upgrade or software patch occur, a team of qualified experts should be available onsite to offer services toward restoring network operations to normalcy. In many organizations, this group of individuals is referred to as the computer security incident response team (CSIRT). These teams are also sometimes referred to as computer emergency quick-response teams, or computer emergency response teams (CERTs). A CSIRT is a team made up of technically qualified individuals who are charged with responding to any computer incident detected by an intrusion detector. Because responding to computer incidents is not a full-time job, the team is generally made up of technically savvy personnel whose main job functions exist outside of the CSIRT. Although a CSIRT's primary function is responding to computer-related incidents, a CSIRT should provide an organization with the following services.

- Computer incident response
- Post-mortem investigations
- Law enforcement liaison
- CSIRT manual
- Event preparedness
- Recommendations for improvements
- Training
- Documentation
- Technical analysis

CSIRT Manual

Whether a committee is involved with company-wide events planning, safety, or computer incident response, a standard operating procedure (SOP) manual should exist to guide their meetings and training sessions. In addition to a copy of the SOPs, each CSIRT manual should also include at least the following.

- A clear chain of command
- Priority of response (the PORT system)
- Standard operating procedures for certain incidents
- A copy of the security plan
- Updated, important company contact information

- Updated, important first responder and law enforcement contact information
- Training notes
- Meeting notes

Clear Chain of Command   The chain of command should have key positions, with outlined responsibilities. In addition, the chain of command should have a clearly defined reporting structure. Each person within the team may have up to five people directly reporting to him or her, however, each person should only be assigned one authority or "boss" in order to facilitate a clearly defined chain of command.

If a problem is massive enough in scope, taskforce teams may be assigned to work with specific problems. For instance, if a server is overcome by a malware attack, one taskforce team might be assigned direct response to the issue, another might be tasked with getting a secondary server up and running temporarily, and another would be given the task of contacting key employees to let them know about the issue, and what is being done about it. As each team finishes its task, their manpower should be folded into the efforts of the next highest priority team, according to the designated priority of response.

Priority of Response Tree (PORT)   During the response to each computer incident, there may be several fires to put out. Upset customers, confused and frustrated employees, broken equipment, physical security, data logging, discussions with law enforcement, investigations and discussions with involved employees, reviewing IDS logs, checking firewall and router history, and so on.

It is the job of the CSIRT to build a priority of response tree, or PORT. The PORT should clearly list what is at stake for each task, and then assign a priority to each task. Priorities should be handled in the following order of importance.

1. Provide Safety for People   The first priority should always be to ensure the physical safety of employees, customers, and anyone else who might have been affected by the incident. If applicable, call the police to help secure the area, search for missing people, or to locate suspects if there are still suspects at large. If a physical disaster has occurred, call 911 and let them know as many specifics as possible, including the nature of the disaster, how many people are involved, what types of injuries (if any) have occurred, and any still-existing threats such as suspects-at-large, downed power lines, flooded areas, spilled chemicals, and so on.

2. Provide Safety for Organization Property   After authorities have been contacted, everybody has been accounted for, and no harm is facing the affected people, the CSIRT can attend to protecting company property. If a digital attack is the source of the incident, the main focus of this step would be to stop the attack. If the incident was physical in nature, it would be best to let the proper authorities clear the area before going back into the building.

3. Focus on Getting Services Running   After providing safety for people and equipment, the CSIRT should focus on getting any downed services back up and running. If power was lost, power generators need to be brought online, and critical systems should be brought up. Network connections to the Internet and between organization campuses will need to be reestablished. Before bringing the network completely online again, be sure to analyze any available logs and current vulnerability levels of the network to determine the best steps for proceeding.

4. Inform Affected Individuals   If customer databases were compromised, the organization will need to contact the customers to let them know. Usually, organizations will inform customers how the incident occurred, the scope of the compromise, and what the organization plans to do to remedy the situation.

5. Incident Review   Whatever the nature and scope of the incident, it should be treated as an opportunity to improve existing policies and controls. The review process for incidents should include thorough post-mortems that illustrate areas for improvement, including changing of personnel, policy, and controls. For all but the smallest of incidents, a formal review with incident causes and suggested future preventions should be created.

6. Follow-Up After a formal incident review has been accomplished, be sure the review isn't simply shelved and forgotten. The CSIRT should do their part to make sure any reasonable suggested controls are put into place, including security policy changes, updating equipment, implementing new training procedures, making appropriate changes to personnel, changing IDS and firewall settings, updating antivirus packages, and whatever else needs to happen to prevent or mitigate the effects of similar future incidents.

7. Legal Implications Whenever dealing with emergency situations, there are often legal considerations. Of course, the safety of people is paramount, and whatever needs to happen to ensure the safety of individuals should happen. Still, make sure that whatever steps your organization is taking in reaction to an incident, proper procedures and laws are being followed. Having a predefined incident action plan with a clearly organized chain of command will help ensure that procedures and legal requirements are followed.

A PORT in Action A CSIRT should be training for future responses. Make sure at least a portion of the time spent training includes going over specific examples, which taskforce teams will be in charge of what, and how the PORT will come into play. For instance, if it is known that somebody has physically broken into the server room, the PORT may be as follows.

1. Ensure physical safety of employees by evacuating the building, calling the appropriate law enforcement agency, and clearing the building of any potential suspects. Make sure people are out of harm's way, but available for interviews as part of a post-mortem investigation.
2. Protect the organization's assets. Examine the physical locks and barriers that failed to protect the server room from unauthorized entry. Be sure to reinstall whatever necessary physical controls are needed to successfully stop similar attempts from being successful in the future.
3. Get services up and running ASAP. Make sure power to the server room is available. If there is a second server room, move

necessary hardware to the other room. Start providing "normal" network services as soon as possible.

4. Protect customer data. Part and parcel of normal network services includes security controls and measures to protect data contained on network databases. Before bringing the server room back online, make sure firewalls, IDSs, and antiviral measures are in place and ready to handle the traffic.

5. Inform customer service employees of occurrence, as well as services affected, in order that they can appropriately communicate to the organization's customers what has happened, which services were affected, what the organization is doing to remedy the situation, how the customer's data are being protected, and how soon they can expect a return to normal service.

6. Follow up with customers, if need be.

7. Involve legal counsel in each of these steps, to ensure proper and legal handling throughout the recovery process.

The PORT is considered a tree, because even though the above list is in numerical order, numbers 4, 2, and 3 can be performed simultaneously, instead of in order. In other words, instead of following a strict linear flow of operations, there may be branches of operations within the tree occurring at the same time.

Of course, the physical safety of people should come before anything else is accomplished during a response to an incident. This includes a break-in or natural disaster. After people have been secured, communications should be next on the list, if they've been affected. Following communications, all critical services, such as power and water should be fixed. Restoring services to operational status while communicating with customers can then be tackled.

Standard Operating Procedures (SOPs)   The time to figure out how to properly handle a disaster is not during the disaster, but prior to one actually occurring. Responses to events should be ready to be put into action once word is received about an incident. The experts tasked with responding to an incident should have rehearsed exactly what to do several times before putting their skills to the test.

Standard operating procedures are what ensure everybody is on the same page of a response. They enforce the chain of command and provide a foundation from which to launch a response to an attack. Without SOPs, responders will be groping in the dark at answers, and nobody will be speaking the same language. Chaos will ensue, and the team might wind up creating more damage than help. Without a concrete plan of attack, the CSIRT will also likely duplicate efforts, and nobody will be in charge of specific task forces. Things will not get done in a timely and effective fashion. With the application of CSIRT SOPs, everybody will know her job, how to do it, and when to do it. A concerted effort will make all the difference when trying to battle a botnet or trace an attacker's IP address.

Security Plan   Included in every CSIRT member's manual should be a copy of the organization's security plan. Again, this is not to be used for reference during a response, but should be used to guide training and meetings. The security plan should dictate how often the CSIRT meets, and with what goals they will meet. It is a good idea to meet at least once a quarter for training, drilling, and discussing current threats. The team should use this meeting time to hone existing technical skills, share knowledge, and review security threats that have occurred since the last meeting.

Updated, Important Company Contact Information   Every conceivable person who might need to be called, including everybody from the CEO to the maintenance staff should have an updated contact number in the CSIRT manual. If possible, home phone numbers and e-mail and physical addresses should also be included. This is especially true for company officers, who will need to be notified immediately of any situation that could place the organization in some sort of liability with customers.

Updated, Important First Responder and Law Enforcement Contact Information   If your organization has experienced a disaster that places people in direct harm, 911 will likely be the only number you need to dial to get hold of the appropriate first responders. Other times, nonemergency personnel will need to be contacted. For instance, if somebody breached your digital security, you'll need to call the police, but not 911, as nobody is in any apparent physical danger. Where possible, include the names and contact numbers of specific law enforcement and first responders. Make sure to include the rank or position of the contact. Just as in the military, it is a sign of respect to appreciate and recognize the rank of first responders. This is especially true of law enforcement and firefighters.

Training and Meeting Notes   Like SOPs, training and meeting notes should be available to CSIRT members for review. The notes created and disseminated during training and CSIRT meetings will work toward establishing improved SOPs, and will be the basis from which to update existing security policies. In addition, training notes will act as an ad hoc reference manual.

Types of CSIRT Teams

The CSIRT can either be an ad hoc team of tech professionals, or they can be a formalized group of individuals dedicated to the prevention of and response to computer incidents. The latter option always provides the most efficient and effective approach to a CSIRT solution. If a team is already formed, then regular training can occur, and simulations can be run. These simulations and training sessions should cover potential attacks, review network security weak spots, and hammer out standard operating procedures for all CSIRT operatives. The time to figure out the chain of command is not during an incident response.

Although a core group of employees will likely make up the main body for most CSIRT activities, including training and simulations, the CSIRT can expand and contract depending on the needs of a particular incident. For instance, a small incident may only require a single task force, whereas larger-scaled events may require the entire CSIRT, plus law enforcement, search-and-rescue specialists, consultants, and legal counsel.

The duration for which a CSIRT responds to an incident will also vary depending on the scope and nature of the event. Smaller events might require only an hour or two of response, and larger events might require several days, weeks, or months of response, including debriefing, physical upgrading and repairs, training employees, handling lawsuits, dealing with customers, and whatever else is required.

Non-CSIRT Responsibilities   Being a member of the CSIRT does not preclude an employee from the requirements of his daily job. In fact, having the technology training and experience made available through active participation on the team will allow team members to bring more value and insight into their jobs. Indeed, having the various departments and locations in the organization represented by team members will give the team a better view of computer security issues that may need to be handled.

For instance, if a team member notices a lackadaisical approach to security, such as employees not locking their workstations, or doors being left open to otherwise secure areas, the team member can bring these issues up during a CSIRT meeting, and proper training and policy changes would likely result. In other words, members of the CSIRT team are likely part of a larger security team, and are not only concerned with measures taken during incident responses, but also with the overall prevention of incidents and protection of data.

Response to Events

Perhaps the main reason organizations decide to implement an official CSIRT is to have a "ready team" that can appropriately respond to digital incidents that greatly adversely affect network security. For instance, if a worm is released on the computer networks, the damage to an organization could be catastrophic. Network throughput speeds would slow to a crawl; computers would be sluggish in their operations, because all the processing resources of the computer would be tied up in duplicating and spreading the illegal worm. In some cases, entire systems might have to be reformatted, and critical data could be lost. In an extremely short period of time the worm would likely spread outside the organization's perimeter and begin infecting other networks. The time to clean up a mess such as this could be as little as a couple of hours to as long as several days, and sometimes even longer.

Or, perhaps a virus containing a keylogger is downloaded unbeknownst to a user. While the user goes about their daily operations, the virus is tracking every stroke punched into their workstation keyboard and remotely storing the data into a database. Because keyloggers are designed to be well hidden, they use very little bandwidth, and often the information sent to their remote hosts "ride" along with outgoing traffic, as to make the sent information nearly undetectable. Network speeds and access to internal databases would therefore likely not suffer. The real damage due to the keylogger would come into play when and if the cyber criminal collecting the data decided to act.

A well-placed keylogger could give a malicious user access to databases and information that could be leveraged against a company for blackmail or extortion. Or, if a cyber criminal simply wanted to be destructive, they could wreak havoc by deleting files or restructuring the network in a manner that would render key systems inaccessible. Keyloggers are especially dangerous when the concealed nature of the attack is considered. The cyber criminal implementing the may just decide to wait until an opportune time to use the information, or may not ever use it.

In the above examples of the worm and a keylogger, we have two types of attacks that can bring an organization to its knees. The worm can slow network speeds to such a pace as to make the network completely useless during the attack. Imagine how much money would be lost due to your organization not having access to customer files, employee records, and any other critical company documents located on an inaccessible network. Although a worm's damage is more immediate in nature, and the effects of the attack can be felt throughout the network, the example of a keylogger attack is a bit more problematic concerning damage caused, due to the hidden nature of the damage and exposure of the attack.

Because keyloggers are generally designed to hide in the background of a computer, users will likely never know they are installed and recording keystrokes. This means a keylogger could be collecting confidential information in the background for months or years, without the knowledge or consent of the user. Most good antivirus programs will alleviate the issue through early detection and elimination, although some can still slip through the cracks for at least a few weeks. Imagine how many pieces of company confidential information are input into your computer during a typical workday, let alone a few weeks.

The problem of a keylogger occurs once the attacker decides to capitalize on the gathered information. Depending on the information gathered, the attacker may have access to company secrets, high-level login information, or perhaps even company credit card numbers. Most keyloggers are used for profit, so you can count on the attacker selling your information or using it for personal gain at some time. Once the time comes for the attacker to use the information, they can do massive amounts of damage to financial accounts, and could possibly even use any personal employee information to request (and receive) credit from banks and other financial institutions. Once they've trashed one person's financial identity, they'll move on to the next.

As far as organizations should be concerned, destroying personal credit is simply the beginning of the issue. Having your organization's employee records compromised by a criminal does little to improve your standing with the public. In fact, when considering the cost involved with such an attack, be sure to factor in legal fees associated with going to court due to the lawsuits your organization will surely face. Once the lawsuits end, your organization will still have to deal with the loss of public trust, as well as the drop in employee morale, if the attack in fact involved employee information.

Further public relations issues include dealing directly with the organization's Internet service provider (ISP) for the purposes of reporting the attack to them, as well as possibly getting records of from where the attacks stemmed. Keeping a good rapport with the ISP is advised, as they are your organization's gateway into the Internet. These issues all speak to just how critical having a group of people assigned to computer security breaches is. The required tasks arising from such attacks range from reformatting disks and reviewing router logs to public relations issues.

Preparedness Is Key

When the proverbial levee breaks, you will need specialized workers to protect your organization from the flood of problems and devastation that will undoubtedly pour in. Make sure your team is ready for attacks and system failures. The time to learn how to respond is not after an attack. Those responsible for the protection of networks should know how to assess the scope of the problem, how to respond, and how to mitigate the issue in the future.

Recognizing Scope

Once an attack is successfully levied against an organization, the CSIRT must be able to quickly identify the scope of the attack. If network speeds are bottlenecking in a particular location of the network, the team should be able to diagnose the problem quickly with appropriate network monitoring software, as well as a review of network traffic logs to determine the origin of the problem. Through the use of network troubleshooting techniques and interviewing employees, the CSIRT should be able to efficiently determine who and what has been affected by the attack. Only once the scope is determined can an appropriate response be developed and implemented.

Management of Occurrences

It is not enough simply to know how to respond to events. It is essential that the CSIRT have the appropriate level of skill and experience to respond to attacks and network problems; however, they must also be concerned with the prevention and mitigation of such incidents.

Prevention   This entire book is aimed at assisting organizations with the design and implementation of proper and thorough measures with the intent of protecting networks through preventive techniques and policies. The CSIRT should be a key component in developing those policies and techniques unique to your organization. The intent of the CSIRT, in regard to prevention, is eliminating access to critical systems from unauthorized entities. For the sake of this intent, we include human entities as well as natural entities such as weather. As long as this purpose is maintained when crafting policy and training employees, computer security in your organization can only get stronger and better with time. If a CSIRT activity is not producing an end that increases the organization's network security, reevaluate the activity to see if it is truly necessary, or if it can be altered or tied together with another process or policy in an effort to meet the goal of improved computer security.

Mitigation   Sometimes, total security of a system is cost prohibitive, or it would require measures that would so substantially affect the operations of the organization that it is simply not a feasible or practical solution to the need for security. In these cases, mitigation of attacks is still possible. In fact, nearly all security measures are simply mitigating the chance of a successful attack. Even military installations could be successfully attacked with enough planning, manpower, and resources. An organization should keep this truth in mind when attempting to secure networks. Never should the false feeling of total security allow an organization to rest, allowing security measures to slip.

On the other side of the coin, CSIRTs should not feel hopeless in their efforts toward creating a more secure network. Admit the weaknesses of the network, but don't resolve yourself to "give in" and accept them as unchangeable facts. If a network is exceptionally large and has very few security measures in place, don't simply throw your hands up and believe that such a large network could never be protected. Don't allow yourself to get overwhelmed by the entire project at once. Instead, focus on one implementable solution at a time. Build a checklist of things that can be done, and then do them. Begin with software solutions, such as router settings, upgraded and up-to-date antivirus software, and current security patches. Then, focus on what cost-effective hardware can be implemented to shore up any weak spots. Build strong DMZs through which all traffic must pass, and beef up security at those points.

Event Postmortems

One of the key responsibilities of a CSIRT team is the thorough investigation of computer incidents. Included in these investigations are the root causes of failure in security, the responsible parties, and how to prevent similar incidents from occurring in the future.

The root causes of an incident include not only the actions taken by an attacker, but the failures of the target organization's security. In this manner, finding the root cause establishes a cause for allowance of the failure, as well as establishing responsibility for the failure. For instance, a distributed denial-of-service attack is an action taken by an attacker through the use of botnets. The success of such an attack is allowed by a failure somewhere in the layers of applied security. It is the job of the CSIRT to determine where the failure(s) occurred. For instance, was the Internet service provider not providing proper filtering of IP addresses? Were the target organization's routers not set up to deny teardrop attacks? The questions regarding how the attack was allowed to happen are as varied as the attacks themselves.

Many people wonder why it is necessary to determine where the responsibility, or fault, of allowing an attack to occur lies. Why go through the trouble of investigating who is responsible, simply to point a finger at them? The point is not the assignment of blame. The reason CSIRTs must in fact determine who or what was responsible is because only then can such attacks be prevented in the first place.

If the responsible party acted out of negligence, then appropriate disciplinary measures need to be taken. If the party responsible truly didn't know any better as a result of poor training, then four main issues must be addressed.

1. *Untraining*: First of all, the employee who was improperly trained must be "untrained" in whatever issue caused him to fail in the first place, and then he must be trained properly.

2. *Retraining:* Second, the training process itself must be reviewed. Was it a process or policy in the training sessions that instigated the improper training? Was it a bad trainer? Whatever the issue is in the training sessions, it must be remedied. This means either retraining the trainer, or changing a policy.

3. *Following the Flow of Training:* The next issue is retraining all of the other people affected by the training issue. If the issue is important enough, then everybody who received the false information should attend a special training session specifically aimed at re-educating them regarding the failed security policy.

4. *The Root Cause:* Last, although most important, the CSIRT must determine what caused the faulty training experience in the first place. If the trainer was improperly informed, where did he get his information? What has changed since the information was accepted to be fact, and what steps can be taken to ensure similar information is properly checked for

accuracy and validity in the future? Some people may insist that CSIRTs should not be employed in this manner. Instead of focusing their attention on past events, they need to be prepared for future incidents. By dissecting and thoroughly understanding events that have occurred in the past, CSIRTs will gain knowledge to more readily understand any new challenge they might encounter.

Collaboration

In addition, some organizations forget that even though divisions and departments exist within the walls of the organization, only a truly collaborative work environment will achieve a culture in which security can thrive. Through a careful examination of the root cause of failure, the CSIRT can help troubleshoot issues that may be occurring in training, which will go a long way toward facilitating a more secure network.

Recommendations for Improvements

Unfortunately, it sometimes takes a disaster to strike before we recognize our failure to properly prepare and protect ourselves from catastrophe. Through the information gathered during incident postmortems, CSIRTs will be able to provide a wealth of information to other IS professionals within the organization they serve. A formal review of incidents should be given to management, along with the CSIRT's recommendations for improving existing security measures.

Law Enforcement Liaisons

If a target organization experiences a direct attack aimed at its server, and the IS professionals within the organization are aware of who is responsible for the crime, it is likely the police will be called. Most of the time, police are genuinely too busy fighting crime on the streets to take time out to respond to your organization's "disaster." Apprehending real, live dangerous criminals on a daily basis somehow dampens the validity of the necessity to involve police in a digital investigation. It is therefore a good idea to foster relationships with local law enforcement. This way, when your organization is in need of assistance, your organization is at least familiar enough with the local police to call the appropriate people. It is always much more reassuring to have somebody you have personally spoken with (and maybe even met a couple of times) respond to your police call. Toward this end, make sure there is at least one person on the CSIRT who has met with somebody in the local police department with the intent of discussing appropriate responses to organization incidents.

10
PHYSICAL SECURITY

If you want total security, go to prison.

Dwight D. Eisenhower

A critical, yet often overlooked aspect of information security is physical security. Entire teams of information technology specialists are employed to monitor networks, configure routers and firewalls, and otherwise provide technical, software-related protection for the networks they serve. These measures are not simply a good idea; they are necessary. More than just technical prowess and digital know-how is needed to provide protection of an entire network infrastructure successfully, though. In order to thoroughly protect all of the data contained on the computers, as well as all of the systems in the network, the computers themselves must be physically protected from harm. A robust physical security program will properly address human causes of network failure including accidents and intentional harm, as well as natural causes such as weather.

Human-Caused Incidents

As long as people use computers, computers and data will always be in danger of being destroyed by accidents. The two categories of accidents, in regard to computer systems, are physical and software-related accidents. Physical accidents occur when a person accidentally causes physical damage to a computer or network system. Software accidents occur when somebody accidentally alters a software setting and destroys or alters data contained on the computer. For most accidental forms of physical destruction, simple controls and policies can be put into place to help ensure better physical security for computers and network components.

Accidental Spills

In regard to physical accidents, food spills are relatively common. Somebody could place his water, coffee, or other beverage next to his laptop or keyboard, and then accidentally spill the drink onto the system. Most spills will not cause major damage, although laptops will likely experience more damage due to a spill because of the compact and delicate nature of the system. Spills can be remedied by implementing and enforcing a "no drink, no food" policy, which would keep drinks and other foodstuffs away from desktops and out of server rooms. Short of such a policy, it would be wise to at least implement and enforce a covered-container policy, wherein any drink in an office area must be in a covered container, so that if the container dropped it would not spill; or at least any spill would be minimized. A good policy, regardless of what is required for rank and file users at their workstations, is never to allow any drinks or foodstuffs, regardless of the container, into a server room. The critical nature of the server room systems, coupled with the fact they contain more opportunities to cause damage than a normal workstation make them uniquely off-limits for food. The potential financial, legal, labor, and network performance losses are just too great.

Accidental Destruction

Although physical accidents, such as a misplaced knee into a computer cart, or a shoulder brush that knocks over a server rack tend to happen a lot less frequently, they can cause much more damage than a spilled drink. If somebody accidentally knocks a monitor off a desktop, the monitor will almost certainly be destroyed by the relatively short fall. Because people are usually careful around computers, stationary systems are not generally in harm's way.

Accidental Transport Damage

Where most accidental incidents will likely occur is during the transportation of computer systems. A policy that works to protect equipment in transit is not allowing people to ever move their own equipment. Moving equipment should always be performed by IT technicians, and always with great care. Even the IT technicians should not ever pick up a PC and simply carry it from one desktop to another. It would be wise to have a transportation cart to move equipment from place to place. The cart should have a strap that securely holds the equipment while in transit.

Server Room Accidents

When crafting a policy for the proper transport and care of computer systems, special attention should be paid to the server room and its contents. For instance, cabling should never be left on the ground, but should be routed carefully behind systems, so that nobody will trip on the cables when walking across the room. Be sure to keep wires organized, too.

Wire organization may not appear to be an issue in terms of preventing accidents, but consider the times when equipment must be moved from one location to another, or when servers need to be replaced or worked on. Too many server rooms have massive bundles of cables underneath, behind, and around the computer systems in the room. A technician may know exactly which cables to disconnect, but because of their knotted and disorganized fashion, disconnecting one wire will likely pull on and loosen, or completely disconnect, a different and unrelated connection. Such an unseen connection might go unnoticed by the installer, and could cause network performance problems. Although wire connections are some of the easiest issues to remedy, they are sometimes the last to be checked, and so a disconnected wire may not be looked into as a possibility until hours of wasted network troubleshooting have already occurred.

Losing network connectivity is never acceptable for systems that need to be continuously running; make sure your organization is doing what it can to prevent such unnecessary disconnects. Many technicians are more concerned with "getting the system running" rather than keeping it organized. Impress upon them the importance of a cleanly run bundle of wires, and they will be thanking you soon enough. The hallmark of a well-run, high-tech server room is a well-thought-out layout and cleanly routed wires.

Intentional Destruction

Disgruntled employees, vandals, and criminals all have the ability and desire to hurt your organization. Whatever their reason for causing your system harm, be sure you plan for their attempts at disruption with thorough physical security measures. Depending on the criticality of the systems and information you are aiming to provide protection for, you may consider security systems, alarms, specialized door locks, cameras, and in some cases paid guards and security checkpoints.

Disgruntled Employees   The best defense against disgruntled employees is a set of robust employee management policies. These policies should include vetting employees prior to employment. The process should be strong enough to catch the vast majority of problem employees before they work for the organization. Make sure the organization uses a combination of background checks, personal interviews, and reference checks as part of the vetting process.

Once an employee is working for your organization, management policies should focus on clear and professional communication with the employee. Many organizations provide annual or semiannual reviews. Although these reviews are important, they can catch employees off guard, and surprise them with bad news of their poor performance. Managers and employees should recognize the need for a continual performance review. Frequent honest communication regarding the employee's performance will improve work performance by building a relationship between him and his manager. It will also head off any negative surprises to the employee during a scheduled review. These "surprises" are often the trigger that sets retribution in motion, and can usually be easily avoided through simple communication.

When an employee is let go, follow the HR checklist. Be sure to retrieve all company property, especially any keys, proximity cards, and dual factor authentication fobs they might have. Close any access to e-mail and change the password for their login.

Vandals and Criminals   For the sake of this text, vandals are considered criminals who just want to destroy things for the fun of it. Criminals are usually more purpose-driven, and have a specific goal in mind. For instance, a criminal may want to break into a building to steal files or computer equipment, or to gather information for later use against a company. Both vandals and criminals can be deterred through the implementation of robust physical security measures, including perimeter fences, security systems, door locks, cameras, checkpoints, and security guards. Of course, how many of these measures, and the degree to which they are applied, will depend upon the importance of what your organization is trying to protect.

Physical Security Measures

Perimeter Fences

Installing a fence around a campus or particular building is a fairly common method of providing a basic level of physical security. For the sake of this discussion, a perimeter fence is any physical barrier, from thick concrete walls to short hedgerows, that can exist as a physical barrier between the organization and the outside world. As is true with most security measures, fences may vary in size and level of security offered. A 20-foot tall, 4-foot thick concrete wall topped with razor wire and machine guns offers a much different level of security than a 3-foot tall picket fence. Both provide security, but the implementation of each installation carries with it different intents.

The example of a gun-laden concrete wall provides an extreme, militaristic level of security. Usually, these walls are provided in an attempt to keep certain people or property inside, and unauthorized individuals outside at all costs. Examples of this type of security include maximum security prisons and military forts. Only the most sophisticated, highly armed, and trained individuals would ever attempt a direct physical assault on such a compound.

Although it may not appear to offer any security, the white picket fence does provide a level of security to buildings. Human nature dictates a certain level of respect for boundaries, regardless of how tall or easy to overcome. A small white picket fence is a clear physical delineation between public and private property. This type of barrier will prevent casual passersby from looking into windows and exploring further. Of course, not everybody will be so polite, and some people will happily step over such barriers in search of excitement. In these situations, the barrier still holds some benefit to security. If other people happen to spot a person stepping or climbing over a perimeter barrier, it will likely be enough to register as odd, and may even cause alarm. Even though someone observing the trespasser may not call the police, the possibility of being seen by others is usually enough to stop most trespassers from venturing beyond clearly defined borders, no matter how easily overcome.

Security Systems

One of the most basic approaches to security is the installation of a good security system. The options are endless, and range from a self-installed Radio Shack system to a professionally installed system that automatically contacts law enforcement, fire services (if appropriate), and key employees when an attack occurs. Consider the security system a foundation of security upon which your organization can build. The most basic system simply sounds a loud piercing alarm intended to scare off would-be thieves. If you don't believe your organization currently needs more than the simplest system, but you anticipate growth that would mandate a more sophisticated approach to security, be sure to purchase your system with the idea of growth in mind. Make sure that if you want to add a live camera system or law enforcement response at a later time, you can do so. Most systems allow for such expansion, so you shouldn't have a problem finding a well-priced solution for your needs, yet still allowing for potential future growth.

Door Locks

It goes without saying that any door leading to a critical system or important equipment should have a secure lock to protect it from unauthorized entries. The most basic approach to locks is the deadbolt. Make sure all of your external doors have one. Any workshop, garage, or storage room that leads outside should be considered outside your main building, so that any door from that storage area leading directly into your main office area is considered an external door. For instance, in a domestic residence, the door leading from the garage into the house should be considered an external door, even though it does not lead directly outside.

Of course any main door that leads outside from the garage or shop area should also have a deadbolt, to maximize protection. This rule has more to do with the relatively insecure nature of garage doors than with anything else. Take time to really look at the security of a garage door and you'll quickly realize how easy it would be for a determined burglar to bust in one or more of the panels. Such doors usually have only a very thin layer of siding, behind which is a one- to two-inch layer of foam. A few hard kicks will break in many of these doors. Although deadbolts offer good single-point physical security at certain doors, they do not offer a complete answer to physical security. Make sure all of your security solutions, physical or otherwise, don't rely on a single point.

Controlling Physical Keys Many larger companies have several campuses. On those campuses are many buildings. Within those buildings are dozens, sometimes hundreds of rooms with myriad uses and varying security levels. Many of these rooms are access controlled through the use of a door lock. Considering how important the contents of these rooms are, controlling keys should be on the top of the list of physical security measures taken by an organization. Properly controlling access to keys presents a few unique challenges, but overall is a straightforward issue of implementing sound policies and following through with them.

The first goal of proper key management is keeping good records of who has keys to which doors. An up-to-date physical key database should be kept, either in Human Resources or the Security Department. Even if the database is not actually kept by the HR Department, a tie-in to the employment status and job descriptions for employees with keys should be a part of the key management database. If an employee is terminated, or her position changes in a manner that affects which keys she should have, the keeper of the physical key database (PKD) should be notified of any changes in the employee's level of access. Key retrieval should be on a checklist for any exit interview, or when the employee moves to another position within the organization that negates the need for their current keys. The bottom line is that whenever changes in employment status mandate corresponding changes in key possession among employees, the PKD needs to be updated as well.

Physical locks present another unique security challenge. Keys can be easily duplicated for a nominal fee at nearly any hardware store. Even the words DO NOT DUPLICATE don't provide any level of assurance to key owners that the key won't actually be duplicated. In addition to the ease of duplication, locks are usually very expensive to change. This is especially true of commercial grade locks, which generally offer better protection than locks intended for residential customers. In addition, the physical nature of keys means authorized users may accidentally misplace their keys, or their keys might get stolen. The truth of the matter is that however expensive or secure a lock your company employs on one of the doors, the ease of duplication, and the possibility of an authorized key falling into unauthorized hands precludes it from being a full solution to physically stopping unauthorized visitors from entering the organization's buildings.

Even though door locks can't offer absolute assurance, they are still a necessary part of any complete security solution. Having locked doors provides yet another level of security, which, when combined with the other measures in this chapter, works toward providing total security for an organization.

Types of Door Locks Depending on the room your organization is attempting to protect, you will need to seriously think about what type of lock you will want to purchase and install. A fairly good level of security can be implemented with common locks, however, the best protection for server rooms, engineering rooms, or other rooms where critical and sensitive organizational documentation is stored is with the implementation of much more secure and specialized locks.

Cylinder Locks Cylinder locks are ubiquitous, and are used to lock most home doors. The majority of deadbolts and door handle locks are cylinder locks. The operation of the cylinder lock includes a cylinder, plug, and a cam. The plug is contained within the cylinder, and the cam is attached to the plug. The cam is part of a mechanism that slides the deadbolt back and forth. So, with the rotation of the plug within the cylinder, the cam turns and as a result the deadbolt either slides into the "locked" or "unlocked" position. Normally, the plug is immobile within the cylinder. This is due to pins attached to the cylinder that are pushed into their respective slots into the side of the plug by small springs. When the correct key is slid into the plug, the key "lifts" each pin the exact distance out of the plug to allow the plug to turn freely. The turning of the plug thereby turns the cam, and as a result the bolt moves.

The problem with the cylinder lock is that it is relatively easy for many criminals to pick. With a few minutes and good set of lock picks, most of these locks can be easily picked by "feeling" the pins and pushing them out of the plug and allowing the cam and plug to spin. Another problem with many of these locks is the creation and dissemination of what are known as "bump keys." Bump keys are essentially special keys designed to "bump" the pins in the cylinder, thereby rendering the lock useless.

Strongly consider the room you are attempting to secure when choosing the door's lock, and realize there is more than one option. For instance, pick-resistant locks are designed to prohibit bump keys and picks from working.

Keypad Locks   The most common next step up from a standard deadbolt is the electronic keypad lock. Although the physical lock of this door is extremely resistant to picking and generally offers more physical strength around the area of the lock due to the bulk of the steel-framed key pad, be aware of social engineering attacks. For instance, criminals could easily piggyback behind somebody who is authorized to enter the doorway, or they could simply stand a safe distance behind somebody with the combination and look over that person's shoulder to learn the password.

Biometric Locks   What is even better than the installation of a key-pad lock is the installation of a biometric lock. Up until recently, this technology was reserved for military and ultra-high-security facilities. Nowadays, it is not uncommon to see these locks used in even the most mundane of locks, including some lockers, and even for entrance into some theme parks. Biometrics are also used on some secure flash devices, which require users to swipe their finger on the top of the USB device before gaining access to the information contained within.

Cameras

Nowadays, high-quality digital cameras can be purchased for under $100. In the scope of an average day, you will likely be recorded on more than 20 cameras owned by private companies, from the local barista to the cameras at the grocery store and possibly where you work. These cameras provide an extra level of security support to your entire system. If you plan on using these cameras as a deterrent, then make sure they are widely visible. If you are simply monitoring what is going on inside your buildings and don't want them to be readily noticeable, keep that in mind when installing them. Be sure also to consider any local laws that may affect the placement of cameras.

Security Guards

Sometimes, security needs warrant the hiring and stationing of full-time guards. You have the option of hiring full-time internal guards, or contracting a third party for such services. If you plan on hiring a third-party firm, make sure you check the firm's references as well as references listed for individual guards. If you don't check references and ensure you are hiring fully qualified, quality individuals, you are essentially placing unknown people in charge of your most critical assets. Regardless of who you hire, make sure you obtain experienced people with a proven track record. Also, be certain to obtain extensive background checks for the people hired. Because of the relatively low cost of performing these checks, it is wise to have them performed regardless of whether a third-party security firm claims to provide them as well. In addition, if your organization feels having security guards is a necessity, be sure to keep local laws in mind before hiring them.

Checkpoints

Security checkpoints can be internal or external to the building being protected. Internal checkpoints will usually cordon off a certain area, such as a server room, or an office area where sensitive information is dealt with or stored. These checkpoints are usually delineated by the addition of a locked door that requires an additional key or code. A key should be considered any item, or token, that will gain a person access through the door, such as an RFID card, a card with a magnetic strip, or even just a regular key that physically unlocks a lock. Other options for obtaining authorized access to internal checkpoints include doors with a coded access pad or a biometric scanner.

Something to consider before placing a checkpoint is the required foot traffic and relative speed with which an individual may pass through the checkpoint. It is important to strike a well-thought-out balance between security and expediency. Don't create checkpoints that cause unnecessary slowing of foot traffic in already congested areas. For instance, if you plan on installing a checkpoint at the main entrance of your building that requires sliding a magnetic strip to gain internal access, consider installing a turnstile system instead of having a door that closes and locks between each person. Turnstiles are generally more expensive, but the added expediency is often worth the cost. Because turnstiles are smaller than a doorway, multiple access points can be installed, further expediting the foot traffic of employees.

Construction Considerations

In some cases, you may have the ability to influence the actual design and construction of the building you are trying to protect. When thinking about the security of the building from the point of concept, consider the external walls, barriers, venting systems, roof access, internal walls, and fire suppression systems. These are the systems that, if well thought out, could provide an extra layer of protection from the outset, without forcing the organization to spend a lot more money to implement.

External Walls External walls can be the source of many security problems. Because they are the first and in many cases the last measure of defense from the outside world, make certain to consider the systems they are designed to protect on the inside. These walls should be thick enough to withstand a physical attack appropriate to the level of security your data and systems demand. In most cases, this simply means a person should not be able to gain physical access through the use of a crowbar or hammer. External doors should have appropriate locks and be built of appropriately strong material, such as steel, to prevent an intruder from breaking in.

Another security issue in regard to external walls is that of protrusions from the wall. Anything that sticks out from the building should be seriously looked at to determine if it could help a criminal gain access into your building. Decorations, and even awnings and lampposts will sometimes provide would-be burglars with footholds and handholds for climbing the sides of your organization's building. Many commercial buildings, for instance, have lateral vertical slats that run the height of the building. These slats can offer grips and footholds for skilled climbers, as can window sills and spaces between brickwork. This consideration is mostly important for much higher security buildings, although it should at least be discussed when designing a new building. Just because an office is on a higher floor than ground level does not mean the contents of the office are secure.

Internal Walls   The external walls are only part of the physical security issue. It is, after all, possible for a criminal to breach external walls of even the most secure buildings. If a burglar does gain access through your external walls, your internal security is your last shot at stopping them, or at least detaining them long enough for the security system to contact law enforcement. Internal walls are one of the main ways internal security can be assured. Many organizations place their servers in rooms walled with sheetrock, or even in large, half-walled cubicle offices. Of these two options, the sheetrock-walled room is better with regard to security. Although the sheetrock option is generally far more secure than the cubicle option, they are both lacking in total security. A cement or brick wall would be ideal for security, however, other considerations such as fire system plumbing, electricity, and ventilation prevail in terms of practicality.

Regardless of whether your organization uses sheetrock, cubicle walls, or even brick or cement, when possible the walls should rise all the way from the foundation to the actual ceiling. Many organizations have false ceilings, above which all the utility wires and piping are run. Consider how easy it might be to push up a ceiling tile and climb up above the false ceiling and you'll quickly realize this is not the most secure setup. Once somebody gains overhead access, it would be a small matter to figure out where the server room is and then drop down into it. Also, many server rooms have false floors, as discussed below. This isn't to say having false ceilings in general is a bad idea. It only suggests that the most critical and secure of systems should have such floor-to-ceiling walling, when possible. Of course, location, budget, and many other contributing factors will lead you to determine the correct internal wall solution for your organization.

Plumbing   Plumbing is a key issue when considering internal walls. Fire suppression systems will be considered in a different part of this book, but in regard to the discussion of physical security, plumbing is considered the introduction of water into and throughout your organization's building. It is important to think about the proximity of computer systems to the nearest plumbing source.

The reason you must consider how close your computer equipment is to water is not just for the sake of cooling it down, but instead to provide enough distance from any potential leaks or pipe bursts. This is especially true when considering externally walled pipes, whose temperatures can, in some parts of the country, reach those that could potentially freeze the water inside and burst pipes. After these broken pipes thaw, water will drip and pour out, destroying any electrical equipment in its path. If a server room must be surrounded by, or in the path of necessary plumbing, consider lifted floors.

Lifted Floors   Lifted floors are common in many high-tech server rooms. Because of the routing of hundreds of different wires, air conditioning, and plumbing, server rooms can quickly become a messy hub of system connections. The most elegant answer for keeping this mess out of harm's way is to bury the wires, pipes, and conduits under the floor. Floor panels become access doors for inspecting, removing, and installing new system components.

If your organization decides false floor panels are necessary, make sure they are not used simply as a way to hide a big mess. Server room technicians should still take the same care to properly route wires as they would if the wires were not hidden from view. If systems are being installed, the correct color-coding and labeling should be installed on each wire as it is placed under the floor panels. In addition, massive bundles and nests of cables should not be accepted, but cables should be cut to an appropriate length for the install, and then tie-wrapped in a clean fashion.

Keeping the space under the floor panels clean with well-routed wires is important on a few different levels. Practically speaking, cleanly installing each system allows for easy and uncomplicated access to every wire. Dozens of systems can be routed along the same path without causing confusion. As long as the systems and wires don't overlap, and are color-coded or consistently labeled at designated lengths along the installation, even a technician who is unfamiliar with the install can easily tell the difference between wires. This allows troubleshooting, installation, and removal of systems to be a lot simpler and headache free. In addition to being easier to work on, these clean installations are often a matter of pride and the hallmark of a well-managed server room. Once technicians see what a difference such an installation makes in regards to their ability to properly care for a network, they will usually pride themselves on building such installs.

Weather/Natural Disasters

Even if it were possible to prevent people from breaching the physical perimeters of your campus and buildings, and physical accidents were not an issue, nature will always eventually throw a curveball into your network infrastructure. This could come in the form of a windstorm, rainstorm, lightning, flooding, earthquake, or any other form of natural damage. Prevention of physical damage and contingencies for such occurrences should be made when considering physical threats against your organization's networks.

Windstorms

There are a couple of possible failure modes when dealing with protection from windstorms. The first, and biggest, consideration is the fact that power can be shut down due to wind damage at the power station. If your system is in an area prone to windstorms, it is also likely that power outages occur frequently. Become familiar with how often these power outages occur and at about what speed the wind needs to be flowing before wind damage causes these outages at the local power station. After gathering data about how often the power in your organization's area is interrupted annually, and for how long, the organization will need to purchase an uninterruptible power supply (UPS). This UPS should be capable of powering your critical systems for at least twice the length of time that power is generally out. This extra buffer will allow for longer-than-normal power outages. Critical systems are usually considered to be any system that would cause undue safety, financial, or legal burden if down for any amount of time.

Another consideration of windstorms is loss of communication. If there is any physical piece of equipment, such as a satellite dish, cell tower, or other device that is external to your building and provides communications either through the Internet or via telephone systems, consider having a backup plan. If you are located away from landlines that provide Internet and are forced to have a satellite dish for communicating, it is also wise to know at what wind speed the satellite dish will be damaged beyond repair. If weather is predicted that exceeds those speeds, have a backup plan in place that will allow for the temporary lack of availability of the services provided by the satellite dish or antenna affected by the winds.

Floods

Some areas are more prone to flooding than others. If your organization is in one of these locations, it is imperative to be familiar with the different flood zones that might affect your organization. How often does the area in which your organization is located flood, how high does the water typically get, and how long do floods historically last? Build a flood response plan based around these numbers, but also plan for a worst case scenario. If your organization is located in a flood zone that floods once every hundred years, don't ignore the possibility that any given year could be the year.

For established companies, moving to a new location is usually not feasible, even when faced with the possibility of floods. There are ways to mitigate losses, however. For instance, moving server rooms to a higher floor is a possibility if your organization is located in a building with more than one story. Even if the server room cannot be moved, at least computers in the server room can be situated at such a height that even in the case of most floods, the most expensive and critical systems will be protected from damage or complete loss. Even if you are just moving the servers to a taller height than most floods, consider placing servers in nonstationary racks or carts for quick transportation.

Fires

One of the scariest issues facing any organization is the possibility of fire. Of course, the loss of human life is, and should be the primary concern of any security policy. People's safety should always, always be the first order of business. Protecting people and property are not mutually exclusive, however. The same types of systems used for protecting networks and computer systems are the same that will provide safety for the people who use them.

Fire Detection Systems   Overheating electronics and electronic shorts can create situations that are conducive to spontaneous combustion. There are two main types of fire alarms. Make sure you have both ionization and photoelectric types installed. Ionization smoke detectors are better at detecting flaming fires with smaller combustible particles, whereas photoelectric smoke detectors generally excel at detecting smoldering, "smoky" fires.

Fire Suppression Systems   Detecting the fires is only part of the fire-fighting solution. Having some sort of fire suppression system is usually required by law or insurance companies. Depending on the size of your organization and the assets you are attempting to protect, you have a few options from which to choose.

Wet Pipe   The most common type of fire suppression system is what is known as a "wet pipe" system. This simply means that pipes overhead are full of water, waiting to burst forth to shower the fire below. These systems usually look like little upside down sprinklers hanging from the ceiling. The basic idea behind these systems is that a plug melts or a bulb breaks at a certain temperature and releases the water from the sprinkler. Often times, if you look closely at these sprinklers, you can see a little colored tube in the middle of them, most often orange or red. The color of the tube (or sometimes, a piece of colored metal) indicates the temperature required to activate the sprinkler. The intent of having individual sprinklers activated solely based on temperature is to prevent unnecessary water damage from affecting nonthreatened areas. Only sprinklers located in the direct vicinity of the fire are activated by the heat of the fire, which minimizes water damage to unaffected portions of the building while maximizing the water pressure over the fire. The added bonus is that these systems are the cheapest to install, which explains one of the reasons why they are, by and large, the installation of choice for most commercial buildings. A drawback of the wet pipe system is that the sprinklers can sometimes drip, causing damage to office furniture and electronics located below.

Dry Pipe   In a dry system, pipes directly feeding into the sprinkler heads are filled with pressurized air or nitrogen instead of water. The pressurized air pushes a valve closed, which keeps water out of the system. Once a sprinkler head is activated by heat, the pressurized air is allowed to "drain" from the system through the activated head, and the water valve opens, allowing water to begin to spray through any activated heads. Dry pipe fire systems offer a couple of distinct advantages over the wet pipe system. To begin with, because they are not filled with water, they won't ever freeze during colder months. This is why these types of systems are often used in empty warehouses, or other buildings in which providing heat is not a major concern. In addition to not freezing, the lack of water in the system prevents the issue of dripping onto electronics and furniture. A major drawback of the dry pipe system is the fact that they cost a lot more to install than a wet system.

Wall Versus Ceiling   If cost is a concern when installing your organization's fire suppression system, consider the option of installing the system in the walls instead of the ceiling. When activated, these sprinklers spray outward into the middle of the room, instead of downward from the ceiling. If the sprinklers are in the walls, they cannot drip on equipment below. Of course, if there are rooms wherein large spans exist between walls, such as in some call centers, this may not be a feasible option, due to the limited range of the outward spraying nozzles. Be sure to take into account your organization's needs when making this decision. Cost, convenience, and safety should prevail in your considerations.

11

PCI Compliance

A great wave of oppressive tyranny isn't going to strike, but rather a slow seepage of oppressive laws and regulations from within will sink the American dream of liberty.

George Baumler

Virtually every organization that has something to sell allows patrons to use a credit card to make a payment or provide a donation. Without the capacity to process these credit cards, companies are crippled and cannot function in a profitable manner. Because of this fact, organizations are often entrusted with thousands of credit card numbers, as well as the customer data associated with those numbers, such as names, phone numbers, addresses, and even (sometimes) social security numbers.

A multitude of security concerns surround the issues of processing and storing these cardholder data. Many people assume only the card numbers themselves must be protected in order to provide proper security; in fact all of the personal data provided by the cardholder should be protected from unauthorized viewers. This requires thorough network security measures such as firewalls, DMZ configurations for customer databases, security plans, and so forth. Not only are all of these rules a good idea, they are now required by a consortium of the big players in the credit card industry.

How can an IS professional determine whether his specific organization, department, or network is following industry standards? Where are these standards found? Recently, these questions were all answered by the Payment Card Industry Security Standards Council (PCI SSC), in the form of the Payment Card Industry Data Security Standard (PCI DSS). The PCI DSS provides a sort of framework within which organizations can build network security to a level that provides a solid level of security for cardholder data.

PCI Compliance

PCI compliance refers to an organization's adherence to the regulations set forth by MasterCard, Visa, Diner's Club, American Express, and Discover. Although the rules outlined by these different credit card companies were created in response to the ever-growing need for technological controls, the measures required for securing credit card data are sound principles for guarding any data. Because most organizations need to comply with these rules anyway, and because they are great security considerations regardless, it is important to be at least familiar with PCI compliance and what is required for different types of organizations.

The PCI Security Council website can be found at https://www.pcisecuritystandards.org/.

Goal of PCI DSS

The goal of PCI compliance is to protect customer information from fraud and theft through the implementation of commonsense applications of security and data storage. Because PCI is primarily concerned with protecting cardholder data, the documentation for PCI compliance often refers to the "cardholder data environment." This broad term simply refers to any computer server or other aspect of the network wherein cardholder data are stored. Keep in mind that credit card companies provide protection to cardholders for fraud and stolen card numbers. It therefore behooves credit card issuers such as Visa and MasterCard to require organizations to protect cardholder data; again, just because PCI compliance is concerned with providing thorough protection for cardholder information, the rules provided for protection are an excellent framework for use in the pursuit of total network protection.

Who Must Adhere to PCI Compliance?

The bottom line is that if your organization accepts credit cards for payment of any services or products provided by your organization, your organization must comply with the rules outlined in PCI DSS in order to maintain PCI compliance. If your organization has Internet-facing IP addresses that collect or transmit cardholder information, your network must have a security scan performed annually. Any path from the Internet into your cardholder data environment is subject to a security scan, or audit. Even if your organization doesn't have such IP addresses or apparent paths, less apparent pathways almost certainly exist within your network infrastructure. For instance a savvy cyber criminal could use your organization's e-mail functions, a virtual private network through which employees have external access to an organization's internal network, or any other possible path to gain unauthorized access to your customers' cardholder information. Be sure to include in a security overview all possible routes to the cardholder data environment, and include a list of all measures taken to protect those paths.

Who Is Authorized to Perform PCI Security Scans?

The Qualified Security Assessor (QSA) companies that have been approved by the PCI Security Council to have certain, certified employees of the organization validate the organization's adherence to PCI DSS. The organization in question does not certify these employees, but the employees must be approved and certified through the PCI Security Standards Council. The certification of both the QSA companies and their QSA qualified employees must be renewed on an annual basis. The PCI Security Council provides self assessments to companies desiring to know if they are in compliance with PCI DSS, but in order to be certified as in compliance, the organization in question must receive validation from either an in-house QSA employee or a third-party QSA-certified individual.

The PCI Security Council maintains an up-to-date list of QSAs on the web at https://www.pcisecuritystandards.org/qsa_lookup/index.html. In addition to the Self-Assessment Questionnaires, the website provides users with many other informative PCI documents, including PCI FAQs, QSA requirements, PCI DSS overviews, and more.

The Five Levels of PCI Compliance

The PCI Security Council recognizes the fact that not all organizations have the same level of exposure to customer cardholder information. For instance, some companies may only have all their customer cardholder information handled by a third-party vendor. Others may have a point-of-sale (POS) machine through which the organization swipes a customer card directly connected to the Internet, with no sensitive cardholder information stored on company servers. Still yet, other organizations may not only physically handle the actual credit cards at the POS, but also maintain an up-to-date database of all cardholder information, in which hundreds of thousands of cardholder data records are stored.

It is clear to see that varying levels of security are required for different organizations depending on how many cards the organization handles, and what the organization does with the information, such as storage, processing, and transmission. Based on these different levels of involvement with cardholder data, the PCI Security Council has come up with five distinct levels of compliance.

Level 1 Compliance

This level of PCI DSS compliance refers to organizations that handle all cardholder data through a third-party vendor. In these cases, the card is not actually physically present for the transaction. For instance, mail orders, telephone orders, and e-commerce are all transactions wherein the card is not physically handled by an organization taking payment through a credit card. Because the organization is relying on a third party to process the card number and keep it in a database off site, the organization doesn't need to follow any network-specific security measures for Level 1 Compliance.

If your organization uses a third-party vendor to process all the cardholder data, the organization must take proper steps to ensure the company handling that information is appropriately certified by the PCI Security Council. In other words, just because the organization pays a company to do the work, the organization has not completely relegated the responsibility of security to the card processing company. Never, never, never forget that the bottom line, in regard to security of the information your organization handles, is up to your organization. Be vigilant in your pursuit of security. Don't leave it to chance!

Level 2 Compliance

Level 2 of the PCI DSS compliance is in reference to organizations whose only source of obtaining cardholder information is through the use of a credit card imprint machine. Although most customers only see these now-antiquated machines pulled out of some dusty and forgotten drawer when electricity is unavailable, or when a computer system crashes at a retail outlet, there are still some organizations whose sole method of storing cardholder data is on these physical receipts. Clearly, the requirements for digital security will be much less stringent for a company falling into this category; however, even though the network security needs will be diminished, the requirement for keeping the physical records safe from unauthorized eyes is not. Proper, secure file storage is required to keep unauthorized people from gaining access to cardholder data, including all of the steps necessary to maintain completely protected files.

Level 3 Compliance

The third level of PCI DSS requirements is identical to the requirements of Level 2. This is because as in Level 2, there are no digitally stored records. Level 3 refers to those organizations whose POS machine is a direct-dial machine, using a telephone line. These machines don't communicate with the organization's network, and therefore do not create any digitally stored cardholder data records to protect through network security, just as with Level 2. Instead, these machines create printed receipts for processing with bank deposits. Like the requirements for proper security as listed in Level 2, compliance with Level 3 does not mean an organization can relax security measures, but must instead strengthen the physical security protecting the stored printed receipts.

Level 4 Compliance

The fourth level of PCI DSS compliance, in regard to cardholder data processing, transmission, and storage, has to do with organizations that process cards through the use of a POS directly connected to the Internet. Although the POS sends data via the Internet to the bank, the cardholder data are not actually stored on company servers. Even though the data are not stored on servers, digital security is paramount, because cardholder information will be processed and transmitted through the virtual wires of the web. In this level, proper encryption of data, and secure firewalls and network security measures are required to properly comply with PCI Security Council measures.

Level 5 Compliance

For all organizations not falling within the definitions of the other four levels, Level 5 requirements for compliance are required. These requirements are the most stringent of all levels, and are outlined below. Level 5 compliance assumes an organization is taking and processing credit cards internally. In addition, Level 5 compliance is for organizations that store credit cards on internally protected databases. Furthermore, Level 5 compliance assumes the organization's network has multiple points of Internet access. Therefore, the requirements attempt to cover all of the digital bases, as it were.

PCI DSS Overview

Twelve key requirements, listed under six different categories, are included in the rules for PCI compliance. These requirements are listed below. Notice that the requirements are somewhat open-ended, although specific enough for an IT specialist to have confidence that she has properly implemented the necessary controls and processes to be in compliance. PCI compliance is a massive subject, and this chapter only gives an overview of the requirements. However, keep in mind there are minutiae and subrequirements that are not listed, due to the massive scale of the subject. This chapter is only meant to be a simple introduction, not a replacement for a thorough study of PCI compliance and how it directly affects and relates to your specific network.

Category 1. Protect and Maintain a Secure Network

The category to "protect and maintain a secure network" may seem a bit too vague, but as we show in the requirements listed below, what is necessary to meet the needs of this category has mostly to do with firewalls and router settings. To begin with, the network must have some sort of secure firewall installed to protect cardholder data. The requirement does not specify whether the data need to be protected from internal or external issues, just that the data need to be properly protected. This is important to keep in mind, as many networks have no internal firewalls protecting critical data from internal attacks. Be sure to consider protection from internal attacks when designing your network and providing data security for your databases.

Requirement 1.1—Install and Maintain a Firewall Configuration to Protect Cardholder Data.   Installation of a firewall is a straightforward concept, but what is required for proper and thorough maintenance? The maintenance portion of this requirement is really more concerned with awareness of the current state of the network configuration, and proper adherence to strictly documented requirements. For instance, a current diagram of network connections, topology, and systems should always be kept on file. Any changes performed to the network or the systems therein must always be clearly and completely documented in the record.

Not only should the record be documented, but so should the processes directing the maintenance of the network. For instance, firewalls are required at specific points in the network, such as at every point where the internal network has a connection with the Internet. The process of how these connections and firewall settings are reviewed and maintained must be documented, as well as the business justifications for the use of each protocol, port, and so forth. For instance, it isn't enough just to document that port X is open because Christine and Jackie like to play Doom on their lunch breaks. Unless a port is specifically required for legitimate business purposes, or a certain protocol such as HTTP, SMTP, FTP, or VPN is necessary for an organization to function, then it should be turned off or otherwise blocked from use.

Even once a business justification is determined, simply having the protocol or port documented is not enough for proper PCI compliance. Indeed, the organization must not only list what protocols are in use (and why), but also what security measures are in place to protect against intrusions. For instance, let's take the most commonly used protocol, HyperText Transfer Protocol (HTTP). HTTP is used for accessing and sending web pages on the Internet. Justifying the use of this protocol is not a problem, as any organization desiring relevance must have some sort of access to or presence on the Internet. The problem is that not every website on the Internet is necessary to access. In fact, your organization will undoubtedly want to block access to the majority of the Internet for a large percentage of your users. It would be useless if Jackie and Christine's computers had the X port blocked so that they couldn't play Doom during work hours, only to have them able to access Doom through an online website.

The answer to this quandary is a properly configured firewall. Through either packet filtering or proxy filtering, the communication between Christine and Jackie's computers and the Doom server will be cut short at the chokepoint of the firewall. The bottom line is that by keeping activity limited to those actions required by daily operation of the organization, while establishing and maintaining secure procedures and methods (such as having securely configured firewalls) for those activities, the critical data, such as cardholder information, are properly protected.

Requirement 1.2—Build a Firewall Configuration That Restricts Connections Between Untrusted Networks and Any System Components in the Cardholder Data Environment.   This requirement is very similar to 1.1, except it specifically speaks to filtering and restricting data to and from the cardholder data environment, with additional requirements for router synchronization and specific configuration settings. Synching routers is a common practice, and can be accomplished by using certain network time protocols, such as NTP. Synchronizing routers means each router has been synched to the same exact date and time. This is important for proper troubleshooting and diagnostics. Ideally, each system, including switches, routers, computers, and all components of the network will be synched. This will allow technicians to more accurately determine when systems crashed, and what the possible causes of certain traffic and performance issues are.

Requirement 1.3—Prohibit Direct Public Access Between the Internet and Any System in the Cardholder Data Environment.   The creation of a demarcation zone, or DMZ, is necessary for secure separation of internal networks and the Internet. DMZs are also sometimes referred to as a perimeter network. The DMZ is a sort of subnetwork that sits between the internal secure network and the outside, less secure network such as the Internet. The DMZ is usually created by implementing two firewalls on either side (internal side and external side) of a point in the network. For instance, there is a data point through which all data must flow to get out of the internal network. This is the internal side of the DMZ, and the router placed at that location should not allow unauthorized traffic to pass through, which could access unauthorized software or websites on the Internet. Such access could cause harm to the services located in the DMZ, or even on the more sensitive internal network. Likewise, on the internal side of the DMZ, there should be a firewall protecting the DMZ and internal network from the incoming traffic from the Internet.

Both firewalls are protecting from traffic originating from their respective sides, however, they should also be configured as though the other firewall did not exist. That is to say, just because an external firewall exists on the external side of a DMZ, the internal firewall should not just protect the DMZ from outgoing traffic originating from the internal network, but also from traffic attempting to access the internal network. It is also important to make certain the two firewalls are not configured the same.

In fact, it is wise to configure both firewalls differently with the intent of providing a layered approach to protecting the internal network. In other words, just because an attacker breaches the first firewall with certain tricks and tools, he will not necessarily be successful in his attempts to break into a dissimilarly configured firewall on the other side of the DMZ. Dissimilar configuration schemes running on the DMZ firewalls mean attackers will need a whole new set of skills to break through an internal firewall. On the other hand, if both firewalls are similarly configured, all somebody has to do is get through the first firewall, and the keys to the internal network are his.

The services needed for accessing the larger, less secure network are also usually contained in the DMZ. For instance, domain name servers (DNS), mail servers, file transfer protocol (FTP) servers, and VoIP servers are usually located in the DMZ. Notice that only servers are located in the DMZ, as no individual node (user computer) should ever be placed outside the protected environment of the internal network. Also notice that database servers, such as those used for storing employee, customer, and cardholder information are never ever located in the DMZ. This is again to protect the data contained within the databases from the less secure, external Internet.

In addition to the protection provided by the creation of a well-designed DMZ, PCI requires organizations to protect the internal infrastructure of a network by hiding internal IP addresses. This is accomplished through the use of what is called "IP masquerading." Essentially, IP masquerading is a process that allows internally connected computers without specific IP addresses to access the Internet via another computer. This is commonly practiced in most work environments, and allows system administrators to monitor traffic going in and out of that single point.

Requirement 1.4—Install Personal Firewall Software on Any Mobile or Employee-Owned Computers with Direct Connectivity to the Internet (Laptops Used by Employees, etc.) That Are Used to Access the Organization's Network. Most corporations employ individuals who require access to the company website through mobile devices such as laptops and personal cell phones. Because these devices are not always attached to the network, they must be specially protected from malware and attackers. This is done through specifically installing software firewalls on each device to ensure the organization's network is protected when the equipment is installed on the network.

For instance, the computer that this book was written on is a personal laptop. I use it to build websites, write e-mails, create small programs, access social networking sites, play online games and so forth during my personal time. The company I work for, Electronics International, allows me to use this computer during work hours. What I do with my laptop on my own time is my business, but it could severely affect the security of Electronics International's business once I hook into the company network. Because I am aware of the dangers of plugging a personal laptop into an organization's network, I have taken great pains to protect company data. I have installed a firewall on my computer, created backups of all company-related files, and installed multiple antivirus and antispyware applications on my laptop. I also never place customer, employee, or cardholder information on my laptop, just in case all of the above measures fail, inasmuch as no security measure is perfect.

Category 2: Protect Cardholder Data

Of course, the goal of all the PCI compliance issues is ultimately to provide for the protection of cardholder data. Category 1 was focused on network security in general, and Category 2 gets more specific and places requirements on systems instead of the network as a whole.

Requirement 2.1—Always Change Vendor-Supplied Defaults Before Installing a System on the Network. This requirement states that any installed network equipment should not use the vendor default settings. For instance, many commercial off-the-shelf (COTS) routers use the name "admin" as the default name, and "password" as the password. This type of default setting is true for virtually all routers and their default settings. It would require far more time during manufacturing and installation of the router to have a unique name and password assigned to each router. Anyway, the manufacturer assumes that the first thing an installer will do is change the name and password, just as this requirement states.

The "name" of a router is referred to as the service set identifier, or SSID. If you are in an Internet café, or at home looking for your wireless router, this is the name of your router as seen on your computer. There will be multiple SSIDs available if there are multiple routers broadcasting in the same area. So if somebody asks about the default SSID for a router, you can bet it is probably the model name of the router.

What makes these default settings especially easy for cyber criminals to locate on the Internet is the fact that the default name of the router *is* usually the model of router, such as "Linksys WRTG54." All the cyber criminal needs to do is intelligently search for routers with default names and she will have easy access to them. If somebody has not taken the time to change the default SSID, the chances are good he has also left the router's password the same as well. Some cyber criminals will literally drive around neighborhoods looking for an SSID with a default name. Once they find one, they will try to hack into the system. Many times, they simply want free access to the Internet, although they may also try to access any computer attached to the network. The solution to this issue is far too easy and cost effective not to be implemented. Just log in, change the password, and implement encryption. The bottom line is that a network router should not be allowed online without encryption, a new username, SSID, and password.

Requirement 2.2—Develop Configuration Standards for All System Components That Address All Known Security Issues and Are in Keeping with Industry-Accepted Methods for System Hardening. The basics of this requirement boil down to eliminating unnecessary protocols and services that could be compromised. In other words, if a protocol or service is not being used, disable it. Also, don't just eliminate unnecessary protocols, but protect those protocols and services being used by providing dedicated servers and associated protection for the ones in use. For instance, if it is possible, don't have an e-mail server also provide domain name resolution. This is a high-horsepower approach to protecting the DMZ, as it requires multiple servers, so smaller companies may not be able to implement this step. Keep in mind these are PCI requirements, which may not necessarily be the most cost-effective solution for overall security in your particular organization. A PCI Compliance QSA may be able to help your organization meet the requirements of PCI compliance and be in harmony with your organization's budgetary and labor constraints.

Requirement 2.3—Encrypt All Nonconsole Administrative Access. Nonconsole access refers to any remote administrative access. This just means the administrator is not sitting at a computer directly attached to the internal network. This requirement is one of the most important, because it assumes administrators may need to access organization computers through the Internet while not physically present. Before transmission of access codes, passwords, or other login data, the connection must be secure and encrypted. It would be easy for an attacker to grab an unencrypted data stream from the Internet and use it to gain unlimited access to an organization's network. The bottom line for this requirement is to make certain critical and secure information is not simply shot out into the Internet without being properly hidden by an encryption scheme.

Requirement 2.4—Shared Hosting Providers Must Protect Each Entity's Hosted Environment and Cardholder Data. Many companies simply don't have the in-house talent or resources to host their own website, and even some larger companies use online databases such as customer resource management (CRM) applications as part of their daily operations. Although online services often provide viable, cost-effective solutions for smaller companies, they introduce a whole new set of considerations in regard to security. Just because the provider is not in-house does not mean he doesn't have to abide by in-house rules. This requirement simply states that if an organization is using a shared hosting provider, that provider must maintain unique security measures for each website or service hosted.

For instance, if a provider hosts 100 websites, it cannot simply provide a firewall generic to all 100, but must delineate each service to provide proper protection as outlined in the PCI requirements. This is not because PCI wants to make life more difficult or complex for the provider or the entity using the provider's service, but to protect cardholder data from all sources of potential threat. A firewall may protect the 100 websites from the external Internet, but it does not protect them from one another. Therefore, when choosing a host to provide service for your website or servers, make certain they have protection in place that will meet the requirements of your organization's security plan, including separate firewalling between vendors being hosted by their company.

Category 3: Maintain a Vulnerability Management Program

After securing the networks, including setting up firewalls, switches, and other network devices according to PCI requirements, it is important to recognize and manage new and existing threats to the network. A vulnerability management program will help accomplish this goal.

Requirement 3.1—Keep Cardholder Data Storage to a Minimum. It used to be that many companies would keep all customer-related, legal, and financial records for up to seven years for tax purposes. Instead of the old method of holding onto cardholder data, Requirement 3.1 states as far as cardholder information is concerned, get rid of it as soon as your organization has no use for it. If your organization has a 90-day charge-back guarantee, there is no need to keep the credit card data for more than 90 days. Even at that, make sure most of the card number is encrypted and that customer service employees can only view the last 4 digits for verification purposes.

In short, make certain your organization only holds onto cardholder data for the length of time required by industry regulations, necessity, and law. After that, properly destroy that information. If it is on paper, have a certified paper disposal company take the shredded files for removal. More likely, the data will be on disk. PCI requirements include provision to dispose of outdated cardholder information at least once a quarter. This process should be at least partly automated, so that it relies on nobody's memory to go through and eliminate the data. In other words, a program of some sort should be set up to take care of the elimination. This could be done by moving outdated files to a storage location once they've expired, where a program will automatically delete them at the quarter's end. Physically stored files should likewise be moved at certain intervals, and then shredded and disposed of properly at the end of each quarter.

Requirement 3.2—Do Not Store Sensitive Authentication Information after Authentication.   Once a card is processed, the information needed to complete the transaction in the first place (i.e., card number, cardholder information, service code, primary account number (PAN), etc.) should only be stored as required by business. Often times, this means that only the cardholder's name, address, phone number, and the last four digits of the card are stored in association with purchase orders and invoices. If the information is extraneous to the requirements of daily business, don't store it. If a cardholder needs to change an order, he can always provide customer service with the credit card number again.

Requirement 3.3—Mask PAN When Displayed.   Whenever the primary account number is displayed on the screen of a user's computer, only the last four or six digits should be readable. The other six to eight digits should be properly encrypted so as to protect the card number from being deciphered. Keep in mind that stricter requirements of industry or company policy will override this requirement. For instance, if your organization's policy requires only the last two or three digits be in plaintext, then the stricter organization requirement will supersede PCI Requirement 3.3.

Requirement 3.4—Render PAN, at Minimum, Unreadable Wherever Stored. There are several methods that can be employed to render a file unreadable at a glance, such as truncation, encryption, and hash-marking, however, this requirement simply requires one of them to be utilized in protecting the cardholder information from being easily read by users. Truncation simply "cuts" the number off at a certain placeholder, such that only the last four to six digits are seen, eliminating the possibility that somebody could duplicate the card number. Encryption and hash-marking replace the actual digits of the account number with a coded alphanumeric symbol, so that the card number is illegible by normal standards. Whatever your organization decides upon, be sure customer card numbers are not readily viewable at a glance.

Category 4: Implement Strong Access Control Measures

Access control measures refer to controls that ensure only specific authorized users are allowed access to particular areas of data storage. When a user logs onto a protected network system, his credentials are authenticated through the use of various methods of authentication. Each user's account is assigned a certain level of access, which allows the user to access files with a matching level of security or classification. Once he has been authenticated and authorized to access the system, the user does not have to restate his login credentials or password until he attempts to access another system, or until he tries to access a level of authorized files higher than the one for which he is logged on.

Access control lists (ACLs) are stored in a database and contain all of the access control information, such as login names, passwords, authority levels, and expiration dates of login information for each user. Every user listed within the ACL should be given a unique user ID, to avoid duplication and confusion of access levels and user login information. ACLs should be maintained by administrators to ensure only those users who should have access are approved. For instance, when an employee is terminated from working at the organization, her authority to access the system should be eliminated from the ACL database.

In addition to the ACL and the digital protection provided therein, access to cardholder data must also be physically restricted. For instance, even if an organization stores all cardholder data on secure database servers in a properly configured DMZ, any physical receipts, printouts, or imprints with cardholder data must be properly protected through the use of secured rooms and locking cabinets. Make sure the level of physical measures implemented is commensurate with the level of criticality of the information being protected. Cardholder information does not have to be protected on a level equal to Fort Knox, but it should be kept in locking metal cabinets that have been approved for such storage.

The bottom line when considering access control is to take all reasonable steps to ensure only those people with authorization are allowed access to cardholder information. Essentially, this is the primary concern of all PCI compliance measures. Everyone, from the casual snooper to the hardened cyber criminal should be dissuaded from attempting to gain access to the secured files. This doesn't mean spending millions of dollars on state-of-the-art technology, but instead means using sensible approaches to security, such as encryption, physical locks, appropriately configured firewalls, and so forth.

Category 5: Regularly Monitor and Test Networks

One of the best methods for locating issues in networks is through constant monitoring of network traffic. With a good network monitor, many issues can be discovered and fixed. After fixing issues, the network can then be retested to determine if the fix was appropriate or if further tweaking is necessary. For instance, network monitoring can assist network administrators with locating such issues as:

- *Network bottlenecks:* Bottlenecks affect the throughput performance of networks. Network performance is directly related to gaining immediate access to data on the networks. Access has everything to do with data availability, which is part of the CIA triad of information assurance.
- *Unauthorized software:* Unauthorized software can be malicious in nature or nonmalicious. Malicious software packages are immediate and clear dangers to your network security. Network monitors should be able to quickly detect and eliminate such software. Even so-called nonmalicious

unauthorized software should be immediately deleted, and the responsible individual should be spoken to, written up, or, if the incident was severe enough, fired. The organization should take a stance that there is no such thing as nonmalicious unauthorized software. Screensavers, font packages, and other nonmalicious software are sometimes just a package in which malicious software resides. This type of software is probably okay, but probably okay isn't a good enough measure of security for any organization.

- *Testing traffic throughput speeds of specific portions of the network:* Throughput speeds affect access to data, and sluggish overworked networks could be indicative of larger issues occurring. Massive amounts of data flowing through the network without apparent cause usually point to the existence of malware communicating to sources outside the network.
- *Troubleshooting network issues:* Network monitors are great for troubleshooting. Because troubleshooting often involves removing, replacing, and testing individual systems, network monitors allow technicians to isolate suspected systems by monitoring their effect on the network as a whole.
- *Determining origins of incoming and outgoing malware:* By monitoring network packet traffic, technicians can pinpoint the origins of malware. Once IP addresses of malware are identified, administrators can block any traffic to and from those addresses.
- *Determining which users are currently on the network, and in what functions their workstations are engaged:* Another issue to keep in mind when considering network monitoring is data logging. Data logging provides a history of what traffic has flowed through the gateway to and from your network. If somebody has launched a virus onto your network, you will have a much greater chance of locating the culprit and isolating the infected systems if you have a history of network traffic on which to look back. Also, during legal cases involving criminal network activity, having a log to back up claims against disgruntled employees, competitors, or other cyber criminals adds weight to the validity of your case.

Category 6: Maintain an Information Security Policy

Having an information security policy is a key part of thoroughly protecting any network. Without a policy dictating how to handle specific issues, security is essentially an afterthought. The security plan should be detailed enough to deal with particular security concepts and still broad enough to cover all network functions. For example, a standard security plan would include the following:

- Specific network topology, including physical layout, number of users, number of servers, operating systems used, and so forth
- Division of authority for specific security-related tasks
- Router settings and configuration
- DMZ configuration for perimeter routers and firewalls
- Computer security response teams
- Security awareness training
- Computer incident postmortem procedures
- Computer forensics methodologies and law enforcement

Regardless of what level of PCI DSS compliance you are required to meet, your organization would benefit from a solid network security plan. Even the most robust security measures cannot ever provide an absolute guarantee of protection for your network or the data contained therein, however, the legal ramifications, not to mention the maintenance and security headaches associated with a lack of such a security plan, make it all but necessary for even the smallest networks and organizations to create and maintain some sort of security plan.

A Good Place to Start

PCI provides a good overview of network security, in plain English. The PCI requirements provide a good baseline of security for most organizations, even if the organizations don't take credit cards from customers. Regardless of whether these rules apply to your organization, they are worth researching and getting to know.

12

Business Continuity Planning

As system virtualization becomes mainstream, IT managers will find a greater need for disk imaging for disaster recovery and systems deployment.

Walter Scott

It is impossible for an organization to foresee and prepare for every eventuality, every disaster. Natural and manmade disasters will continue to wreak havoc upon our world, and organizations cannot ignore this unfortunate reality. If there is any doubt about the effectiveness of proper planning, just look at organizations that survived floods, fires, and other disasters to see that they had plans in place to handle the worst-case scenarios. Although management cannot and should not try to put into place controls and backups that plan for every single contingency, an organization should at least have some idea of what to do after disaster strikes (see Figure 12.1).

The goal of continuity planning is to keep organizations afloat in as much the same manner in which they operated prior to the disaster occurring in the first place. Good continuity planning will provide for proper and immediate emergency response to most types of disasters and major incidents. It will seek to provide safety for all people involved, and will keep normal operations humming along as close to normal as possible. Minimum impact to business operations is the target. If your organization needs further assistance determining the proper steps, a good guide for creating a business continuity plan can be found at the National Institute of Standards and Technology (NIST) www.nist.gov/.

Business continuity planning can be broken into the following steps.

1. Evaluation of critical systems and resources
2. Prioritization of critical systems and resources

175

Business Continuity Planning

EVALUATE CRITICAL SYSTEMS
Determine all systems relevant to basic continued service for the organization

PRIORITIZE SYSTEMS
Decied which systems take precedence over others, in regards to gaining basic operational functinons of the organization.

IDENTIFY THREATS
What threats face each resource?

ASSIGN RESPONSIBILITIES
Who is in charge of getting each resource back into operational status?

DESIGN THE PLAN
Create a plan which will do the best job of effectively and efficiently putting your organization back into operational status.

IMPLEMENT THE PLAN
The Business Continuity Plan should be official policy. Make sure people are not guessing or planning during a crisis, but instead using the existing plan already put into place.

TRAIN PERSONNEL
Make sure key employees know what is required of them and how best to achieve it during different crisis scenarios. Use training as the time to trim unnecessary steps to recovery, and to refine existing ones.

Figure 12.1   Business Continuity Planning

3. Identify threats posed to critical systems and resources
4. Assign business continuity responsibilities
5. Design business continuity plan
6. Implement business continuity plan
7. Train according to business continuity plan objectives

Evaluation of Critical Systems and Resources

This step decides which systems and resources are absolutely necessary for the continued operations of your organization. Be sure to talk with departmental managers, administrative staff, and data owners to determine which systems are critical to the daily operations of the organization. Among the list of required systems and resources, most companies will include key servers. For instance, most companies would consider customer databases and employee records among some of the most important databases to have access to during normal operations. Whatever firewalls, routers, servers, and other network hardware are necessary to achieve access to these servers should be included in the list of items needed for basic operations.

In addition to any physical equipment and network hardware, remember to list all necessary labor and whatever else is required for such labor to function at required levels. Just because a customer database is up and running does not mean customers can be processed. For instance, in order for the customer database to be of any value, customer service and sales representatives must be available to answer phones, and a safe location must be provided for the representatives to perform their jobs. Therefore, for each necessary resource, be sure to include all auxiliary resources required for the normal function of that resource.

Prioritization of Critical Systems and Resources

Once the list of necessary resources is created, prioritize them in order of greatest importance. For instance, although access to an IMAP e-mail account may be important to the daily function of a particular job, it is not as critical as getting power to basic systems throughout the building.

Something to take into consideration when deciding the criticality of a system is alternate methods of achieving the same service or resource. For instance, take the IMAP e-mail account as an example. If the IMAP e-mail database is located offsite, but Internet access is not available to the organization during the recovery process, myriad other options are usually available for accessing the Internet. If users can gain secure access through remote sites, e-mail can be checked, and customers can be alerted to any existing problems being dealt with during the recovery process. Most resources will have alternate modes of accessing them during a crisis, so be sure to list those possible access methods in the continuity plan.

Identify Threats Posed to Critical Systems and Resources

For each necessary resource, there exist corresponding threats. After making a list of the resources necessary for the daily normal operations of your organization, list the threats specific to the resource. For example, telephone lines can be accidentally cut or otherwise disrupted, e-mail databases can crash or be infected with malware, servers can fail for many different reasons, routers can be hacked, and so forth. Perform thorough research to determine how each resource could possibly fail, and list that failure as a threat posed against the system. Most of this work is included as part of a risk management analysis.

Assign Business Continuity Responsibilities

Each resource should have a manager, or "owner" who is in charge of managing the process of seeing the resource back to normal operations. For instance, if water floods a server room, a system administrator should be named to manage the incident, including cleanup, removal of destroyed equipment, evaluating damaged equipment, reinstallation of fixed equipment, and the purchasing and installation of new equipment. Without clear, predefined decisive management, people will assume certain responsibilities are being taken care of, and details will be overlooked. Whatever the mode of failure, make sure someone has already been named in the business continuity plan to manage the failure.

Before a business continuity plan can be built, it is common practice to craft a planning policy statement. The statement will be more than a standard mission statement. It will include a list of actions to be taken during the recovery process, and a short discussion of general principles that will guide maintenance, responsibility delegation, and systems evaluation during the business continuity planning process.

Develop the Continuity Planning Policy Statement

Much like the organization's mission statement, a continuity planning policy statement must provide a concise set of guidelines for the development of a thorough continuity policy. This document is not the place to ask for the newest technology or provide budgeting for certain items. Instead, this statement is essentially a formal document that grants authority to the IT managers in charge of the continuity planning process.

Ideally, a C-Level executive such as the CIO or CISO will be directly involved with the creation process. The support of top-level executives is absolutely critical when crafting such an important document, as it provides both the authority and funding to back up the intent of the document. Of course, those who will be directly in charge of implementing the policy, such as directors and managers of the IT Department, should also have a hand in the creation of the statement.

What Should the Continuity Planning Statement Include?

Think of the statement as a roadmap of accountability. At any time, an IT professional should be able to pick up the continuity plan and compare it against the existing continuity planning statement to see if the goals are being met. The statement should include such things as the following.

- *Titles of law or industry standards:* It is a good idea to list in the statement exactly which law, industry standard, or requirement to which your organization is attempting to adhere. For instance, the statement may start out, "In accordance with ACME Industries IT standard, all organizations will develop contingency plans for all major systems, etc." By spelling out the standard your organization is aiming to meet, you will be able to quickly pull up that original requirement to see if at each step of the policy creation process you are appropriately meeting the requirements listed by that standard.
- *Key employees and roles:* Listing key employees doesn't mean saying, "Jaime in IT will be in charge of backing up the files in Accounting, and his good friend, Tammy, will be in charge of IT training." The policy statement is simply a touchstone against which your organization will compare the actual policy. Therefore, instead of actually listing specific employees in the statement, the statement should simply say something like, "The plan will assign specific duties to key IT personnel, such that the policies listed within the plan can be appropriately and thoroughly carried out to ensure success," or something along those lines. Remember that the statement is simply that, a statement about the security plan itself. The

place to list key employees will be in the actual plan, instead of in the statement.

- *Training implementation, including type and frequency:* Again, the statement is not the place to get specific. The statement will not list who is in charge of training, but instead make the statement that provisions will be made for recurrent training, and that proper resources will be provided to the training personnel to ensure success. This is also the place to indicate whether simulation exercises for the purpose of training will be performed to ensure response readiness and preparation.

- *Auditing information:* Some information regarding auditing the actual continuity plan should be included in the statement. This portion of the statement might indicate the frequency of intervals during which the specifics in the plan will be audited. For instance, it might be indicated that the measures in place for business continuity will be audited annually or biennially, quarterly, or even "frequently." It would be wise not to be open-ended, such as with the use of the word "'frequently." If such a vague word is used in the policy statement, make certain you tighten up the language in the actual plan when discussing auditing procedures and frequency.

- *Backup frequency and storage media used for those backups:* Be sure to include the frequency of backups, as well as which type of media will be used for those backups. For instance, a statement may include the goal to back up all major systems nightly on a backup server. Again, remember that this is simply the statement that precedes the actual plan. The place to describe the server used, as well as who is responsible for updating the server, is inside the document, not in the statement.

- *Which systems are subject to the contingency plan:* Although the policy statement is vague in nature, try to indicate which systems will be subject to the contingency plan. It is important to include which systems must adhere to the plan, however, don't list each system, as the list of affected systems should be included somewhere inside the security plan. If the statement indicates all major systems, applications, and software bundles will be subject to the contingency plan, make certain that somewhere in the total document a definition is listed for exactly what a "major" system, application, or software bundle is.

- *Resource requirements for successful contingency planning:* This portion of the statement ensures the organization will provide the resources necessary for implementing the security plan. Specific resources required to successfully implement the plan are not listed here. Instead, include a simple statement indicating that such resources and provisions will be made available as necessary in accordance with the actual continuity plan. Be sure that this statement is followed through, even if it means setting aside a portion of the annual budget to maintain systems, provide backups, train personnel, or whatever other resource is required within the security plan.

- *Maintenance scheduling:* This is simply a statement that indicates maintenance of the systems covered by the plan will be properly and frequently carried out, as required for the proper success of those systems in accordance with the plan. No specific maintenance scheduling is listed in the statement, although some reference to required maintenance should be included, such as, "Regular and thorough maintenance, as required by the specific systems covered herein, will be provided for on whatever schedule deemed most appropriate for those protected systems."

- *Conduct the business impact analysis (BIA):* Conducting a BIA is similar, although not identical, to administering a risk analysis. Risk analysis is concerned with documenting all assets in the organization, as well as the likelihood of those assets being lost or damaged by certain threats posed against them. A business impact analysis has less to do with the chances of an asset being lost or damaged and more to do with how losing listed assets will affect the organization. For instance, when considering a telephone system, if an organization were to lose this asset it would be devastating to customer service relations and communications throughout the organization. Even though the chances of losing the system may be very slim, the loss of that asset should be documented in the BIA. Another difference that the BIA has when compared against a risk analysis is the fact that a risk analysis lists assets and the BIA is strictly concerned with functions. For instance, with the telephone system the function in question would be the ability to communicate with customers and vendors over the telephone. Although the functionality is made available by the presence of the telephone system, the BIA is more focused on the function rather than the asset. When performing a BIA, it is wise to have a questionnaire that can be used to gather information from middle management. The reason middle management will likely be the best candidates for answering the questionnaire is because they are familiar enough with the bottom line functionality of the resources in question, yet they are also tied into upper management enough to understand the larger impact losing a particular company function would have on the organization.

Listing Critical Functions

When investigating the various functions of your company, be sure to include the following for each function researched.

- *Function name:* Make sure the listed function name is appropriately specific. Instead of *phone services,* be sure to list *Technical Support Telephone Service* separate from *Legal Department Phone Service,* for example.
- *Function description:* What department services this function, and what service does it provide to the organization? For example, "The customer information database provides sales, customer service, and technical support personnel with immediate access to existing and potential customers. The organization relies upon this information for shipping/receiving operations, generating new sales leads, and following up with existing customers."
- *Dependencies:* What resources are required in order for this function to be fully operational? Power, water, utilities, heating and cooling, personnel, and phone lines are among the resources. On what other resources does this function depend?

- *Steps for recovery:* If this function failed, what steps would need to be taken in order to get it operational again? What resources are necessary to continue this function?
- *Organizational impact*: What impact would the loss of this function have upon the organization? What other functions would fail as a direct result of this function's failure?
- *Financial impact:* How would a loss of this resource affect the organization? When would those effects first be felt, and how long would they be anticipated to continue if a total loss of this resource occurred?
- *Workflow impact:* How would the loss of this function affect workflow? Would other manpower resources need to be pulled away from their primary duties to support the function?
- *Necessary resources:* What resources are required to support the function immediately after a disaster hits that destroys the function? Think of phones, computers, software, and hardware; don't forget labor, too.
- *Records:* What workflow records, such as reporting structures, work procedures, build processes, database files, login information, and any other important document is needed for the successful operation of the function?
- *Inflow and outflow:* What inputs does this process or function need, and what outputs does it send out? For example, a production floor needs components and subassemblies as its inputs, and when it has completed a product it outputs finished goods. Find out if the necessary inputs and outputs are operational in order for the function to succeed.
- *History of loss of function:* Has this function ever been lost or disrupted in the history of the company? What were the expenses involved with bringing the function fully back online? How long did it take? Learn from the past by putting stronger controls and better resources in place to facilitate a quicker and more thorough response time, if such a loss were to occur again.
- *Return to service time:* Make sure you document the estimated time you believe the function will take to be back in service. Also include the maximum time to return to service and the reasons for such a requirement. For instance, if electricity

absolutely must be brought back on within four hours of a disaster, be sure to include not only the required time for return to service, but back it up with clearly listed reasons: for example, in order to prevent equipment damage due to uncontrolled air temperatures in the server room, backup power must be instated within a maximum of four hours from initial loss.

- *Any other relevant issue:* Remember, you are more intimately familiar with the operations of your organization than any book or detached process could be. Simply because a book may recommend bimonthly testing of your network, your technicians may know that monthly testing is the more appropriate approach. Be sure to tailor every process and document to meet the specific needs of your particular organization.

Develop Recovery Priorities

After a thorough BIA is performed, a clear picture will begin to form regarding the functions and resources that are imperative for the continued livelihood of your organization. List in order of importance the most critical functions your business continuity plan aims to protect. In this way, if a disaster does ever strike your organization, no time will be lost in fruitless discussions, wherein individuals attempt to justify the priority of the function of their resources. Instead, all of the prioritizing will have been already handled, and people can simply get to work trying to save those resources most important to the survival of your organization, in order of predetermined priority.

Identify Preventive Controls

A well-written business continuity plan is not simply an attempt to remedy a situation that has already gone bad, but also provides preventive measures. Most companies already have a massive inventory of preventive controls, but they just haven't thought about it. For instance, security systems and door locks are preventive measures aimed at protecting a building or secure room from being penetrated by an unauthorized individual. Firewalls perform the same function on a software level.

Preventive measures and controls don't just offer prevention, but also attempt to deter and detect issues prior to their becoming disasters. For instance, fire suppressors and smoke alarms don't necessarily prevent fires, but they offer early detection in an effort to allow a response to the issue prior to a building burning to the ground. Some other important preventive controls include the following.

- *Fire detection systems:* There are two main types of fire alarms. Make sure you have both ionization and photoelectric types installed. Ionization smoke detectors are better at detecting flaming fires with smaller combustible particles, whereas photoelectric smoke detectors generally excel at detecting smoldering, smoky fires.
- *Fire suppression systems:* Detecting the fires is only part of the fire fighting solution. Having some sort of fire suppression system is usually required by law and/or insurance companies.
- *Approved containers for data storage and backup media:* Backup media should be contained in water and dustproof containers for long-term storage. Even though onsite storage of data is okay, it is wise to have at least one offsite location where critical data are duplicated and stored. This could be with a certified third-party vendor, or at a different campus of the organization. It is far too easy to copy and move data these days to justify having all backup files in one location.
- *Master power switch:* If there are systems that need to be shut down during or immediately following a disaster, make certain there is a master power switch to shut down all required systems.
- *Uninterruptible power supplies (UPS):* These are the power supplies that sit between the main power supply and whatever computer equipment you desire to maintain consistent power during a disaster. Make certain to be aware of the current requirements for each UPS device.V
- Power generators: If a total loss of power is experienced, be sure to have some gas or diesel generators on hand to provide adequate power for the critical systems needed for the minimal continuous operation of your organization. Don't

forget phone systems, computer systems, minimal lighting, and security systems when considering power needs.

• Air conditioning: Electronics need to stay cool in order to maintain effective operations. Make certain your organization has an appropriate amount of air conditioning for the most critical functions of your network. Be sure to factor in some excess capacity.

• Backup lighting and security: Be sure that your organization has backup lights installed in the most traveled locations, in the case of a power outage. Also be sure to keep in mind that security systems require power to operate and plan accordingly by having backup power supplies for both lighting and security.

Develop Recovery Strategies

Even the most thorough planning and implementation of preventive measures cannot stop disaster from striking. Eventually, certain situations will arise where key functionalities are temporarily lost. This is when the recovery strategies put into place in the business continuity plan will come into play. When considering recovery strategies, don't forget to consider the cost of each strategy also, as well as alternatives. For instance, if using a hot-swappable server room in the case of a failed main server room, consider using a warm or cold server room instead. Compare and contrast all strategies in an attempt to arrive at the best, most cost-effective solution for your organization. Be creative!

Develop the Contingency Plan

Once a thorough BIA is accomplished, you are ready to start crafting the contingency plan. This document is the touchpoint for all contingency operations. In order for a plan to be complete, it must document key personnel and resources required for the safe and successful operation of your company during the interim period between disaster and full recovery.

Key Personnel

There are a few considerations that must be taken into account when discussing key personnel. To begin with, it is important to designate internal and external personnel.

Internal personnel Internal personnel are the key players within your organization. They are the employees most necessary to keep the organization running at the minimum requirements for continued operations. The people on this list should only include those positions without which the organization simply cannot run. Be sure to include everybody whose job fits this description, but do not unnecessarily include positions that do not warrant inclusion. Having more employees to assist with a postdisaster situation may seem like a nice idea before a disaster strikes; once you are in the thick of a major problem your organization will want to operate as lean and flexibly as possible. Having extra people around simply means more people will need to be managed.

External personnel External personnel are people who your organization depends on for daily operations who are not directly employed at your organization. These may include a third-party accountant or lawyer, or some other contracted professional not physically available during normal operations. Because they are not employed at your organization, be sure to list as many of them as you may need for a recovery process, and be sure to keep a file of updated contact information and hours of availability. It is easy to forget these folks when creating a list of essential personnel, so be careful that you are thorough in listing who they are.

Telecommuters Telecommuters are internal employees who work away from the office. Don't forget to list them as potential resources to the company during recovery. Unlike the internal personnel, these external personnel can't cause more "on the scene" stress by being present and needing direct management. However, they are still employees and will expect to know what their role is in the recovery, so be ready to assign them tasks that will add value to the process. In regard to telecommuting, it would be wise to make a list of which roles in your organization could be successfully accomplished from a remote location. For instance, a satellite sales office could be put together at an offsite location for those key roles needed to operate the organization and sales could be run at the offsite location. So could customer service. Any job that only requires a telephone and Internet connection could potentially be performed offsite. Think of the critical roles your organization would need to fill during and immediately following a crisis and determine who could and could not telecommute. Having the flexibility to operate away from the office not only adds value during normal operations, but allows for quick responses to disastrous events if and when they occur.

Key Resources

The list of key resources required to run your organization will likely be much larger and varied than the list of key personnel. Don't overlook anything when considering the key resources of your company. Sometimes it helps to work backwards from a key resource to determine all of the support it will require. Take a company database, for instance. The software necessary to access the database is required, as well as the computer to run the software. The database server is necessary, as well as the file that contains the actual database itself. Naturally, you will require the computers, networking equipment, and peripherals that are needed to gain access to the database. Power supplies will also be needed to provide power to the computers and necessary equipment.

If we list everything needed for the database example it might look something like this.

- Computer
- Database application
- Server
- Monitor
- Peripherals: printer, keyboard, mouse
- Network cabling or wireless communication device
- Documented passwords and login information for the database
- Continuous power source
- Employee to run the program

Implement Business Continuity Plan

Once the business continuity plan is finished, appropriate personnel should be notified of their parts in the process. Each departmental manager, administrative personnel, and data owner should be made aware of the priority of recovery for their systems, the steps that will occur if their systems ever fail, and what is required of them to achieve the quickest and most effective recovery effort.

Part of the ongoing implementation of the plan should include allowance for maintenance of the plan. If something isn't working during training, the plan should provide steps for changing the plan to reflect better practices. This allowance for change should include the name or position of the person in charge of the plan and the appropriate channels for changing the plan, such as a request-for-change form, including:

- *Affected resources:* Which resources will be directly affected by the requested change? Have resources been added to the network or are established resources at risk?
- *Potential threats:* These are the threats posed to the affected resources. What has changed about the threats posed against the affected resources that would require a change to the business continuity plan?
- *Proposed maintenance or control:* What is the maintenance or control required to make this change? What patches need to be installed, and on what frequency? Is there a specific control, such as a router setting, that needs to be set? Are new procedures required, or does the process already exist in a different department in the organization?
- *Cost of proposed change:* What labor, software, and hardware are required, and how much will the total change cost?
- *Associated data or resource owner:* Who is in charge of the data or resource required to make the change? What will be required of the data owner once the change is made? Which other employees will be affected, and how?

Maintain the Plan

As mentioned above, the business continuity plan is a living document. Do not simply write this document and forget about it. Use it as a tool to learn from, and develop it and change it often. As new technologies and resources become available to your organization, reconsider prior alternatives. For instance, if your organization builds a second campus, you should consider what resources can be at least minimally duplicated at the other site, for continued operations in the case of a disaster.

In the efforts you expend to maintain the plan, get to know it! The plan is not a document that should need to be reviewed during a disaster. It is not a reference that should be physically referred to in the moment of crisis, but instead should be part of the atmosphere of the workplace. In other words, there should be no question of who is in charge of obtaining copies of backup data, or who needs to ensure the security system is working, or what procedure is required for securing the building after a disaster.

All of these procedures and protocols should be learned and become second nature during the many training sessions and maintenance efforts directed at keeping the plan relevant. Don't just make the business continuity plan something your organization creates simply to comply with an industry or insurance requirement.

Train According to Business Continuity Plan Objectives

All well-developed business continuity plans are tested to ensure their thoroughness. Don't simply trust that your strategies work. Instead, run through specific scenarios, simulating the shutdown of key services and resources. Of course, these tests should never interfere with the daily operations of your organization. For instance, don't actually shut down systems and power required to run your business successfully. Document everything during these training exercises.

Keep track of any failures in communication or support structures. For instance, if a backup power supply doesn't work, or if the simulated failure is not properly communicated throughout the organization, document the failure. Use the documented failures to examine and improve the process. After fixing the perceived problem, plan another time to train with a similar scenario, and continue to document the results. Consider the business continuity plan a living document that is constantly changing in order to better protect the lives and equipment that are housed within the organization's walls.

The business continuity plan should be a document that provides guidance for preparedness training. If the plan sits on a shelf and is never read, it is useless. The organization should hold regular training sessions to ensure key personnel are aware of their roles in the recovery process, and what to expect if the system ever goes down. Make sure the training tries to replicate real life as closely as possible. Use live servers if possible, and bring in key personnel from departments to communicate as though they were in a recovery situation. Be careful not to spend too much time training, but also be sure not to train too little. If done regularly and as close to realistically as possible, issues with the recovery process will be illustrated during training. These issues can be dealt with far more easily and for a lot less money than when they are real-life problems being responded to as part of an actual system failure.

Although key management and technical personnel should be included in the training, it is likewise imperative that rank and file employees be made aware of their roles in the recovery process. Part of the employees' expectations should include what is required of them during this process. If all that is required of them is to vacate the building and let recovery personnel start the recovery process, employees should know how to properly exit the building, and where to assemble once outside. In the case of a physical emergency requiring such an exodus from the building, a manager should be assigned the duty of counting heads. Coworkers can be relied upon to discuss who showed up for work and who did not. Even if someone didn't show up for work, it would still be a good idea to try calling them on a cell phone, just to be sure they aren't trapped inside the building.

13

USER AUTHENTICATION METHODS

People have to have access to information in order to do their jobs, and we need to make them understand what is secure and what is an unsecured venue for information transmission.

Allan Rodgers

There is a consistent need in cyberspace for multiple entities to communicate securely and privately. Among many other scenarios that necessitate secure communications, organizations need to communicate with employees and clients need to communicate with organizations. All manner of personal data, including payment cards, social security numbers, and so on, are transmitted daily throughout the Internet between various parties. Before communications can be relied upon for security, all of the parties must be trusted. There needs to be a method of verifying users who wish to contact each other over the Internet while maintaining a high level of security. Once users are authenticated, they will need to maintain a secure transmission of data. The data can be authenticated and remain secure through the use of various cryptosystems, as outlined below.

User Authentication

At the core of both the web of trust and public key infrastructure is the need to authenticate users. User authentication is the process by which a user joining a particular domain is verified, so that every other user trusts the new user is who he or she claims to be. This can be accomplished through a process of "users authenticating users," or a single trusted source authenticating all other users.

Cryptosystems

One of the main issues of secure communications has to do with protecting data while in transit. If networks are hacked, communications can be monitored by digital eavesdroppers. The answer to protecting data from such eavesdropping is the employment of various cryptosystems. A cryptosystem is an entire package required to provide proper encryption and decryption of a plaintext piece of information. The necessary components include the keys, protocols, software, and algorithms used to encipher and decipher plaintext messages.

In addition to these components, cryptosystems provide confidentiality, integrity, authorization, authentication, and nonrepudiation. Confidentiality is provided through rendering the message unreadable, except for parties who hold the key. Integrity is maintained with the use of a checksum, ensuring the data have not been altered from their original state. A checksum is essentially an algorithm that is applied to data prior to transmission, and after being transmitted. If the algorithms don't produce the same result prior to and after being transmitted, then the data have either been lost in transmission or corrupted. Authorization is maintained through the use of a key; if a user does not possess the proper key, her computer cannot decipher the encrypted message and communication does not occur. Nonrepudiaiton ensures that the sender's mark is on the message; if the message is sent through the services of a cryptosystem, the receiver will know who sent it.

Cryptographic Hashing

In most computing circles, hashing is an indexing function, which takes a certain datum point and indexes it to a number, usually an integer (see Figure 13.1). This hash number is used to quickly find certain indexed records. Although cryptographic hashing can be used for such indexing of records in a table, it is most commonly used for more secure functions. In most cases, hashing is used to take a message of an indeterminate length and return an encrypted string of a fixed length. The four characteristics of a cryptographic hash function are as follows.

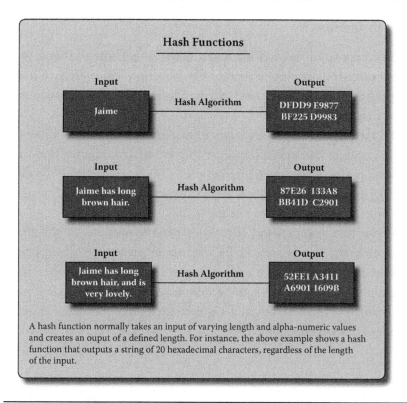

Figure 13.1   Hash Functions

1. A hash output can be easily computed for any input of any variable length.
2. Even if a hash output is given, the original message cannot be determined.
3. A message cannot be changed without changing its corresponding hash output.
4. Two messages will never have the same hash output.

Hash algorithms can be used as checksums, because the original and transmitted data, if identical, will produce the same hash output. This checksum feature is often used to verify message integrity. In forensic cases, digital forensic investigators will often use hash algorithms to build a hash output during the data gathering stage of the investigation. During a potential trial, that same hash algorithm can be used to determine if any of the data recovered in the investigation have been altered.

Data Compression

Data compression takes a file and applies an encoding scheme that compresses the data into a smaller file footprint. There are two main categories of data compression schemes, lossless data compression and lossy data compression.

Lossless data compression uses statistical redundancy to allow for more accurate decompression later. Statistical redundancy does not provide perfect decompression, but uses statistics to analyze the data during decompression, which allows for accurate "guessing" at what the missing data would have been.

Lossy data compression eliminates certain portions of the data, such that the decompressed file retains its main use while being smaller than the original file. This is most commonly used with video and digital pictures. Although decompressed pictures and videos may be smaller than their original counterparts, they maintain enough quality for acceptable use.

Symmetric and Asymmetric Keys

Keys are used for encrypting and decrypting messages. The simplest keys are substitution keys, which simply substitute one alphanumeric value for another. For instance, A = 1, B = 2, C = 3, and so on. These are not the types of keys used in computer security. Instead, algorithmic keys are applied to messages, such as the aforementioned cryptographic hashing algorithms.

Two main types of keys are used in computing, symmetric and asymmetric. A symmetric key implies a message is encrypted and decrypted using the same key. Symmetric keys pose an inherent security risk, because if the key is discovered by an unauthorized user, he can read encrypted messages, and also pose as another user.

Historically, secure cryptographic communications have relied primarily upon the existence of one secure key existing between two entities desiring to communicate in secret. The problem with this system is that if the secret key were ever to be compromised, any communication between the two parties would be able to be translated by whoever held the key. It also means more than one person would have access to the same key, which eliminates the possibility of nonrepudiation. Nonrepudiation requires only one person to have access to a password, key, or in this case, an encryption algorithm.

Asymmetric algorithms use two keys: one for encryption, and the other for decryption. One key is a public key, and another is a private key. Each user on a network has both a unique public key and private key. Both keys are generated at the same time and are mathematically related, although it has been determined impossible for a hacker to determine what one key is simply by looking at the other. Private keys are only available to their respective owners, however, all public keys are accessible by every user within the assigned public key infrastucture (PKI).

Public keys and private keys can be used to both encrypt and decrypt messages. For instance, if User A wants to send a secure message to User B, User A would first encrypt the message using User B's public key. When User B receives the message, he can decrypt it using his private key. Because the message was encrypted using User B's public key, only User B has the ability to decrypt the message.

Certificate Verification   Not only can the asymmetric keys be used to send encrypted data securely over an unsecure network, it can also be used to verify someone is who she says she is. This is accomplished through the use of the asymmetric key, as well as a digital certificate. Every user within the PKI system also has a digital certificate, which contains all pertinent data of the holder, such as a copy of the holder's public key, her name, the serial number of the certificate, and so on. This information is publically available and is usually stored in the same publicly accessible database as the public keys.

Public Key Infrastructure

The target of two parties exchanging any type of sensitive, classified, or critical data is secure and trusted communications. The goals of PKI include the administration of this secure and trusted communication between two parties. The security portion of the communication occurs in the use of digital cryptography. Both parties' computers use a predetermined set of keys, or encryption algorithms, to encrypt and decrypt each other's messages. When Computer A sends a message to Computer B, it first uses a key to encrypt the message. When

Computer B receives the message, it uses an agreed-upon key to decrypt the received transmission.

The other part of the equation is trust. It is essential to keep in mind that a PKI is not a complete solution, but instead a construct, or concept, within which solutions can be executed. Perhaps the biggest hurdle in the PKI system is the establishment of trust. Both Computer A and Computer B must trust that the other is whom it claims to be. It could be disastrous for a computer masquerading as Computer A to contact Computer B, only to have Computer B provide Computer A with some otherwise secure and secret information. But how are the two computers to verify each other's identity, especially if they have never shared a prior connection?

Consider the multiple e-commerce transactions that occur in the millions per day. Although customers who enter a store do not necessarily need to authenticate themselves at the time of purchase, in order for an e-commerce site to provide successful security to its customers, it must provide the confidentiality, integrity, authentication, and non-repudiation as needed for complete security to exist.

Availability and integrity are important factors for any website, but more security is required for e-commerce websites receiving orders from customers and processing credit cards. Such sites must not only establish and maintain integrity and availability of the marketing information to be posted on the site, they must also authenticate customer data and provide confidentiality for customer records. In addition, the system must provide a method of nonrepudiation, so that an online customer cannot dispute he actually made the purchase. In essence, for an e-commerce site, all four characteristics of information security are required: confidentiality, availability, integrity, and nonrepudiation.

In addition to the aforementioned e-commerce transaction, there exist many more situations wherein such a concept would apply, such as the following.

- Remote secure transfer of files between two or more parties
- Symmetric key distribution and management
- Digital voting booths
- Verification of an individual's identification
- Secure login for website manipulation and updates
- Virtual private networks

Certificate Authority

One of the answers provided by PKI, in regard to establishing trust between two entities, is the use of a certificate authority (CA). A CA is a third entity who essentially vouches for both parties attempting a secure connection. This trusted third party (TTP) verifies that the two communicating parties are both who they claim to be. The CA is trusted to provide this authentication of the two parties because of prior and independent authentication. Each communicating party has previously and independently authenticated the CA, so any connection made through the CA is automatically trusted. The prior authentication can occur using several different methods, and may vary in stringency, depending on what information you are trying to protect and which protections need to be afforded it.

Registration Authority

Before a user is assigned a key, the PKI process must first verify her identity. Depending on the importance of the data being protected, this can be achieved online or in person. Because of the efficiency of online transactions, the vast majority of systems verify identities via online processes. The role of PKI responsible for providing this authentication is the registration authority (RA). The RA ensures the proper binding of asymmetric keys, and provides assurance that the keys are associated with the correct and authenticated user.

X.509 or PKIX

X.509 is a version of PKI that provides users with a hierarchal, single sign-on (SSO) environment. A root certificate authority is usually distributed to an organization's employees, so they can access the organization's PKI system. The CA can be bound to a distinguished name, an e-mail address, or a DNS entry. One difference between X.509 and other PKI systems is the ability to create and maintain a certificate revocation list (CRL). The CRL is a list of certificates that have been revoked or are no longer valid.

Key Management

All of these keys and certificates require proper and careful management. The management of asymmetric keys, including verification of individuals and the creation, dissemination, and storage of the keys, is perhaps the biggest and most costly portion of a PKI system. The people, hardware, and software required is huge, and should be thought out thoroughly prior to deciding your organization needs to implement a PKI system.

The good news is that your company does not necessarily need to create the entire system from scratch. If, after reviewing certain e-commerce or secure online processes, your organization decides it is in fact necessary to implement some sort of PKI system for protecting data, there are third-party vendors available who already have the required software and infrastructures in place to provide you with PKI management.

PKI Vendors

Because of the costs surrounding such a massive undertaking, involving personnel, server equipment, policy creation and implementation, training, and encryption schemes, just to name a few, it might behoove your organization to look to a PKI vendor for assistance. The costs to hire another organization already set up to perform the necessary tasks to implement PKI are generally far less than designing, building, and maintaining your own.

An added bonus of working with a PKI vendor is scalability. If your organization takes the project on in-house, it may be difficult to increase the capacity of servers to accommodate growing bandwidth and storage loads. Conversely, if your organization purchases too much capacity, but the anticipated traffic doesn't materialize into reality, getting any kind of return from the money invested in the infrastructure will be next to impossible. Having a third-party vendor with a tiered approach to services offered will allow your organization to pick and choose the needed components for your PKI solution.

There are many PKI vendors, although perhaps the most commonly used is VeriSign. Their services range the gamut of the entire

PKI world and their name is usually seen on bank websites and other major commercial sites where security and e-commerce are concerns. Another major player in the PKI industry is RSA. RSA provides many of the largest companies in the world with security solutions, including applications of PKI solutions. CyberTrust is a company that offers PKI services, and was purchased by Verizon.

No matter which company you choose for your PKI solutions, be certain it has a proven track record. It may be wise to give the IT departments of some of their customers a call to find out how easy the companies are to work with, what solutions they offer, cost of products, and any other important information that will help your organization in determining which vendor to choose.

VeriSign
Website: www.VeriSign.com
Contact Phone: 650-426-5310

RSA
Website: www.RSASecurity.com
Contact Phone: 800-495-1095

Verizon (CyberTrust)
Website: www.verizonbusiness.com
Contact Phone: 781-693-3570

Web of Trust

An alternative method of verifying users within the same domain is the web of trust (WOT) model. The web of trust model is a flexible form of authenticating users, which can change depending on what the users require. User authentication for an established WOT usually occurs in three stages: not trusted, partially trusted, and fully trusted. Unlike PKI, WOT does not use a certificate authority to verify users. In most cases, a fully trusted member of the WOT can verify another user. It commonly takes three partially trusted members to verify another user. The specific parameters, for instance, whether partial trust is allowed at all, can be changed by the users of a WOT. Because the requirements for this verification scheme are so flexible, true security cannot be guaranteed with certainty. Users should therefore use caution when communicating in a WOT. Web of trust operations fall under the category of data transmission known as pretty good privacy.

Pretty Good Privacy

Pretty good privacy, or PGP, is an authentication program often used for signing, encrypting, and decrypting e-mails. PGP exists in many different forms. Some implementations of PGP provide symmetric keys, others asymmetric. It is not generally accepted as being as secure as PKI, although PKI methods have now been adopted into some implementations of PGP.

14

COMPUTER AND
NETWORK FORENSICS

In today's world, people put most everything on computers. We
need the forensics capability to go in and retrieve that information off the company's networks.

Earl Devaney

In the physical world, people use doors, locks, and walls to store and
protect private items and important documents. If somebody outside
those protected walls desires to gain access to a protected area, he
can do so with a little skill and luck. If he is really skillful, he can
even cover his tracks so that nobody even knows he was there. This is
especially true if he doesn't actually break anything during the illegal intrusion. If somebody wanted to take photographs of important
documents contained in an office, and had the skills to pick a lock and
pass by security without being detected, she could achieve this feat
and nobody would even know the documents had been compromised.

The same concepts are true in the digital world of crime. With the
right equipment, skills, and time, a digital criminal can gain access to
your system and copy, delete, manipulate, or otherwise destroy your
important data. This chapter reviews what steps can and should be
taken by an organization once it learns its data has been successfully
attacked. As in the physical world, reliance upon basic forensic principles will prevail in regard to best practices.

Because of the emergence of computers in our everyday lives, a
thorough approach to digital forensics has surfaced as the *de facto*
guideline (see Figure 14.1). The first approach to accomplishing this
guideline was mentioned at the First Digital Forensics Research
Workshop. Much like its physical world counterpart, digital forensics is concerned with appropriate handling of evidence for admissible

---

Three "A"s of Digital Forensics

ACQUIRE

During the acquisition of evidence, investigators must be certain the integrity of the data is protected, so that when the data is entered into evidence, its integrity is not questioned. This is accomplished by adhering to the procedures of chain of custody.

AUTHENTICATE

Because digital data can be easily duplicated and altered, it must be authenticated as genuine at the time it is collected. Later, during a trial, the same process can be used to ensure the data has not changed and is in fact authentic. Usually, a checksum or hashing sequence is used to verify the authenticity of a piece of data.

ANALYZE

Data must be analyzed to determine the nature of the data. Is the data itself criminal in nature, or was the data illegally obtained?

Figure 14.1   Three "A"s of Digital Forensics

use in court. Although digital forensics as a whole is a complex and meticulous methodology, the entire process is sometimes referred to in terms of the three "A"s: acquire, authenticate, and analyze.

Acquire

One of the most difficult parts of solving any digital crime is locating the evidence. For some crimes, discovering evidence will be as easy as looking on the hard drive. Others will require the investigator to look at the computer's RAM, as might be the case in some network intrusions where the computer being used to accomplish the crime is external to the network, but traces of the attack can still be found on local RAM.

When acquiring evidence, it is absolutely essential to keep in mind the integrity of the data being retrieved. The investigator must always be mindful of the fact that evidence must hold up in a court of law as being complete and not tampered with, as it was when first discovered by the investigator. At no time during a trial can the original data's intactness come into question, as it will cause serious doubt as to the quality of data being presented later in court. Keeping this in mind, there are certain procedures that must be followed in order to ensure the integrity of the data being acquired is in its original state, as found during the investigation. Most of these procedures are part of what is known in the forensics world as the chain of custody.

Chain of Custody

The term *chain of custody* has been used for years in law enforcement when considering evidence. The data recovered from a computer used in facilitating a crime is considered evidence, and therefore the chain of custody for each bit of information gathered during the investigation must be properly documented. In essence, anybody should be able to look at a piece of evidence's documented chain of custody and determine the following information.

Evidence ID   This is the unique identifier, or name, assigned to the piece of evidence. This can be a serial number or name, but should be unique to each piece of evidence so that each piece can be tracked separately. This information can be entered into a database for easy searching. Note: Even though it is wise to place information about the evidence into a secure database, make absolutely certain the piece of evidence has an actual physical document that is attached to it from the time it is considered evidence. Databases can easily change to reflect different information about evidence, but messing with a document with an unchangeable ID number stamped on the top, although possible to fake, is a lot more challenging.

Evidence   Although a physical description of the item is not necessary, the chain of custody should briefly discuss what the evidence is. For instance, "HR Records for XYZ Organization, dated January 4th through March 31st, 2008." If an investigation is large enough, different pieces of evidence will begin to look alike. Even if there is only a handful of evidence, if an investigation is lengthy, investigators may forget what each piece of evidence was. This is why it is important to describe each piece of evidence in the associated chain of custody document.

Who Found the Evidence?   In case the evidence is used in trial, the person who originally found the evidence may need to testify about the methods used to uncover it. Be sure to include contact information, or at least the department the person works in as well as their complete name.

Who Has Handled the Evidence?   One of the most crucial aspects of the chain of custody is the metaphorical "chain" of people who have come in contact with the evidence. Each piece of evidence should be officially handled and documented by one person at a time. This creates a detailed paper trail of where the evidence has traveled, and forces accountability upon those who have touched the evidence. If the evidence is in a different state after being handled by a particular individual, that person better have a good reason why.

There should be absolutely no gaps in time, to the minute, of where a piece of evidence has been. If Person A is handing off the item of evidence to Person B at 12:53 p.m., the log associated with the evidence should reflect the exact time. This portion of the concept of chain of custody is absolutely imperative! If gaps exist in a piece of evidence's chain of custody, the evidence could be thrown completely out of court no matter how compelling it may be. The defense can always argue that evidence was altered during those undocumented gaps in the history.

Where Was the Evidence? This refers to the location where the evidence was originally situated before it was entered as evidence. For instance, if a disk was found in the drawer of a suspect, the chain of custody document might say, "Top right drawer of suspect's desk in room number 324." If the evidence is physical in nature, such as with a physical hard drive, computer, or peripheral, take snapshots of the evidence, making sure to get the "big picture" of the physical context in which the evidence was found (for instance, the desk in the office), as well as close-up photos that might later reveal more information about the evidence. If the evidence is strictly digital in nature, screenshots may be necessary. Often times, screenshots are not enough to capture the entire scope of digital evidence, and entire computer systems will be physically taken into evidence.

When Was the Evidence Found? This refers to the time and date the evidence was found and entered as evidence. Remember that from this time stamp onward, the chain of custody begins.

Why Is the Item Considered Evidence? This covers a brief description of why the item was entered into evidence; that is, somebody's login history could be entered into evidence because certain network sabotage only occurred during the times this individual was logged on.

How Was the Evidence Collected?   List any tools, software programs, and methods used to gain access to a suspect's computer to gather and store data considered evidence. It is critical to meticulously document these methods, because if the evidence ever makes it to court, defense lawyers will rightfully question the methods used to collect it.

How Was the Evidence Secured?   It is important to list on the chain of custody document the methods used to secure the evidence. For instance, if a PC is taken into custody, what physical locks were placed on the disk drives, how was the tower or computer case physically secured, and what if any container was the PC placed in to ensure nobody tampered with the evidence? If the chain of custody document states disk drives were removed or physically locked, and the PC in evidence has accessible disk drives installed, either the document was incorrectly filled out or the PC was tampered with in the interim. Either way, the validity of the evidence is called into question.

The bottom line is to essentially document the entire process of collecting evidence, including all details. Be sure to have only the highest level of accuracy in your documentation of evidence. Do not guess at times or dates, and do not make assumptions. Only document that which you know to be true. To do otherwise will compromise your integrity as a professional, and will destroy any credibility otherwise offered by the evidence in a potential trial.

Identification

The process of identifying evidence is without a doubt the most difficult part of the entire process. This is especially true if the suspect being investigated is computer savvy and has taken steps to specifically hide, delete, or otherwise obfuscate evidence. Looking for evidence in a computer is like trying to find evidence in the physical world after a crime has been committed, only physical crimes are usually limited to one scene. If a crime is digital in nature, the investigator must possess the skills necessary to scour hundreds of gigabytes of data in the attempt to discern evidential information from other files that are innocuous in nature.

Evidence locations may include the following.

- Computer hard drives
  - Registries
  - Hidden files
  - Unallocated space
  - Password-protected files
  - Encrypted files
  - Application files (saved documents)
  - System logs
  - Firewall logs
  - Router logs
  - Internet service provider (ISP) logs, if made available with subpoena
  - Slack space
- Floppies, CDs, flash drives, and any other removable data storage media.
- PDAs, cell phones, gaming devices, and any other portable storage devices

A thorough digital investigation requires myriad specializations and vast areas of knowledge. Just as in the physical world, many investigators may be necessary to obtain the evidence. Some of the areas of knowledge required to successfully acquire evidence might include the following.

Operating Systems   These include all versions of Windows, variations of Unix, Linux, and Mac OS, and also embedded operating systems such as Palm OS, Embedded Windows, and many more. As more cell phones and mobile devices arrive on the scene, the number of operating systems is constantly increasing, placing more demand on the digital investigator.

Hardware   A digital forensic investigator will also be tasked with knowing precisely how all of the various pieces of hardware operate within the computer. This is not the same as being a technician who is an expert at building and maintaining computer systems, but requires a whole different set of skills. These skills require investigators to do the "impossible," which may involve gathering information from a physically broken hard drive, retrieving and reading deleted information from a disk, decrypting encrypted files, and discovering a digital "trail" among millions of logs and records. The list goes on, although it is apparent that a good investigator must have the ability to find "a needle in a stack of needles."

Software The term *software* covers a massive scope of knowledge. For instance, router firmware, viruses, and accounting software packages are all considered software. Each relevant manifestation of software in a criminal investigation will need to be understood, to the point where an investigator can properly dissect the software and determine exactly how it was used in the commission of a crime.

File Retrieval Files associated with digital crime will likely be deleted, especially if the criminal knows law enforcement has discovered his criminal actions. Criminal investigators must be familiar with current methods of extracting deleted files from hard drives. In addition to deleting files, some criminals may corrupt incriminating files so they cannot be opened. Corrupted files are often harder to open than so-called deleted files, and require a special set of file retrieval skills.

Cryptography

Digital investigators should be familiar with current hash algorithms and cryptographic methods. In addition, investigators should be able to work with the latest available decryption packages.

Digital Forensic Tools

Depending on whether investigators are attempting to decrypt a file, retrieve deleted files, or "fix" a corrupted file, they must understand which tools are available and appropriate for each task.

Evidence Preservation

As stated throughout this chapter, the preservation of the gathered evidence is essential, as without such preservation the integrity of the evidence is called into question. Sometimes, gathering the information to be used as evidence is not so simple, however. Investigators may need several hours, days, or weeks to dissect the evidence in an effort to build an accurate picture of the information. In an ideal investigation, the investigator could simply sit down at the PC or system in question and type away until he or she located the desired information. This is not always possible; for instance, with some key organizational servers required for continued daily use, a file or system may not be able to be removed from service for analysis because of its criticality to the operation.

In these cases, an investigator can use specialized software to create an exact copy of the original evidence needed for analysis. This process of copying the data bit for bit is often referred to as "imaging." Because of the ease with which data can be copied and altered, only special forensic software should be used for these procedures. This software provides assurance, through special algorithms and methodologies of marking original files, that the imaged version of the file is absolutely identical to the original. The bottom line, as with the chain of custody documents discussed above, is that the investigator must prove that the data being considered evidence have not been tampered with in any way.

Authenticate

If the ultimate goal is to submit evidence to a court, the data being submitted must be shown to be identical to the original. This is done through a process using a time stamp at the time of evidence collection, and is referred to as "hashing." Hashing uses an algorithm through which the data are processed, along with time and system information. This process creates what is referred to as a "checksum," which is a number that only the specific processed data can repeat when put through the same hashing algorithm. When the evidence is later submitted, special hashing software must be used to compare the hashed software with the copied version. The algorithm will come up with the same checksum, if the data are identical. MD5 and SHA-1 are two of the better-known hash functions.

Analyze

After the investigator has retrieved the digital evidence, she must pore through all the data in an effort to build a complete picture of the criminal activities. This is much easier stated than accomplished. If an investigator has incomplete data, it is often difficult to draw conclusions and connections between key pieces of data. Sometimes, investigators may even know or have a good idea where data are located, but simply cannot get to them. This is true of data on hard drives that have been overwritten. Although it is very difficult for a person to overwrite data at the same memory locations on a hard drive, it can be equally or more difficult for an investigator to retrieve data from a drive that has been mostly or partially overwritten. Again, this is where specialized software comes into play.

The Digital Investigator

Relying on experience, ingenuity, and a growing arsenal of forensic tools, the digital investigator can often be the linchpin in a solid case against a criminal. Your organization may not employ a specialized digital investigator, however, it is important to be aware they exist, and can help your organization if you need data retrieved or analyzed. In fact, it may add credibility to your organization if a certified third-party digital investigator is hired to assist during digital forensic examinations of your organization's networks. If Sally in Accounting is being fired for embezzling money from the company, it may be wise to hire somebody outside your company to gather the evidence if you intend on pressing charges, or if you simply want to document the evidence in its entirety to protect your organization from possible repercussions.

Apart from hiring or subcontracting digital investigators for assistance with your organization's attempt to locate and analyze forensic data on your network, it is critical to understand how they operate, in order to preserve the credibility of the evidence they collect. By knowing the importance of the chain of custody process and obeying its general concepts, your organization will not only add to its credibility in the courtroom, but you will also be a help to law enforcement and any outside contract labor you wish to hire.

15
MALWARE

I can't imagine a secure system that wasn't difficult due to the ongoing war with hackers and malware.

Charles Kramer

The Internet is like a modern-day Wild West. Because it is impossible to create law and order among the vast horizons of data on the Internet, malicious software and cyber criminals roam, for the most part freely, among the vast throngs of innocent digital denizens of the Internet. Most people who venture onto the digital plains of information will likely come into contact with some ill-intentioned software. This software is generally designed by cyber criminals and then "released" into the "wild" to perform destructive, invasive, and otherwise illegal actions.

These malicious software, or malware, programs are varied in their approach to destruction, so the defenses against them must be equally diversified. In order to properly protect a network against the different strains of malware, we must first have a look at many of the different types of malware and digital attacks. There are viruses, worms, Trojan horses, keyloggers, denial-of-service attacks, botnets, and more. Malware is also always intended to do harm. That is to say, malware should not be confused with "buggy" software, which fails to perform as designed due to mistakes rather than planned malicious intent.

Viruses

Many people use the terms *malware* and *virus* interchangeably, although there is a differentiation that can be drawn between the two. The term *malware* can be applied to any form of software that causes damage to other software or hardware. This "damage" could take form in any variety of ways. The most commonly accepted definition of a software virus is a piece of malware that self-replicates. Therefore, a virus is a subset of the larger term malware.

As stated above, a computer virus is any program that self-replicates. This means the software can copy itself onto another system without the knowledge or approval of the system's owner. This process occurs whenever one system comes into contact with another system, and the virus embeds itself in data transferred from one to the other. For instance, this happens when an infected computer accesses another computer on a network with the user's knowledge. During an IRC chat session, for example, a virus could access the open and connected port used for IRC (usually port 6667) to transfer itself to another computer.

Most commonly, the instructions within a virus will attempt to copy it onto a server, as this gives the virus the largest access to new "host" computers. Once on the server, the virus can simply wait for other computers to access the server. As soon as a new chat session is started with another computer, the virus will copy itself through the new connection. The virus cannot, however, open communications with another computer on its own in order to duplicate itself on another computer. In the IRC example, a virus could not initiate an IRC session on its own and then propagate itself onto the IRC server, but would require the IRC session to already exist.

Worms

Worms are one of the biggest single threats to the Internet as a whole today. If a large-scale Internet attack makes it into the news, it likely has something to do with a worm. The reason worms are so devastating to the Internet is because they have the ability to open connections with other computers, unlike traditional viruses. This may not seem like a much bigger problem, but consider the fact that this gives the worm virtually unlimited scope. Whereas most viruses are designed to affect certain servers, networks, or protocols, such as the IRC example mentioned above, worms will exploit any other computer attached to its current host. If we follow those connections out to the extremes, we quickly realize this encompasses the entire Internet!

Famous Worms

Virtually every computer will be connected, in some fashion, to the Internet. Because of the resource drain a mass-propagated worm would place upon every system connected to the Internet, it is easy to see how a well-designed worm could bring the world to its knees.

In order to gain an even clearer picture of the devastation dealt by worms, let's discuss some of the more famous cases that have affected massive amounts of the Internet. These examples have occurred over the span of the Internet's history. Worms are not new, nor have they diminished in occurrence or ability to ruin networks. It is crucial to understand their history in an attempt to more accurately determine their future. Imagine the chaos at retail locations, military installations, hospitals, and any other organization that depends upon daily operations of computers, if those computers could not function.

The Christmas Tree Worm—1987   The Christmas Tree Worm sent messages to users and asked them to type the word, "Christmas." Once the user typed Christmas, the worm would use the list of names stored on the user's computer. So great was the drain on resources that IBM's mainframe crashed on Christmas Day of 1987 due to the resource drag.

The Internet Worm (aka Morris Worm)—1988   One of the earliest worms was quite simply called the Internet Worm. The longer name of the worm is sometimes the Internet Worm of November 2, 1988, in reference to its original launch date. This worm was created by a PhD student at Cornell University, although it was sent from MIT to disguise this fact. The student who wrote it wanted to know how large the Internet was, and the worm was written to propagate through the whole Internet to determine its size. At that time in the Internet's history, most networked computers were still at universities across the nation, and security was scarcely considered. Because of the inherent lack of security on the networks, it was easy for the student to create a piece of software that would simply open connections with other computers and then duplicate itself onto their hard drives.

Because there were no "checks" in place to prevent the process continuing ad infinitum, the worm continued to duplicate again and again until virtually all of the resources of each computer were dedicated to reduplicating the worm. In addition to the gaping holes in the Internet's inherent security, a general lack of password security helped allow the worm to spread to damaging proportions. This brought computing speeds and connection throughput to a crawl (even by that day's standard). Communications were slowed so much that when the student attempted to inform every infected computer how to properly remove the worm, the message could not be sent. It took many months to undo the damage, and estimates report the costs were between $1 million and $10 million.

The intent of the Internet Worm was not malicious, but it crippled the existing Internet infrastructure because of its simple, yet powerful and unrelenting nature. An interesting note about the Internet Worm is that the original source code is still contained on a floppy disk, now at the Boston Museum of Science. Another fact is the coder of the worm, Robert Tappan Morris, who originally disguised the code to appear as though it came from MIT, is now an MIT professor.

The Love Bug Worm—2000   In May of 2000, the Love Bug worm struck. Victims were emailed an MS Word file, with the Subject line of the e-mail reading "ILOVEYOU." The e-mail would always be sent from another user's hijacked e-mail account, so the receiving user would see an e-mail sent from somebody they knew, along with a deceptive note requesting them to open the letter. The user would open the file, and immediately their e-mail would be hijacked as well. The worm would use all of the e-mail addresses in the user's contact list to duplicate the message over and over.

The Love Bug worm is historically notable for more than a couple of reasons. Because e-mail was still gaining popularity around the world, users were not yet educated about the dangers associated with opening file attachments without scanning them for viruses if they weren't sure of the origins or intent of the file. This worm would help push education regarding such precautions. Another reason the Love Bug worm is important to consider is the fact that it propagated itself onto the computers at the U.S. White House, Congress, and even the Pentagon! The relative simplicity of the program allowed it to masquerade as a friendly file in order to gain access into the supposedly most secure networks in the world.

Historically speaking, the existence of the Love Bug worm brought to light many of the shortcomings of our legal system to deal with such attacks. Although the perpetrator was located in the Philippines, and proof was sufficient to determine he was the culprit, no laws existed to prosecute him. Philippine law protected against accessing computers without the knowledge of users for fraudulent use, but provided no measures regarding the intent to cause damage. Therefore, the cyber criminal responsible for the act was never prosecuted, and the billions of dollars of damage it cost nations around the world were never recovered. The Philippines have since enacted severe cyber laws, but of course cannot go back and charge the culprit with the original crime.

The Sasser Worm—2004 The Sasser worm exploited security issues in some installations of Windows XP and Windows 2000. This worm replicated itself and spread through predetermined, unprotected ports (most commonly TCP ports 445 and 139, used for SMB and NetBIOS, respectively). The worm utilizes a buffer overflow exploit in Microsoft's Local Security Authority Subsystem Service, or LSASS. Thus, the name "Sasser" (after LSASS). If installed on unpatched and unupdated Windows XP and Windows 2000 machines, the Sasser worm will spread quickly and cause massive damage, but the worm can be stopped easily with a downloaded and installed security update from Windows.

Conficker (aka Downadup)—2009 In early 2009, the Conficker worm spread throughout the Internet via guessing at passwords, and hitching rides on USB sticks and other portable devices. Once the flash drive was inserted into a new host, the virus planted itself. Unlike many of the earlier viruses and worms, Conficker planted a file onto its host computers that turned computers into bots, which can be made to send information, such as keystrokes, passwords, e-mail contacts, or whatever other information the sender of the worm wants to see.

Protecting Against Worms

Worms are allowed to propagate through holes that exist in the security of applications and operating systems. The best protection against worms is to make sure your software is up to date. Vendors of these systems and applications are continually reviewing their code and issuing software updates, or patches, to protect against these attacks. Sometimes patches are not created or installed quickly enough, and Zero Day attacks occur. Zero Day attacks are attacks that attempt to exploit holes in an application's security before a patch is issued to prevent potential exploits.

Keyloggers

Keyloggers are hidden malicious programs that are installed on a user's computer to monitor, record, and transmit user keystrokes. In this manner, a cyber criminal can collect all sorts of personal information from users. This includes passwords, login information, browsing history, and more. Because keyloggers don't require a lot of overhead in terms of processing speed, it is generally not easy for the casual user to detect their presence. That is why keyloggers usually will be installed and remain undetected for very long periods of time, if an appropriate antivirus application is not used frequently.

Rootkits

The primary purpose of a rootkit is to hide the presence of malware on a computer. Rootkits are designed to take control of operating systems with the intent of tricking the OS into ignoring the rootkit and malware. This can be done by "hiding" the malware, or by convincing the OS the software being run by installed malware is approved, thereby raising no red flags.

Sometimes rootkits include entire suites of malware. For instance, rootkits might include a Trojan horse, which is a program that appears to be an authorized process, such as one that is related to the operating system or a known and authorized application. Often, these Trojan horses include backdoors, which are hidden entry points through which a cyber criminal may enter any time after the rootkit has been deployed and successfully installed. This allows the cyber criminal complete access to the system at a later date. Cyber criminals will also sometimes install adware and spyware as part of the rootkits (see below). Usually, an attacker will pick one type of malicious program, because bombarding an otherwise healthy OS with the requirements for running all of the extra software will raise flags and increase the chances of discovery. Because rootkits almost always contain software to hide their tracks, these additional malicious programs are rarely seen or noticed by users.

Spyware

Spyware is a type of malware that usually does more than simply "spy" on users. Spyware generally collects data from users' computers such as personal information, Internet surfing habits, and so forth, however, many spyware programs actually change settings in the computers on which they are installed. For instance, some of them redirect web browsers or change the user's homepage to another site, and then remove the ability to change it back without considerable work. Because spyware creates such havoc with browsers, one of the key indicators of whether your computer has been affected is a sudden and large drop in browsing speed.

Adware

Although some adware actually exists as stand-alone malware applications, others are part of complete spyware installations. These irritating packages generally start flashing advertisements whenever a user's browser is run, and many of the adware packages actually go a step further by downloading other advertisements. Like spyware, many of these malware packages are first noticed when browsing speed drops. Of course, the unending stream of unwanted ads flashing up on a user's screen is usually a good indicator too!

Trojan Horses

Trojan horses are viruses that specifically leave what is known as a "backdoor" in the operating system of the victim's computer, for later easy access by the cyber criminal. These files are usually masked inside other files and programs that appear to be legitimate. For instance, some Trojans piggyback on small computer games or desktop themes. Users download and install the desktop theme or game, and the Trojan installs itself too. The user never sees the Trojan, but all the while the cyber criminal who launched the attack has access to that computer. Because these viruses appear to be benign, but offer criminals such potentially devastating access, they are particularly dangerous to computers. A good antivirus program will have an up-to-date catalogue of known Trojan horse virus attacks, and will perform periodic hard drive sweeps in an attempt to locate and remove such malware.

Types of Antivirus Programs

Regardless of how vigilant an administrator is in regard to monitoring internal and perimeter network traffic, it is nearly impossible to prevent every single malware file from breaking through the network firewalls. There are many steps that need to be taken to ensure proper mitigation against software viral attacks. Just as with good firewall policy, protecting networks from viruses should be considered as a multilayered approach. The first layer is the protection offered by the firewall, although for the sake of argument, the following information applies to protecting the network against malware that has already breached your network's firewall systems. The holistic approach to antiviral protection includes at least a couple of different antivirus types, as well as up-to-date software patches for each layer of potentially affected software.

As software attacks have become more complex, so too have the methods deployed against them (see Figure 15.1). Original antivirus programs only scanned the hard drive for known viruses, but there are now myriad antivirus program types, including signature-based scanning, malicious behavior detection, resident-memory detection, start-up detection, and inoculation. No matter which antivirus applications you choose to employ on your network, be certain you have covered at least all of these types, with redundancy in at least the start-up detection, inoculation, and signature-based scanning arenas.

Signature-Based Scanning

Most antivirus programs have a massive built-in catalogue of software viruses for which they search on hard drives, floppy drives, and any other chosen data storage device. Every virus has a unique associated

---

Signature vs Behavior Detection

SIGNATURE BASED

Many viruses have a 'signature,' or a recognizable series of ones and zeros. Signature-based antivirus programs can spot these signatures and stop the files before they wreak havoc in your system.

BEHAVIOR BASED

A behavior-based anitivirus monitors system processes to determine if a program is attempting to engage in malicious behavior against the operating system.

Figure 15.1   Antivirus Types

string of code from which it operates. This unique code is known as a virus signature. The signature is essentially the virus itself, meaning if the signature can be found and stopped, the virus will be rendered ineffective. Sometimes the signature is embedded in another nonmalicious piece of software through a process known as code injection, and other times the virus is attached to portions of the operating system or an application.

Behavior-Based Scanning

Although many antivirus programs scan files in storage, other virus detection methods include active monitoring of processes. This active monitoring attempts to "catch" malicious code as it is being executed. For instance, some malware will attempt to format drives, inject malicious code into existing files, corrupt registry files, or replace good files with infected ones, along with several other types of malicious behavior. An active monitor will alert users or administrators to this type of behavior, and will not allow it until it is specifically approved and allowed. Because this type of active monitoring requires constant perusing of system files, there may be a slight but noticeable degradation in system performance.

Another sometimes irritating side effect of this type of monitoring is the occasional appearance of false positive reports. These occur when the monitoring system decides that a normal program or otherwise authorized process is potentially malicious. If a user essentially runs the same processes and programs every day, this irritation can be significantly mitigated, because there is often a checkbox option that can be selected, which tells the monitoring application that the process is approved and not to alert the user ever again of the process. As each process is approved, fewer false positives should occur over time.

Memory Resident Detection

Memory resident detection virus scanning software is triggered based on specific events, such as whenever an application is initially run or during operating system shutdowns. This style of detection will increase the chances of preventing a virus attack, inasmuch as many viruses are initialized based on such triggers. The downside is that because the scanner is attempting to scan a file at the same time the file is executing, system performance for the scanned files will likely be degraded. Of course, if the tradeoff is too much, certain files can be excluded from this type of detection.

Inoculation

In addition to detection and removal of malware, many antivirus applications will also provide malware prevention in the form of inoculation. Inoculation of boot sectors and program files essentially involves an antivirus program taking inventory of files in regard to size and contents. If the antivirus program finds a file changed on any subsequent scan, it will alert the user. Chances are good that if a user has not authorized changes to a boot sector, a virus may have committed the change.

Detecting and Removing Viruses

Whatever the method of attack is used in a virus, an antivirus package has a few different options to stop the virus, including quarantining, repairing and deletion. Quarantining is the most common first step that an antivirus software application will take. For this, the antivirus program simply moves the malicious file to a protected area on the hard drive, separate from any other file that could activate the malicious software. Another method of quarantining is simply encrypting the virus, thereby making it unreadable by any running process. If the virus caused some files to become corrupt, another step offered by some antivirus programs is the option to repair the corrupted file to its original state. Beyond quarantining and repairing files, antivirus programs will also sometimes simply delete infected files. This can be dangerous, because it is impossible for an antivirus program to determine with 100% accuracy which files are malicious and which ones are authorized. Many times, antivirus programs will inadvertently target other antivirus programs as potential malware. This is because of the many "behind the scenes" processes being run by the antivirus programs, which oftentimes are embedded into system registries and sensitive system processes. Therefore, be careful which programs you allow your antivirus programs to delete. Quarantining is always a good initial step, but be sure to delete any file once it is a known piece of malware.

Make sure the antivirus program you use allows you to perform all of the aforementioned actions on suspicious files. Also, it is wise to ensure that whichever antivirus packages the administrator chooses to have installed, the programs should include the option to scan based on a manual startup, or automatically at designated intervals. Because the list of viruses is perpetually growing, these updates will ideally be performed daily. Some programs require a large amount of CPU power to search the entire contents of the computer hard drive and associated floppies, and processing speed can sometimes suffer as a result. Therefore, be sure too that any automated process is scheduled during downtime, such as during the middle of the night, after workers have gone home for the day. In situations where a computer is used by three different shifts and has no official "downtime," such as in a 24-hour call center, it would be wise to schedule the scanning during lunch breaks.

Start-Up Detection

A limited form of malicious behavior, or signature-based scanning is start-up detection. Antivirus protection applications that perform this type of scanning are specifically aiming to stop the initialization and spread of viruses during the start-up sequence. The added bonus of running this type of virus scan is performance-based, because the scan only monitors boot-up functions, instead of scanning the entire system for viruses. Of course, the drawback is the incompleteness of the check.

Restore Points

When all else fails, there is always the restore point to fall back on. Operating system restore points provide administrators with a known working point to which to restore the OS settings. Keep in mind that restore points do not back up files or any user data. In addition, it is possible that going back to a previous restore point will corrupt files or make existing applications impossible to run. Because of the potential risks of losing data associated with restoring systems to a previous point, be sure users have backed up all necessary files before attempting to restore a system.

Antivirus Restore   Many antivirus programs will take a snapshot of a user's registry files. If the registry files or boot sectors have been maliciously changed by a malware attack, the antivirus program can reinstate a previously saved copy of approved boot files.

Recommended Antivirus Programs

There are hundreds of antivirus programs, so which ones should be installed on the organization's network? As always, most administrators prefer any software installed on the network computers to be as cost effective as possible. It doesn't get any more cost effective than installing a program that works well and is free. The following programs are not only free, but they have proven themselves to work well time and again on several of the author's personal and business-related PCs and laptops. Just as with all security issues, it is ideal to install more than one antivirus program in order to provide overlapping coverage of potential threats.

Spybot - Search and Destroy (Spybot-S&D)

This program is one of the author's favorite spyware and antivirus detectors. It has been around for years, and has earned its reputation as one of the best privacy software packages available today. As a bonus, it's completely free! Spybot detects and eliminates many thousands of spyware files, viruses, rootkits, and virtually any type of malware. When combating a suspected malware issue on a computer, use Spybot in tandem with Hijackthis in an effort to locate the issue.

Although Spybot may not always be able to successfully remove every malicious item, it will almost always at least detect it and name it. Once an administrator has the name of the culprit virus infecting the computer, he can look it up on Google to find out how other people removed it. Spybot-S&D is available for free download at www.safer-networking.org/en/index.html.

If you download Spybot-S&D and use it to defend your computer, please consider making a donation, as the company that designs and maintains the product doesn't offer any upgrades or other packages for purchase, and the only apparent stream of revenue (that I can find, at least) for this product is through voluntary donations.

Lavasoft's Ad-Aware

Years ago, the author had a laptop that got infected with an adware virus that effectively brought the computer's browsing capabilities to an end. Every time Firefox or Internet Explorer started, ads popped up at a rate that made it impossible to actually navigate anywhere effectively on the Internet. After downloading Ad-Aware on a noninfected computer, the laptop was started in Safe Mode and Ad-Aware was installed. Ad-Aware not only removed the annoying virus, it located about 80 other hidden and malicious files affecting the browsing speed of the computer. The slow rate of uploading and downloading through the Internet was accepted as poor computer performance, and it was very surprising when the connection substantially improved afterward. Ad-Aware has several different packages available for download, including a free version, at www.lavasoft.com.

Hijackthis

Hijackthis (HJT, for short) is a powerful tool that performs a scan of all critical system files that are most commonly affected by virus attacks. The installation doesn't require an installer, but is simply a compact executable that can be run directly from your computer with no installation, which is important if you run Windows and any files associated with the Windows Installer have been corrupted.

HJT examines all manner of files, looking for anything other than what would be installed in a "clean" version of your computer, without all of the extra applications and programs present on any working computer. For instance, most antivirus programs, browser add-ons, or any other process or file that could potentially interfere with an unadulterated version of your operating system will be suspect. Therefore, HJT will nearly always include good files along with the "bad."

With the power of Hijackthis comes the possibility of destroying potentially critical files, so be sure you know what you're deleting before deleting it. If you are unsure if a file is malicious or benign, you can create a restore point from which to reload anything previously "deleted" by the HJT. Likewise, you can also add known "good" files to an "Ignore" list, so that your scans don't continue to list these files. You can download Hijackthis, along with several other antivirus and malware detection and removal tools, from Trend Micro's website at http://free.antivirus.com/

AVG Technologies' Anti-Virus Free Edition (AVG Free)

Another free and effective antivirus software application is AVG Free. This package has several of the requisite bells and whistles to make it a powerful tool to use against malware. Automatic updates and scans are among the benefits of this program, and it can be downloaded for free at www.avg.com/us-en/homepage.

Software Updates

Regardless of which antivirus packages are installed on your networks and computers, it is imperative that security patches and software updates be installed on a regular basis. Although daily downloads provide the best measure of security, these updates should ideally be performed on at least a weekly basis.

The software updates in question are not just limited to antivirus software. Security patches also exist for e-mail management applications, web browsers, hardware drivers, operating systems, and more. Don't forget to include all possible software updates when creating a checklist. It is also a good idea to create a restore point for any major updates, such as those that might affect your operating system or e-mail management application.

16
CRAFTING A
SECURITY POLICY

You're not game-planning for your defense. You're just trying to install your base protections, your base running plays, your base passing plays.

Randy Edsall

Planning Versus Reactionary Response (Or—Why It's Important to Have a Security Plan)

Although security response teams are an essential component of any organization's complete security solution, a thorough security policy will go a long way toward preventing the need for such a team. Ideally, security policies will provide an operational roadmap for employees to follow, in order to avoid ever having to be involved in a recovery effort after a crisis hits. In a recovery effort, costs will necessarily involve more than just misallocated labor. Not only will critical organization resources need to be reallocated to damage control, but proper measures and controls will need to be put into place to prohibit, or at least mitigate, the chances of such a breach ever occurring again. A *reactionary response*, as opposed to a well-thought-out plan, creates three main issues in terms of higher cost and incomplete solutions. Reacting to an incident allows for no cost analysis of implemented solutions, forces incomplete controls to be put into place, and compounds existing security issues,

No Cost Analysis

First and most directly associated with cost is the fact that a reactionary response robs an organization of the time for appropriate cost analysis and comparison shopping. In a normal situation, a security team will have the necessary time, materials, and budget to develop a robust holistic solution for potential threats against the organization's network infrastructure. After designing a thorough approach to security, appropriate tools and solutions can be applied following careful consideration of requirements, cost, and performance issues. In contrast, a crisis response situation will not allow for such slow and thoughtful planning. Because of this, the situation may mandate immediate implementation of a security process or control that may not be the most cost-effective solution, which will result in loss of revenue.

Incomplete Controls

The second issue that will indirectly affect revenue is that a reactionary response comes with the higher likelihood of having incomplete controls put into place. Without the foresight and planning time afforded in normal circumstances, a team of professionals reacting to an event may be forced to sacrifice the best solution for the quickest remedy to the problem. Let us take the following example: A server is the backbone of a network. If one is compromised either physically or by a virus in such a manner that it can no longer function, a new one must be brought online. Four options are available in this situation:

1. Bring in an old server that has been sitting in storage. The benefit of this solution is it will generally be quicker than the other three options and won't cost you the money required to purchase a brand new server. In addition, it will allow your network to "limp" along while you work on getting a permanent, acceptable solution in place. The drawbacks associated with this solution include:
   a. *Antiquated Equipment:* The equipment was retired for a reason. Was it too slow, did it have problematic temperature issues, was it too small to handle all of the organization's records, or was it just too noisy? Whatever the reason was for getting rid of it, you will be immediately reminded of what the issue was once the server is plugged in.
   b. *Wasted Labor:* Unless the server is hot-swappable, meaning your IT Department can quickly physically remove

the damaged server and swap it with the older server, just the physical change out of the servers could take several hours. Even if the required server rack size is the same, and the units are hot-swappable, there will usually be considerable time requirements to reconfigure network settings to accept the older server back into the infrastructure. Eventually, you will either purchase a new server or reinstall the downed server once it's been repaired, so any labor spent on this swap-out will essentially not add any value to your network.

2. Purchase a new server and put it online as soon as possible. The main benefit of this is that once the new server is up and running, your organization will have a brand-new, fully functioning server that you know for certain is free of defects and viruses. The obvious downside is the massive costs associated with:

   a. *Purchase Price*: The cost of the new server will put your organization back several thousands of dollars. This is a huge purchase, and your budget simply may not allow it.

   b. *Upgrade Costs:* If your servers are older, your new server may require newer cabling, faster switching, new operating systems (OS), upgraded uninterruptable power supplies (UPS), new rack mounts, and the like. Because the server is the central core of your organization's network infrastructure, it affects every piece of network equipment and software, which means added costs with installation.

   c. *Inefficiency:* This is caused by the slower network speeds due to the extra load put on the other servers until the new server is up. This is assuming the network is still at least functional in a general sense, even with the downed server.

   d. *Misallocated Labor:* Bringing a server online is no easy or small feat, and it usually requires hundreds of hours of labor. Even if the installation is quick, this can add up very quickly. Until it is completely up and running, an unscheduled server installation will place an undue burden upon the IT Department.

3. Do nothing. Most organizations have multiple servers, so on the surface, it can sometimes seem like a reasonable solution to count on the existing servers to carry the server load. Of course, this is not the best solution unless the server that was downed was superfluous to the design of the network. If your IT Department has installed extra servers that are not central to the primary functions of the network, your organization either has too much money in its coffers, or you need to re-evaluate where your IT dollars are spent. The bottom line is that organizations don't purchase and install extraneous servers, so getting another one up and running will eventually be required.

4. Take the server offline, fix it, and reinstall it once it's up and running again. At the end of the day, this is the solution with which most IT Departments are left. Budgets don't generally allow for the purchase of another server unless in an absolute emergency, and most organizations donate, destroy, or sell antiquated equipment, so older equipment is not available to install in most cases. Of course, as with the other options, there are the drawbacks associated with downtime, misallocated labor, and slower network speeds until the server is back up.

Compounded Security Issues

This brings us to our third issue: a reactionary response will sometimes create more security issues than it solves. Because the implementation will be reactionary in nature, the solution will likely not be as thorough as when the luxury of time and forethought are available. Without this luxury, key areas of concern may be overlooked, which only leads to higher costs down the road to either fix the holes or repair damage caused by exploits allowed by those holes.

Don't Wait to Plan

Having a server fail is just one major issue that will eventually hit any unprepared, unprotected, server room. Although this is definitely one of the larger setbacks an organization could experience in terms of information security, any number of issues at various levels of severity can and will occur at most organizations. The best solution is to carefully plan beforehand, and provide thorough and appropriate security measures to protect the server before you need to make such a decision.

Don't wait until the best solution is no longer available and every concerned party is reacting to the problem instead of focusing on the best long-term plan. Even once the reactionary solution has been implemented, when a better solution is finally implemented sometime farther down the road, the costs associated with implementing that better solution will be much higher when taking into account the amount of money in unnecessary labor, network cabling and equipment, and system downtime.

Importance of a Security Policy

Designing and implementing your organization's security policy is perhaps the most important step you can take to ensure the safety of your networks, computers, and the data stored therein. This policy will serve as the touchstone against which to measure success or failure of security goals and achievements. It will serve to protect the network and its contents during daily operations, and will provide a means to globally increase security awareness within the organization. If a security breach occurs, the security policy will be used as a reference to determine the proper steps to remedy the issue. The steps contained in the policy should be broad enough to cover all aspects of network operations, but also include a level of detail that will allow personnel to act with specific deliberation.

Setting Goals and Measuring Success

Where possible, the security policy will provide specific metrics. These metrics will serve as a measurement of security needs, successes, and failures. Security needs can be quantified in risk and cost analyses, number of attacks against the network, percentage of downtime, and any other quantifiable measurement of network performance and security. Make sure the security policy is not simply put on the shelf, but is used as a tool for continuous improvement. Once a baseline is created after the first measurement, subsequent successes and failures can be monitored, and policies can be tweaked to further improve security within the organization.

Daily Operations

More important than having the policy sought during crisis, it should also serve as part of the daily operations of the organization in regard to network function and security. The concept of a well-crafted security plan asserts that if all the ideas and procedures from the security policy in question are put into place and adhered to, there will be little to no need for reactive measures during a breach because the policy will have pre-emptively protected the information and equipment from attack.

Security Awareness

A good security policy also serves as a tool to infuse the workplace with security awareness, which goes a long way in protecting equipment and software within your organization. When creating your organization's policy, remember to bear this concept in mind. Although disaster recovery and continuity planning are important issues that should be referenced in any thorough security policy, they are not the focus of the policy.

This chapter leads the neophyte policy crafter through the steps of creating a thorough security policy for the organization. Keep in mind that every organization is different from the next, so there is no set method or list of specific parameters that can be applied to every network infrastructure. Some organizations may have thousands of computers spread across myriad geographic locations, whereas others may only have three computers set up on a LAN in a home office. Most organizations will sit somewhere in between these two examples, but it is easy to see how every system will require different levels of security and complexity in its plans.

Resources for Crafting Security Policies

Many organizations have already gone through the process of creating a security policy, so why start from scratch? Most policies are crafted with specific guidelines in mind. Starting off with a template for crafting your organization's security policy will save an incredible amount of time, ensure key security components are remembered, and keep the policy relevant. Several certifications and standards already exist. Some of the more popular ones include the following.

1. *The NSA Security Guidelines Handbook (www.tscm.com/ NSAsecmanual1.html):* The National Security Agency is at the forefront of all things information assurance-related, so when they provide a handbook for security guidelines, it is well advised to get a copy and read it. According to an introductory paragraph in the document, the handbook introduces NSA employees to some "basic security principles and procedures with which all NSA employees must comply." The handbook may not be a complete treatise on the subject of information security, but it offers considerations of physical security, classification of data, access controls, hiring, management, firing, and much more.

2. *COBIT 4.1 (www.isaca.org/Knowledge-Center/COBIT/Pages/ Overview.aspx):* The Information Systems Audit and Control Association (ISACA) created, in their words, "an IT governance framework and supporting toolset that allows managers to bridge the gap among control requirements, technical issues, and business risks." Through an online interface, COBIT will assist you with creating security policies specific to the needs for the scope and size of your organization. At the time of the writing of this book, COBIT version 4.1 was the latest being offered, although plans for a 5.0 version were in the works, according to their website.

3. *ISO 27001 and ISO 27002 (www.iso.org/iso/catalogue_ detail?csnumber=50297):* The International Organization for Standardization (ISO) has created a Code of Practice for Information Security Management. This document outlines the accepted best practices for Information Security Management. ISO 27001 and 27002 are very closely related, and replaced ISO 17799 in 2007.

4. *CERT–CC (www.cert.org/certcc.html):* The CERT Coordination Center (Cert–CC) was originally designed and implemented as an incident response team, but has evolved into a team whose functions include advising system administrators regarding existing and potential threats. The Cert–CC

provides many documents and online media for professionals seeking advice on how to best protect networks and data.

5. *FASP (http://csrc.nist.gov/groups/SMA/fasp/index.html):* Federal Agency Security Practices (FASP) apply to governmental agencies, but are still a wealth of useful and relevant information for any security professional thinking about crafting a security policy for an organization.

After you have researched the various security practices and frameworks available, and have chosen which policies will best serve your organization, the actual crafting of your organization's security policy is the next step.

Crafting the Policy

It's time to craft your organization's security policy! Regardless of whether you are working for a Fortune 500 Company, or you are at a small family-owned business with 15 employees, the basic steps you take to craft your organization's security policy will be the same. First, a team of security policy crafters will need to be assembled. The team will then need to gain the support of management. At that time, they can begin the actual security policy crafting process. The policy will need to include standards, behaviors, policies, and controls. When writing the policy, the crafters will need to write the document with accessibility, supportability, and clarity in mind. Once the policy is crafted, it will need to be distributed and presented to the various individuals and departments in the organization. After policies are put into place, there will also need to be a process for review and updating of the policy.

The Team of Policy Crafters

Within your organization there should be someone, or a team of people, in charge of security issues. Sometimes this person is known as the security coordinator, security manager, or some other title related to security matters. This person might even be you, which would explain your reading this book. The point is, somebody should be in charge of guiding the process of creating a security plan tailored to your organization's specific assets and needs. Once that person or team is identified, the process of assessing your network should begin. From this assessment, the needs and subsequent policies will easily flow.

Management Support

After the security policy team is assembled, and before the framework is chosen, management must be on board. The security policy team will need to convince top-level managers of the importance of having a security policy. When presenting the ideas to management, the security policy team should remember to be concise in the message, and include specific metrics and monetary values where possible, providing risk analysis information and potential costs for failing to implement policies when available. Remember, the people in charge of the organization (specifically the bank account) will be concerned with how the security policy is going to affect the bottom line of operations. By focusing on the long-term savings implementing a security policy offers an organization, the security policy team will successfully illustrate the need for the policy.

Standards, Policies, Procedures, and Controls

A good security policy is not simply a list of rules. Such a list would be cumbersome and irrelevant, and would not get used by the vast majority of the employees at any organization. Human nature would prevail, and users wouldn't read such a list. In order to win over the end users and managers, a comprehensive approach should be taken when considering the policy. Instead of simply listing policy after policy, distinguishing the policies into separate categories, which can be further explained, helps readers understand the whole picture. A widely accepted set of delineations for security polices includes standards, procedures, policies, and controls.

Standards

In terms of information security and computing in general, standards are the technical specifications of the hardware and software comprising your network and systems. These standards might be proprietary, or they may be industry-accepted norms. Whatever the source of the standards, they are the measurable accepted basis from which your policies will be derived. Standards must be considered dynamic, in order to meet ever-changing systems technology and the threats facing a network. Of course, any employee whose job is to provide compliance to a particular security standard must be made aware of the standard, and any subsequent changes to that standard.

Policies

Policies are the documents dictating what is expected to occur throughout the organization, insofar as information security is concerned. Policies are centered on goals, not the methods for achieving those goals. For instance, a retail store's policy may dictate all customer records must be encrypted and stored for up to 90 days after a purchase is made. This policy does not discuss the particular methods to be employed toward the end of achieving the goal, but instead focuses on the outcome of encryption and storage. The standards portion of the security policy will discuss the standards of encryption, how the files will be stored, and how they will be purged from the system after 90 days.

Procedures

Procedures are specific actions required by users. The procedure will describe detailed instructions for how an employee will execute a particular policy. For instance, a policy may state that all server room employees must be sure to secure the server room when they leave for the day. The associated procedure would include details about locking the server room door, setting the alarm, locking workstations, and whatever other specific steps are required for appropriately securing the server room.

Controls

Controls are the tools put into place to ensure the policies are being properly followed. For instance, users may be instructed not to download particular files, visit certain websites, or upload programs onto their workstations. Monitoring the network with a network sniffer could be a control used to ensure the policy is being followed.

Accessibility, Supportability, and Clarity

Sometimes, when corporate documents are written, the authors forget that the document needs to be read by other people. Make sure to remember certain portions of the security policy will be read by various departments, and some people within the organization will need to pore over the entire document. When writing the policy, it is therefore important to keep in mind accessibility, supportability, and finally but most important, clarity.

Accessibility

Not only must the security policy be physically and digitally accessible throughout the company, but it must also have "accessible language." Although there is an accepted taxonomy of technical jargon that exists among many IT employees, this document should be considered globally accessible in terms of not only actual physical access, but in regard to its readability. Remember the key is to promote security awareness throughout the organization, and specific portions of the document will be written for each department. Accounting will have specific file management protocols that will not apply to Customer Service personnel, and vice versa. For instance, for the portion of the policy being sent to Human Resources, nowhere in the document should specific router settings, schematics of network interfaces, or other technical information be included, inasmuch as that information doesn't pertain to their job. Without a clear understanding of what is being protected and why, awareness will diminish, not increase. This will make the job of an IS professional much harder.

Supportability

The second requirement of an excellent security policy is supportability. Supportability has a double meaning regarding security policy. First of all, and perhaps most important, the document must be supported by the upper management of the organization. Without this support, the policy will certainly fail. Support from executive-level managers brings with it all the financial and political follow-through required for success. If you question this mandate for executive-level support, just consider how many times in your organization a company-wide policy has been successful when designed and implemented without executive support. My guess would be that it rarely, if ever, has happened.

The other requirement regarding supportability is the fact that the policy must be a dynamic document, and should be supportable in the same manner an engine or machine should be supported. If an engine needs an oil change or an overhaul, there are mechanics and owners who can perform the work. Likewise, the organization's security policy should be allowed to be maintained and overhauled, if found to be necessary. Remember, this is a living document. A stagnant security policy is a certain recipe for cyber disaster. Because security is a constantly moving target, the individuals in charge of maintaining the security policy must always be refining their aim.

Clarity

In addition to being worded in order to provide accessibility to all employees in the organization, the wording must also have a level of clarity that seeks to be unambiguous in the execution of the requirements set forth in the document. For instance, the document should not simply state that "routers must be used for security," but would provide more specific procedures for how those routers would be used. An example might be briefly describing the use of routers to isolate the organization's internal servers within a DMZ, through which only certain digital traffic may pass each way. Although the document should provide procedures, don't let it get bogged down too much in technical detail.

Assessing the Organization's Network Infrastructure

In order to provide adequate and up-to-date coverage of the network, the security team will need to perform a thorough network asset assessment. This step requires simply creating a list of all items and data your organization desires to protect. Categorizing the network hardware and data will help you determine what needs to be protected and what measures need to be taken in order for proper protection to be in place. For instance, protecting computer workstations requires physical measures for protecting them from accidental and physical damage, as well as extensive software measures to protect against all manner of digital attacks and accidents.

Assessing/Categorizing Assets

Most techs and IS professionals have a decent grasp of what is in their network, however, without actually making an inventory list, details will surely be forgotten. This is why it is absolutely critical to physically walk through the server rooms, computer labs, and workstations located throughout your organization to determine precisely what you are trying to protect. Many retail organizations perform an annual inventory, in order to obtain complete knowledge of all items in stock. Think of this walkthrough as a technical and security inventory. Having a thorough and all-inclusive picture of your network will make the design and writing of your security plan much easier. Be sure to include cabling, routers, computers, peripherals, and all other details of the network.

Not only is this process essential to creating a well-written policy, it immediately gives you a heightened sense of awareness concerning the topology of your network. For instance, a technician could sit in his office and have a fairly good idea of where the network cable leads from his desktop to the rest of the company's network infrastructure without ever getting out of his chair to actually put his hands on the equipment contained within the network. The technician could even probably sketch a fairly accurate network map, including all workstations and peripherals, however, there is a big difference between sitting in the office abstractly drawing network maps and actually getting out of a chair and physically visiting each workstation. If he takes the extra time to walk around and investigate the network, he will be accomplishing several things at once.

First of all, when traveling from office to office in an effort to gain a precise picture of the network, the technician will be in the mindset of physical network infrastructure. He will be paying special attention to details that might otherwise escape his attention.

Interface with Network Users   Another wonderful opportunity that presents itself to the IT professional who embarks on a physical evaluation of a network is the chance to interface with her customers. Take the time during the "network walk" to ask the end users (the customers) if they are experiencing any issues with which the security team can assist them. If a bottleneck is occurring on one of the servers—if the e-mail server is having issues, or if the proxy server isn't allowing them to access needed sites—the security team needs to know about it. Most people are prone to work around issues in order to accomplish the tasks required for the successful completion of their jobs, and will not usually take the time out of their day to inform the proper people of problems. By inviting information from the end users during your walk, the security team will get even more detail about the network.

Categorizing Items   Once you are finished creating your list of network items, you will have just that, a long list of items that don't have a lot of meaning yet. In order to organize these items into a manageable database, we first need to categorize them into the three headings of software, hardware, and information. Some professionals suggest adding a fourth category of processes and procedures, or methods and policies, although any proprietary methods, processes, and procedures are essentially just a subcategory of information.

Security Policy Structure Outline

Remember, the process of crafting a policy for an organization is unique to your organization's needs, so make certain the outline designed for your organization fits the preferences and requirements for your organization. In other words, if the security team needs 15 different categories to properly filter the items on the list, create them. Use the *Security Policy Structure Outline* located here to help you categorize items, but be sure to modify it according to the specific needs of your different departments and organization requirements.

I. *Mission Statement:* Writing a mission statement is a bit of an art of balancing specificity and broadness of goals. The mission statement should be a broad enough umbrella to cover all security needs within the organization, but specific enough to measure success. Before writing a mission statement, take the time to review existing mission statements of security companies, technical departments, and any other relevant organization or department. The mission statement includes both specified and unspecified security goals.

A. *Specified Goals of the Mission Statement:* The mission statement is a written repository for broad goals of network and data protection. These goals will usually not address specific ideas of protection, but will instead discuss short thematic concepts of how best to protect the networks of an organization.

B. *Unspecified Goals of the Mission Statement:*

   i. *Promote the Policy:* This part of the mission statement is a sales pitch to the organization to promote security awareness, and should make an honest evaluation of why such a policy is necessary at your corporation. Instead of simply having a goal of promoting security awareness, a mission statement might include a statement such as, "Providing a global sense of Security Awareness, in order to better protect physical, digital and procedural assets of the organization." This statement both provides a goal of 'providing security awareness while offering a reason, better asset protection.

   ii. *Establish Executive Support:* The mission statement will ideally be written by the CEO, CISO, or some other top executive whose hand is directly guiding the organization's direction. Without the personal involvement of these company leaders, the policy will not succeed. In order to craft a successful mission statement, these individuals must first accept the necessity of the security policy, and will sell themselves on the idea of providing the necessary support in terms of finances and authority.

II. *Reporting Structure:* As with any document in which authority will be given and maintained, the security policy of your organization should appropriately divvy out the tasks of protecting the network. This hierarchal structure will be referenced whenever a change in security policy occurs, or when a computer security incident occurs. In addition to providing responsibility for particular issues, this structure provides a roadmap of necessary relationships for successful implementation of security policies. Without realizing the interdependency between the different departments and people in charge of the organization's security, confusion and chaos may be the result when security issues arise.

A. *IT Personnel:* List all IT personnel or IS professionals, and their specified area of reporting. This reporting structure will serve to direct your employees to an appropriate IT representative for particular issues that may arise during their job. Some examples of areas of reporting may be:

    i. *E-mail and Internet Issues:* All issues related to e-mail and Internet issues will usually be facilitated by helpdesk personnel. If your organization has no helpdesk, list the appropriate IT personnel to contact in case an issue with e-mail or Internet access occurs.

    ii. *Installation and Testing of Software:* All issues related to the purchasing, installation, troubleshooting, and updating of authorized software will be determined by specific company policy. Different responsibilities, such as monitoring networks to ascertain whether unauthorized software is installed, installing authorized software, updating patches of existing installations, and deciding which software is authorized and unauthorized, should be allocated among qualified IT personnel.

    iii. *Hardware Issues:* All issues related to purchasing, installation, and maintenance of network hardware will be facilitated by personnel in the IT Department. Like software issues, be sure to list which IT teams and individuals are responsible for specific tasks.

III. *Areas of Security:* Because "security" is such a massive topic, it serves us well to delineate the issues of security into subcategories. This not only helps an organization deal with the larger topics at hand by breaking them into smaller subcategories, but through the creation of these subcategories, gives management an outline of the required tasks to properly handle the implementation of a thorough security program.

  A. *Human Resources:* The hiring, management, and firing of employees usually falls, at least in part, to the personnel in Human Resources. When we consider how many attacks against the network are perpetrated by existing and former employees, the issue of how to manage employees is critical in the fight against network failures and security breaches.

  i. *Hiring Employees:* Network security, with regard to personnel, begins prior to an employee actually working at the organization. Thorough vetting of employees is necessary to ensure proper security is achieved.

  a. *Background Checks:* The cost to perform background checks on incoming employees is nominal and many online services exist that often provide monthly or annual service fees for unlimited checks. This step is all too often discarded in favor of reference checks and interviews. Of course, reference checks and interviews are also important parts of the entire vetting process, however, background checks are just as critical. This is especially true if the potential employee is going to handle any company banking or customer credit card information. The costs associated with hiring an employee who subsequently steals information can be monumental. Don't skimp on this step, as it could be cheap insurance against future calamity.

  b. *Check References:* Just because someone passes a criminal background check does not assure you they are stellar employees. The author has personally known people who have been let go from their workplace for criminal behavior, and yet the employer did not report them to the authorities out of kindness. For higher-level positions, it is a good idea to obtain written authorization from any applicant, allowing you to ask detailed questions about past employment history from all listed references. Sometimes, previous employers will still not provide any information. In this case, most former employers will still answer truthfully, "Would this person be eligible for rehiring at your organization?" If an incoming employee doesn't have references, you shouldn't consider hiring him.

c. *Thorough Panel Interviews:* Sometimes, applicants will embellish their resume to include more than truthful statements about their work history, education, and experience. For positions requiring technical knowledge or specific knowledge of a particular field, if your organization has the manpower and time to facilitate a panel interview of incoming applicants, it would be wise to do.

d. *IT Skills Assessment:* It is important to ascertain whether applicants possess not only the integrity to be allowed to have access to company information, but the skills to handle it as well. If somebody is applying for a network technician job, they better have the skills to replace a router, install cable, and monitor network traffic. Take the time to test the applicant and make sure she can perform at the requirement level of the job for which she is applying.

e. *Drug Screening:* An applicant may have all the skills necessary to install and maintain networks, but if he is using drugs, do you really want him to be performing work on your networks? Probably not. Considering the massive amount of sensitive data available on most corporations' networks today, it goes without saying that the liability of knowingly allowing an individual on any illegal substance access to your networks should preclude their employment with your company.

f. *Cataloguing of Critical Items:* As employees receive laptops, cell phones, and other items that may be used to store confidential information, a log of which employees have what items should be maintained and updated as new items are loaned or given to employees.

g. *Administering Company Keys:* The process of cataloguing important items not only applies to digital equipment, but should also be used to administer the management of keys. A "Key Log" should be kept up to date, and should include:

1. *Employee Name*

2. *Department(s):* List all departments to which the employee has physical access.

3. *Contact Information*: A personal e-mail and phone number should suffice, but include all methods available for contact.

4. *Keys Administered and Accessible Areas:* This includes the campuses, rooms, and departments to which the employee has physical access.

5. *Activated/Terminated Dates:* Information regarding the date the employee was hired, as well as whether (and the date) the employee was terminated should be included. If the employee was terminated, data logs should show she has not been active on the network.

ii. *Cataloguing of Login Information:* Similar to administering physical key allocation, employees are given digital access to many different portions of the organization's network. Access credentials, including user ID and files to which they have authorization should be kept on file.

iii. *Termination of Employees:* Just as, or perhaps even more, important than the hiring process is the termination process. It is essential to treat employees as human beings during this traumatic blow to their lives. With the proper amount of kindness and communication during the termination process, many mistakes can be avoided, and the chances of reprisal attacks from disgruntled employees will drop.

iv. *Exit Interview:* Regardless of why an employee is being released, management should always take the time to listen to an employee upon termination of employment. The exit interview process should include questions aimed at improving the work environment and security at your organization. This will serve many functions, including:

a. *Providing a Forum for Criticism:* Sometimes, the employees who have some of the worst attitudes simply don't feel as though there exists a forum within which to state their opinion or voice a concern. Also, regardless of how much an employee loves his or her job or the people he or she works with, everybody sees firsthand how processes could be recalibrated to provide the company with better efficiency or oversight. Even if an employee is being fired, his or her voice and input should be taken into consideration.

b. *Discussion of Justification for Termination:* One of the number one rules in good management is keeping in mind that no employee should ever be taken by surprise when he is spoken to about performance issues, written up, laid off, or fired. If the employee asks for justification in regard to why he is being let go, it is not unreasonable to offer a diplomatic, but honest response. If the employee has been written up three times prior for a particular issue, a simple reminder that production standards have been consistently missed would suffice. Try to stay away from personal comments, and keep the discussion as factual as possible. This is not the time to criticize, as the exiting employee has already been told he has lost his job; no further evidence of his failure to perform at company standards need be given. Even if an employee is being let go due to personality conflicts, relate specific incidents where conflicts occurred, and work suffered or failed to happen as a result of those incidents.

c. *Positive Commentary When Appropriate:* Far too often, companies neglect to inject any positivity into the layoff, or termination process. If the employee being terminated really excelled at getting along well with her colleagues, but simply couldn't perform to the standards set forth by the organization, it is fair also to discuss the fact that "Everybody will really miss" having the employee around and that despite performance issues, "We are sincerely sad to see you go." In regard to security, having a disgruntled ex-employee is one of the worst security issues to have to handle. Note: Of course, this does not mean you should lie to an exiting employee. It simply means, during the exit interview there is no hurt in highlighting the positive traits, the ones that will be missed.

d. *Retrieval of Sensitive Material and Items:* In addition to any physical keys, some employees will have had access to confidential company paperwork and files during their tenure. Make certain that all sensitive items are retrieved. Create a checklist of all possibilities. Some of the more common items to secure during the exit interview include:

1. *Building Keys:* This includes keys to door locks, proximity cards, and digital tokens used in conjunction with login information for use in sessions requiring two-factor authentication.

2. *Files:* Both physical files and files contained on disk media that are company property should be recorded as received. Any missing files must be catalogued and recorded, with an emphasis on efforts of immediate retrieval.

3. *Disk Media:* USB sticks, hard drives, tape drives, and any other storage device should be returned.

4. *Laptops and Cell Phones:* Some companies provide key employees with laptops or cell phones. Make sure the laptop or cell phone is retrieved and logged back into company inventory. If an employee uses his own laptop or cell phone for company use, make certain all company confidential files are wiped from the device.

5. *Severance and Consideration:* If appropriate, offering severance to your outgoing employee is a good idea. Not only does it help soften the devastating blow of losing a job, it tells the employee he or she are still valued, despite the fact the organization is letting him or her go. This goes a long way in protecting a company from a possible reprisal of an angry ex-employee. Besides, treating people like human beings is simply the best way to do business, and showing someone they are not simply expendable pieces of company equipment is just good policy. Another step in the termination process that can provide an extra layer of security is that of providing a contract of nonreprisal and consideration. Basically, in this type of contract, a terminated employee signs an agreement to accept the severance being offered by the organization, but in exchange the employee agrees he or she has no grievances or claims against the organization, and will not speak any ill against the company. Such a contract is a complicated legal document and should not be undertaken or written without the advice and counsel of an attorney.

6. *Changing of Locks and Passwords:* Just because during an exit interview all keys are retrieved, this does not mean all methods of gaining entrance to the building or network data have

been removed from the employee. Make certain the employee's login access has been terminated in any data access log.

7. *Legal Counsel:* The author is not a lawyer, and you should always consult a lawyer when crafting policy that will affect how you handle personnel issues. This book is not a source of legal advice, but instead reflections from years spent in an executive role, coupled with an education in information security. The author is not in a position to offer legal advice, but instead, offers observations that may help you in administering certain aspects of managing security issues. Many states have different labor laws, which may preclude you from performing certain steps, or which may direct you to administer them differently. If there is any issue in regard to managing personnel for which you should contact a lawyer, termination policies are certainly among the top. Prior to adopting any formal method in dealing with your organization's employees, talk with your lawyer.

IV. *Network Security:* Most of the issues that surround the topic of information security could really be referred to as network security. Although there are myriad issues outside the scope of network security, this is where most of the nuts and bolts of security of your digital assets are contained.

A. *Routers and Firewalls:* The gateway to your digital atmosphere, the router and firewall, keep unwanted guests out and proprietary information in. Make sure proper security measures are followed, such as:

   i. Don't use "out-of-box" security settings, such as passwords and security encryption settings.

   ii. Make sure security patches are up to date.

   iii. Create a schedule to remind IS personnel to update security settings.

   iv. Close and restrict access to unused ports and protocols.

    v. Establish data logging procedures for router traffic.

B. *E-mail Policy*

    i. Use filtering software to get rid, or at least grossly diminish the existence of, SPAM received.

    ii. Don't open any attachments from unknown individuals.

    iii. Virus check all attachments before running them.

    iv. Don't use work e-mail addresses to write to personal contacts. The e-mail provided to end users by the organization is for business use only.

    v. Personal e-mail accounts should not be accessed during work hours. If there is a workstation provided for personal use, use it only during approved breaks.

C. *Unauthorized Software:* Create and distribute policy regarding proper use of computers, including description of unauthorized software, so that employees understand the organization's stance on installation of such software. Be sure to include reasons for why the policies exist, the possible ramifications of failing to follow the policies, and the consequences facing any employee who chooses not to follow the policies.

    i. Use network monitoring software to determine which services and programs are currently running on all nodes. If unauthorized software is being run on internal computers, take appropriate action to cease operation and prevent subsequent installation and operation of the unauthorized software.

    ii. Create a list of authorized software for employees, but allow them to make requests for installation of previously unapproved software, after an expedited review process. With a written request and explanation of why the software is needed, an approved manager should take no more than a couple of hours to authorize or deny the request.

       The point is to provide security while still maintaining efficiency. If the software proves to be unnecessary, or if it presents new and unanticipated security risks, the authorization can always be revoked later. In this regard, it is better to be lenient with internal requests. Of course, if an employee is requesting installation of software for purely entertainment purposes, the request should always be denied, as it adds no benefit to the organization to have such software installed.

V. *Password Management:* Too often, organizations follow strict security protocols, except when it comes to password management. This is usually because properly managing passwords can be a hassle. Just remember, if an employee or customer has personal information stolen, the organization may be asked to provide the steps taken to prevent such an attack. If security policy was lax in regard to solid password protection, the associated liability for such inaction is far worse than had good password policy been administered and followed.

  A. *Change Passwords Frequently:* It is advisable to have at least quarterly changes in critical passwords. It is human nature to "borrow" somebody else's login information, and from time to time this will probably occur, regardless of what policy is in place. The problems with this occurring are that the borrower is by definition an unauthorized user, inasmuch as she herself likely doesn't have an assigned password. By frequently changing passwords, the security issues presented by such a practice are greatly diminished.

  B. *Don't Write Passwords Down:* This one is a no-brainer, although many people still do it. Some people even write their login information on a sticky-note and put it on their monitor! Although the password may still be hidden from external users, anybody casually walking by could easily see the login information. Even if the password is not posted on a monitor, the paper it is written on will eventually find its way into a trash bin, and could wind up in the hands of someone external to the organization.

VI. *Access Control:* A good access control policy should ensure only authorized employees have access to key files. For instance, with role-based access control (RBAC), users are assigned access to files based on their role in the organization. Each user has a set of login credentials, which allows him access to the portions of the network necessary to perform the functions of his job, without allowing him access to other portions of the network not needed for his role in the organization. For a complete discussion of access control, see Chapter 18, "Access Control."

   A. *Hiring of Employees:* When employees are hired, their role within the organization should be assigned, and their unique set of credentials activated. From that assigned role and associated set of credentials will flow their ability to access the portions of the network.

   B. *Termination of Employees:* When users are terminated, the Accounting Department is automatically notified so that the employee can be removed from the organization's rolls. In addition, the IS Department should also be notified. When the IT Department receives notification that an employee's tenure has been terminated, the employee's credentials should be placed into "Inactive Status," to prevent him from further access to the organization's network.

VII. *Power Supplies:* Be sure all network equipment is continuously supplied the appropriate amount of power to run at normal operating levels.

   A. *Surge Protection:* Allow for surges during power-up in the morning, and also for spikes and surges due to inconsistencies in the power supply from your power source.

   B. *Backup Power:* Make sure all appropriate systems have appropriate uninterruptable power supplies (UPS) attached. If lives are literally dependent upon the continuance of access to the systems, such as in hospitals or 911 call centers, a power generator should be a part of the backup power solution. If your organization decides a power generator is necessary, make sure it is regularly maintained, gas is available, and it can easily hook into the necessary systems. Most power supplies have sockets to simply plug systems into directly. Make sure the power output of your power supply can handle the current draw necessary to run whatever systems are critical. Make sure you have a good margin of available power, such as 20% or more than is absolutely necessary.

VIII. *Server Rooms:* Server rooms are the heart of your network. All traffic must pass through this room to enter or exit the network, and many key facets of your organization's security are contained within the server room walls.

   A. *Ventilation:* Operational electrical equipment outputs a massive amount of heat. It is no surprise that a fully functional server room will often be the warmest room in a building. For the continued health of the server equipment, look up the optimal operating temperature for the equipment and obtain the appropriate ventilation equipment to ensure that temperature is achieved and maintained during operations.

   B. *Physical Security:* Proper locks should be installed on the server room doors, to ensure nobody without explicit authorization will be let in. Cameras may also be monitored, in case the room is broken into in spite of whatever measures exist to prohibit unauthorized entrance. In addition to traditional security measures, simply limiting the number of people in and around the server room will make a big impact on server room security. Don't locate the server room in an easily accessible location, but instead tuck it away so that only people who are intentionally attempting to access the room will walk to the location. It should not be a room, for instance, that customer service personnel pass through on their way to the cafeteria.

   C. *Backup and Maintenance Measures:* If your server fails, or must be taken down for upgrading and maintenance issues, what is your organization's contingency plan? Do your servers have hot-swappable drives that can be removed and maintained without interrupting critical services, or must the entire service be shut down to calibrate and troubleshoot issues? Keep these questions in mind when purchasing and installing server equipment.

IX. *File Management:* Best practices for securely managing files need to be consulted for both physical and digital files.

   A. *Shred Unwanted Sensitive Documents:* A cross-cut shredder is reasonable for most documents. Some governmental agencies perform multiple cross-shred operations, and even burn documents to ensure the contents will never be discernable. If the organization's documents are of a very high security level, but the cost is too high to process them internally, check your local area to see if there is an inexpensive, bonded document shredding service for extremely confidential documents.

B. *Keep Confidential Documents in Locked Cabinets:* The cabinets required to store confidential information don't necessarily need to be a safe, but there should exist a level of security for documents that would preclude access by an individual determined to break in. Although these cabinets don't need to be impenetrable, they should offer reasonable security. If a criminal would need to actually break something in order to gain access, such as with locked metal or wood cabinets, they are secure enough in most cases. For essential company documents that cannot be backed up in digital format, a safe or fireproof locking cabinet should be considered. Most companies specializing in cabinets will know what is appropriate, but be sure to consult industry standards to be sure.

C. *Encrypt Confidential Digital Documents:* For confidential information contained on company servers, encryption is standard practice. Database records and even entire databases can be encrypted to ensure malicious users aren't able to access and view confidential information. Partitioning a portion of a server's hard drive for encryption purposes is a good idea in order to store large amounts of secure data. For more information on encrypting files, see the chapter about encryption.

D. *Regular Backups:* Backing up key information on a weekly basis is strongly recommended. Incremental backups will provide quick and efficient backups of only those data that have changed since the last backup, so that entire files don't need to be downloaded and backed up. This saves time and bandwidth during backup operations.

E. *Off-Site Digital Backup:* For essential data, a third-party data storage service should be considered. If your organization's campus burnt to the ground, or if circumstances occurred in which the campus was not physically accessible, having the data secure and accessible online will make the recovery process much easier. Be sure such vendors have a good reputation. Internet searches will usually yield reviews of public opinion for most businesses.

X. *Cryptography:* Cryptography can be used to transmit or store data securely. The goal is to hide the true signal or contents of a file.

    A. *Wireless:* 128-bit encryption schemes are the minimum for security, although multiple applied schemes will add to the level of encryption. With wireless encryption protocols, this usually entails a key that changes every hour or so. For the most commonly used, secure protocol, use WPA.

    B. *Tunneling:* Virtual Private Networks (VPN) are networks that allow people to communicate securely over the Internet. They are extremely handy for remote desktop and server access. As one could imagine, security issues need to be considered when deploying such technology. Be sure to look into proper tunneling and VPN protocols before implementing a VPN.

    C. *Data Storage:* When storing confidential information, it is a good idea to provide proper protection. It is not only important to keep people physically away from storage media such as disks and flash drives, but also to keep them from accessing the file even when it is in hand. This is done with the use of encryption algorithms. Whether your organization chooses to encrypt certain files or a portion of a hard drive, it is important to have a method for encrypting and securing sensitive data.

XI. *Training:* It doesn't matter what policies your information security professionals draft, you must train the employees within the organization on those policies if you hope for them to take hold within the fabric of the daily operations. The creation of a proper and thorough training program is the way to accomplish this. The security plan should not get specific about the training program's course materials, methods of delivery, or training venues, but it should address frequency, certification, and evaluation.

A. *Frequency:* The security plan should mention how often employees will be trained on key security topics. For most issues, a semi-quarterly training should suffice, in addition to training received at the onset of employment.

B. *Certification:* Will the organization internally certify employees who have completed certain security training seminars? Will a database of the certified employees be created and managed, and if so, who will be in charge of keeping track of and managing the information in the database?

C. *Evaluation:* Simply training an employee does not offer the organization a guarantee that the employee has absorbed and will apply the information presented in the training seminar. How often will employees be evaluated on their security knowledge, and what steps will be taken to assist employees who don't meet the benchmarks?

XII. *Laws and Industry Standards:* Regardless of what services and products your organization provides to the world, there is undoubtedly a federal or state organization that oversees your operations. Some of these standards will likely apply to the security of your customer and vendor information. Be sure to incorporate any requirements, such as handling cardholder information, protecting your website, or ensuring customer confidentiality are completely satisfied in accordance with the laws and regulations that govern your organization. Incorporate those laws and regulations into your security plan to make certain they are documented and followed by all employees performing the affected processes.

XIII. *Computer Forensics:* How will your IT personnel handle any criminal cyber activity occurring on your organization's network? Whenever a cyber incident is handled after the fact, the investigation into what happened, how it happened, and why, is referred to as a postmortem. The professionals tasked with the investigation will remove and scan hard drives, review network monitoring logs and firewall configurations, interview employees, and examine processes and procedures, all in an attempt to ultimately discover the cause of the incident. Afterwards, a successful postmortem will yield an action plan to alleviate future causes of similar incidents. There are a few choices available, depending on the expertise and budget of your organization, when considering digital postmortems. The organization can either choose to take in-house management of the postmortem process, hire a third party, or ignore the cyber crime, assuming it was a fluke. They may also choose to involve local law enforcement, if necessary.

A. *In-House Management:* If the expertise is available in-house, handling an issue internally is usually more cost effective. Efficiency is always a consideration, because the individuals charged with the responsibility of investigating a cyber crime will almost certainly have other tasks they are responsible for, which will have to be put on hold during the investigation.

B. *Third Party:* Sometimes, the resources are simply not available to spare for a large-scale research of an internal cyber crime event. In this case, hiring an outside firm to assist your organization is a viable option. A good firm will not only locate the culprit individual or process responsible for the security failure, they will provide you with a total breakdown of your network security picture, and inform you of steps you could take to prevent similar actions from taking place in the future. Though hiring a third party consultant or security firm frees up your professionals to continue with their daily operations without the hindrance of needing to also manage an investigation, the cost involved can be quite large. Complicating the matter even more is the fact there may be no foreseeable end to some investigations, so most firms cannot give you a solid quote when you are researching price. If you decide to hire an outside firm, at least get a signed ballpark quote.

XIV. *Privacy:* Privacy is a hot topic in security circles. Make sure your organization is performing all of the necessary steps to protect vendor, customer, and employee information from prying eyes. Ensure all HIPAA rules are being met and maintained, as well as any other regulatory requirements mandated for organizations in your industry.

Improperly handled privacy issues alone could sink an otherwise successful organization. Customer goodwill, employee morale, industrial fees, and liability suits could all be affected by poorly maintained privacy rules.

Imagine if your organization made headlines by having some cardholder information stolen by a disgruntled employee, who in turn sold it to an online illegal trading house for illegally obtained credit data. Customer goodwill would likely plummet, as your existing customers realize their information might have been compromised, and potential customers shy away from your organization in fear of suffering a similar fate. Your employees would get a bad taste in their mouths from the whole experience, as they receive angry phone calls from customers, and they begin to wonder how your organization handles its personal information. Industry fees might be levied against your organization, depending on whether the matter was due to improper handling of sensitive customer information. Then, of course, there are the customers affected by the actual event. They will likely come after your organization in an attempt to receive at least a few years of credit monitoring paid for by your organization. In addition, your organization will also be liable for any actual financial losses suffered due to the mishandling of information, as well as any punitive measures decided by the courts.

XV. *Disaster Recovery:* Although the plan may be for the organization to remain on its feet without any troubles, chances are great that some event will throw your organization for a loop. When this occurs, management structures, procedures and contingency plans should be in place. Backup files and equipment should be easily accessible and online in as short a time as possible. If your organization provides critical levels of support, such as in a hospital or emergency response center, you should have backup systems in place, or have a reciprocity agreement with an agency providing equal services to yours.

XVI. *Management Structure:* The time to discuss who is in charge is not during an emergency. A clear management structure should exist prior to an event. Be sure to list who is in charge of specific technical issues, as well as who will handle coordination of larger picture considerations. For instance, when dealing with legal issues, be sure a specific person or team is assigned to ensuring chain-of-custody considerations, and another individual or team is assigned to work with local law enforcement.

XVII. *Physical Security:* Aspects of physical security should also be addressed in the security plan, including:

   A. *Fire Suppression:* What type of fire suppression will be used? How often are the fire extinguishers and alarms tested?

   B. *Door Locks:* Do all doors have appropriate locks for the level of security?

   C. *Guards:* If necessary, are guards posted at key points internal and external to the organization'S building?

   D. *Cameras:* Cameras are a relatively inexpensive method of providing an advanced level of security support. Are cameras capable of being monitored via Internet access, or do they simply record the pictures taken and save them on a file server for later retrieval in the case of a break-in or other physical security breach?

   E. *Computer Locks:* Are physical security locks attached to computers containing highly sensitive data? Are servers locked into stations, making it difficult for a casual burglar to simply lift the hard drives or other expensive equipment from the server room?

Distribution of the Policy

After completing the security policy, it must be distributed to the users throughout the organization. Remember that this policy will not simply be used by information technology gurus, but will be a guide for all employees within the organization. The goal, when disseminating the security policy throughout the organization, is to make sure it is as easily and readily accessible as possible. The two options for distribution are physical and digital.

Physical Distribution

Physically distributing the security policy has a few benefits, and a few major drawbacks. Perhaps the main benefit is "forced accessibility." Although other forms of the document give a potential reader the option of accessing the document, providing employees with a physical document forces them to contend with the contents. Regardless of an employee's inherent interest with regard to network security, having a document handed to them forces them to deal with the issue. Because we live and operate within the physical world, people will invariably have a stronger reaction to the physical manifestation of an idea, rather than seeing it on a computer screen. Instead of requesting the employee to go to an internal website and read about security topics, they must physically deal with the document placed on their desk or put into their hands by the security team. It is psychologically harder to put aside and ignore a multipage document, which is a major benefit of providing a physical document.

In addition to the benefit of forced accessibility, two physical signatures of an employee receiving the document could be taken by the security team. One signature could be taken to document that the employee took possession of the document, much like a mail deliverer does for certified mail deliveries. If an employee argues she never got the document, a signature would be on file to show the date and time the document was hand delivered to them. Another signature could be taken once the employee has read and understood the security policy. The employee's second signature will provide two assurances for the organization. First, it will ensure policies are universally accepted and understood within the organization. Second, it will provide evidence, signed by employees, that each employee read the document, and cannot argue ignorance of policies.

Although there are some unarguable benefits to distributing physical copies to the entire organization, there are two main drawbacks that every organization should consider. The first drawback is the massive amount of paper required to disseminate a policy to every single person within an organization. For smaller organizations, this may not be a major consideration, but for corporations with more than 50 or so employees, the investment of time and paper to create the policies starts to add up quickly. In addition, whenever the policy needs to be updated, a substantial amount of paper must be discarded, which can add up to a massive amount of waste.

Another issue physical copies face is the update process itself. Security policies will and should change as the company grows and security needs change. The logistics of physically updating every employee's security policy can be a massive challenge. All of the options available for the update process are cumbersome. The considerations for the physical update process include who will be responsible for physically updating the policy, how often updates will occur, and whether updates will be incremental, or will entail entirely new revisions be handed out each time the policy is updated.

Who Will Update the Physical Copies of the Security Policy?   For the issue of who is responsible for updating a physical policy, either the security team can hand out the policy each time it is updated, or employees can download appropriate updates and replace the updated information within their copy of the policy. Having the security team hand out the policy whenever there is an update allows for signatures to be taken from employees, but the amount of time required to physically distribute the updates will be a major consideration. If employees are responsible for updating their copies of the policy, your organization will need to provide a method to ensure they have received the document, such as a company-wide e-mail with a "Read Receipt" indicating when an employee has received the download.

There are other issues with having employees update their own copies of the policy. First of all, there is no guarantee they actually read the update, even if an e-mail receipt is sent back to the sender. Second, there is no assurance the employee will print the update, or even place it in the correct location of her copy. These issues, in addition to a lack of concrete proof of receipt such as an employee's signature, make having employees update their own security document a poor choice for most organizations. It is therefore usually a good idea to either have the security team or departmental management provide the updates, ensure the updates are placed in the right order into the existing policies, and obtain signatures of receipt from each employee.

How Often Will Security Policy Updates Be Delivered?   As a result of the everchanging environment of digital security, security policies will necessarily change in order to remain relevant and up to date. For physical security policies, the update process should not be taken lightly, due to the logistics, waste, and labor involved with such updates. Some corporations decide to provide quarterly or semiannual updates, whereas others update the policy with every change as it comes up. The issue with updating the policy on a schedule is that necessary changes may need to wait to be updated. With continuous updates, security policies will always be up to date, but the inconvenience of frequently updating the policy may cause an undue burden on the security team, and may cause users to ignore the updates entirely.

Will Revisions Be Incremental or Replace Existing Policies? Another consideration when updating physical security policies, is whether each update will include only those portions of the policy needing to change, or if the update will completely replace the existing policy. For users receiving incremental updates, human nature will likely prevail, and the new pages of the security policy will likely be shoved in the back of the policy, at the front of the policy, in a separate and unrelated file, or in the trash. If an entirely new policy is created to replace the existing document, users will likely not read the updated portions, because it would entail rereading the whole policy.

Digital Distribution

Perhaps the most widely used method for distributing any policy, including an organization's security policy, is through the use of an internal company website. An e-mail memo can be sent out from the security team announcing changes in the policy, and users can log in to see what has changed.

Myriad benefits exist for this digital method of distribution. To begin with, the policy only needs to be updated in a single location on an organization's server. Once it is updated there, it is updated for everyone. In addition to being easy to update, any employee who is directly affected by a security policy change can be e-mailed with a link to the appropriate changes in the policy. Once they have read the changes and understand them, they can click on a link to let the security team know the changes have been properly distributed.

17

PERFORMING SECURITY ANALYSES AND AUDITS

I don't think there's a company, a management, an audit committee that hasn't gone back and re-looked at what they're doing.
. . . People are really scrutinizing and (want to) really make sure
their houses are in order and clean.

William Esrey

An information security audit is a formal process, performed by a
qualified unbiased entity, that analyzes the current state of network
security. More than just passively observing network characteristics
and then checking off boxes to ensure certain technical measures and
controls are in place, an audit should be an active process, offering
solutions to current network issues. Auditors are not in the business of
catching people failing at their jobs, but instead they are there to provide answers to unsolved problems and questions of security. In addition to providing a complete analysis of the current state of security
with suggested improvements, the auditors will need to provide system administrators with methods for integrating any policy changes
or new controls that may need to be implemented in answer to existing security holes in the network.

The Necessity

Because IT solutions are so ingrained in organizations today, having properly secure systems is not simply a luxury, but an absolute
necessity for continued network system operations. Business continuity plans, security plans, computer security incident response teams,
network traffic logging, security training, and many more facets of
the security paradigm are all critical components of an organization's

security solution. These pieces of the security puzzle should be considered as important to the success of a business as proper financial practices in the Accounting Department. Without proper controls in place for either Accounting or IT practices, the organization will be at risk of losing control of critical business functions. Audits ensure that everybody within the organization is playing by the same set of rules. Having different sets of security standards for each department within an organization essentially creates an environment where the least secure method of doing business prevails. With regard to auditing security, the organization's security policy is the set of rules with which employees must comply.

Audit Committees

Before an audit can take place, a committee of qualified authorized personnel must be assembled with the intent of providing accountability and consistency for corporate audit operations. These personnel should be familiar enough with the network, as well as the processes and procedures they are auditing, so that they can properly determine whether these processes and procedures are in compliance. In addition, the regulations they are auditing should be well known by the audit committee.

The committee will not only be in charge of the process of an actual audit, but the scope of their responsibility may extend to include pre-audit functions, such as helping to establish an organization's security policy, and the subsequent list of security rules against which all security functions will be measured during an audit. The audit committee may be the same individuals in charge of auditing, or they may be an advisory committee, formed to assist with the process of deciding on important security issues relevant to the auditing process.

Internal Versus External Auditors

External Auditors   One of the keys to a successful system audit is the ability of an auditor to remain removed from the network, inasmuch as she can provide an independent unbiased review of a system's state of security. Specifically for this reason, some organizations elect to hire a third-party vendor to assist in the creation of their security policy, and for the subsequent auditing of network systems. External auditors are able to provide an outsider's view of the network, and have no vested interest in the initial state of the network, at least during the auditing process. If something is not in compliance, the outside vendor usually has no pre-established relationships with the client being audited. This impartiality is critical to proper and thorough auditing the state of any system, and is a definite consideration when choosing who will be charged with the task of auditing the state of an organization's network security. In addition to the benefit of being unbiased, third-party auditors are usually more aware of trends occurring in the security industry. Because the main function of their job is to audit companies in all different industries, by necessity these auditors must be aware of the latest threats to security and how best to protect against them. The auditors will likely have seen more implementations of different security measures than an individual whose daily scope is limited to a single organization's network security issues.

Third-party vendors do come with some drawbacks that need to be considered. First of all, a third-party audit will nearly always be more expensive than an audit performed by internal auditors, because even when external auditors are brought into an organization, large amounts of internal labor are still required.

In addition, the incoming auditor does not work year round with the organization's network, so he will need to be brought up to speed on the ins and outs of the particular systems. Because of this lack of knowledge of a specific organization's network, external auditors will need extra time to become familiar with the particular systems within the network before performing an audit. This not only presents extra costs in time paid to the external auditor, but means the auditor will need to accept the word of system administrators with regard to normal network operations, inasmuch as he is not privy to the performance of the network as a matter of his daily job.

Internal Auditors   The other option available to organizations is having the audit process performed by internal auditors. One of the benefits of having an internal auditor is the lower cost generally associated with utilizing available in-house labor. Internal auditors can be assigned to other parts of the company, such as the Accounting, IT, or IS Department, in roles that are necessary to the daily operation of the organization.

Having auditors in these roles adds value to their total function in the organization, and means they are available for audit functions without subtracting from an organization's bottom line.

In addition to the cost savings often realized with internal auditors, employees of an organization are always more familiar with the operation of the network than somebody from an outside firm. Internal auditors are able to constantly review systems and their performance, just as a part of their daily function. For instance, an auditor from Accounting would work directly with secure databases everyday as part of her job function. Any performance or security issues related to the network would be experienced by the auditor as she accomplished the tasks related to her job in Accounting. Whenever a formal audit is performed, the internal auditor would already be aware of issues, both good and bad, affecting the networks.

A major consideration of having internal auditors is the elimination of nonbiased reviews. No matter how much internal auditors attempt to distance themselves from the people and processes being audited, it is impossible to completely remove any bias in the audit process. The auditor will have pre-established relationships with people in all other departments, and will have preconceived notions about which measures need to be altered to improve security.

Internal Auditor with a Consultant   A possible solution to the internal versus external question is the inclusion of both an internal auditing team and an outside consultant. This solution provides answers for most of the drawbacks to either a completely internal or completely external solution. Instead of paying a large amount of money to have an outside vendor come into the organization and perform a complete audit of the organization's entire network, organizations should consider using inside talent to perform most of the audit, relying on an outside consultant to assist with portions of the process.

Having the primary function of the audit process handled by internal auditors allows organizations to realize much of the savings that are part of an internal audit process. In addition, the audit team will have a familiarity with the network that an outsider can not. As far as remaining objective in regard to the results of an audit, an external auditor will bring with him an unbiased view of controls and security solutions.

Preaudit Considerations

Before jumping into the process of a formal security audit, several issues must be considered. First of all, is the auditor internal or external to the company? Next, an auditor cannot appropriately or thoroughly perform an audit of any system without understanding several issues, including the scope of the network, common technical issues facing every network, unique technical issues facing the specific organization's network, the physical security and networking needs of the organization, current security issues, and the industry the organization is serving. All of these issues will likely be discussed and considered in detail in the organization's security policy.

Security Policy

The security policy is the document to which all security audits must be accountable. The security policy should include an overview of the organization's security philosophy, a formal and complete risk analysis, and a list of all currently implemented security controls. These security rules will be the touchstone to measure network security against during the audit process. If the organization does not have a security policy, the first step of the auditing process must be to create this document. Reference Chapter 16 on creating a security policy for more information.

Defining Security Rules

After the organization has created a security policy, a base of rules should be established. Where the security policy provides broadstroke treatments of security topics, the security rules should include further definition. For instance, the security policy may include a broadstroke statement such as, "Only authorized traffic will be allowed to access network databases." A more defined security rule might be:

1. Firewalls will filter network traffic at the packet level to ensure incoming traffic to the network databases is arriving from predesignated IP addresses.
2. The IP addresses from which inbound traffic is allowed will be logged in a secure table, and will be accessible by perimeter routers.

Notice that although the rule offers a more in-depth requirement, it does not get bogged down in specific details, such as encryption methods to ensure the database of allowable IP addresses is secure, or on what server or router that database or table is stored. These details are up to the system administrator to decide, and should not be listed in the security rules.

This level of depth can be a bit of a balancing act when first deciding upon the definition of security rules for an organization's network security. The goal is to be as general as possible while still providing adherence to the intent of the security policy. There should be a reasonable margin of freedom within which the system administrators can operate to achieve security. For instance, a security rule should never list specific vendors, but should allow the system administrator to use his knowledge of current industry products and solutions to bring to bear the latest and most effective security solutions for the organization's network.

Definition of User Requirements

The next step in the security audit process is the creation and definition of user requirements. These requirements are high-level requirements, and are often created in cooperation with key management. Instead of providing specific rules to follow, the requirements are categorically defined. This step of the process is creating the hierarchy of security, which will be filled in fully at a later time. For instance, some of the categories may be:

1. Proper classification of information
   a. Sensitive
   b. Confidential
   c. Administrative
   d. Sales and tech support
2. Access controls
   a. Login credentials
   b. Password management
   c. Token management
   d. User groups
   e. PKI

3. Physical security
   a. External walls
   b. Internal walls
   c. Access doors
   d. Deadbolt locks
   e. Passkey lock
   f. Checkpoints
   g. Piggybacking, tailgating
   h. Providing physical privacy
   i. Storage of sensitive physical files
   j. Server room security

This is by no means an exhaustive list of categories, but simply a short outline of categories within which more descriptive and detailed requirements will be filled. It is important to include both users and managers, in order to ensure all relative categories are discussed. Make sure all user groups and departments are allowed to have input into the process.

Definition of Mid-Level Requirements The next step in building the requirements is to fill in more details under each category. For instance, if we took just part of the category of access controls, it may look like:

Access controls
   1. Login credentials
      a. To ensure dual-factor authentication, login credentials will include both a password and a token.
      b. The token will be an electronic fob which will display a 10-digit key. The key will change every 10 minutes.
      c. For nonrepudiation purposes, the password required for login will only be available to the end user. Managers will not maintain a database of user logins.

Some organizations choose to perform even further distilling of network security rules, and include a third tier of low-level requirements in the rules. This is not necessary, and often results in wasted time trying to dissect a mid-level rule further. The point of creating these rules is not to provide such detailed requirements users and network administrators have no liberty to make security-related decisions. Instead, it should be a framework of security guides, within which users and administrators have reasonable leeway to operate. After meeting this goal, the next step is to perform a network risk assessment.

Performing a Risk Assessment

Once the mid-level requirements for network security are completed, auditors can begin a formal risk assessment of the network and systems. Assessing risk is addressed in further detail in Chapter 7, "Risk Management." The network risk assessment should cover all of the following steps.

Identify All Network Assets

Create a list of every network asset. Be sure to include hardware, software, labor, and physical assets. Remember to include campus buildings that house network systems. For each asset, include the asset's function and cost. Unless the product is vendor-specific, inasmuch as only a particular vendor can provide a product that fulfills the functionary needs of a particular asset, do not list specific vendors, but instead just the asset type and cost. For instance, a hard drive may have a function of providing storage for operating system, application, and other files, and may have a listed cost of $150.

List All Threats

Threats can include anything from windstorms to kidnapping. Make sure to list all possibilities, regardless of how unlikely they are. Once a comprehensive list has been created, filter out the threats that are so unlikely to happen, they border on the realm of impossibility. For instance, a meteor strike is possible, but so far out of the realm of normalcy that it can be regarded as improbable enough so as not to plan for, specifically.

List Vulnerabilities

For each network system, unique vulnerabilities exist. Operating systems are vulnerable to viruses, databases are vulnerable to hackers attempting to access the information they contain, and even the physical cabling of a network is vulnerable to being tapped. Be sure to include each vulnerability facing every component of the network.

Determine Threat Occurrence Frequency

How often is each threat likely to come to fruition? Is the threat an annual occurrence, or is it something that will likely not happen but for every 25 years? Be sure to research historical records to make the best determination of frequency, and consider discussing occurrence of threats with an industry consultant. Oftentimes, hours of research and discussion can be cut short by involving an outside computer security professional.

Perform Threat Analysis

A threat analysis takes the cost of each asset and divides it by the annual loss occurrence (ALO). The result is the annual loss expectancy (ALE). The equation is:

Cost of Asset / Annual Loss Occurrence = Annual Loss Expectancy

For instance, if an asset is worth $100, and is expected to be completely lost or become obsolete every 25 years, the equation to determine the ALE would be:

$$\$100 \ / \ 25 \text{ Years} = \$4$$

Therefore, it is expected that the company will lose $4 annually due to destruction, obsolescence, or otherwise required replacement of the $100 asset. With this information, an educated decision can be made as to which countermeasures are cost effective against the loss of each asset.

Determine Countermeasures

For each threat, multiple countermeasures may exist. For instance, the threat of viruses affecting operating systems can be countered with thorough antivirus measures. Antivirus programs come in several different flavors. Some offer better coverage than others, and prices will vary depending on how extensively each package protects networks. After determining the ALE of the systems needing antivirus protection, budgets for purchasing and implementing protection can be created. For instance, if the ALE of the network as a whole, given zero antivirus measures applied, is $30,000 in labor and equipment replacement, purchasing a $250 antivirus program is easily justified.

Determine Uncovered Assets

Some threats are simply either too difficult to protect against, or available countermeasures may not be cost effective. In this case, the option of purchasing insurance for the asset to which the threat is posed might be the best solution. Even still, some assets might be too costly to insure, and may remain uncovered entirely. These assets and their projected cost of loss should be considered when the audit process is undertaken.

Build the Security Architecture

The security architecture is the culmination of the security rules, asset considerations, and countermeasures discussed earlier. This is the architecture within which all network operations must operate. As mentioned before, the rules, countermeasures, and discussions of relevant system assets should be specific enough to provide clear guidance for system administrators and end users, while still allowing some room for reasonable judgment for compliance.

Migration of Security Architecture

Once the security architecture has been completed, the new rules and security upgrades will need to be implemented. System administrators and auditors need to consider how the implementation process of the new security architecture will affect current operations. This process will directly involve expenditures of labor, finances, and network performance. Labor will be required to uninstall outdated software and equipment and upgrade systems to the standards as required by the security architecture. Finances will be used to purchase systems, both hardware and software. In addition, money will be paid out for consultants and time spent researching best practices. Network performance will suffer temporary downgrades as new systems and software are brought online. This performance drop will be the result of actual downtime as systems are temporarily offline during installation, and will also be related to the learning curve as users get used to the new software, hardware, and policies required by the security architecture. Auditors should make sure trainers are aware of the changes in system operations.

Evaluate Security Measures

As each new network security measure is implemented, a network security and performance test (NSPT) should be performed to make sure the implementation is achieving the desired security requirements while not adversely affecting the performance of the network. This should be considered an ongoing process that allows for users and system administrators to report how relevant changes have affected the network performance in regard to their job function. Modifications should be made as necessary to ensure security measures are being met, and that network performance is not altered to the point it prohibits people from effectively performing their jobs.

Managing Security Implementations

A controlled record must be kept for each change performed to the network. These records must be controlled to ensure complete and proper documentation of each change. The record of change should include the following information.

1. Type of system affected (software, hardware, procedural)
2. Location of installation (where in the network topology is the installation located)
3. Specific system affected (router, operating system, procedure for logging in to a database, etc.)
4. Date of change
5. State of system prior to change (version number or model number used before the update)
6. State of system after the change (the updated version number or model number)

The importance of this documented list of changes will come into play whenever changes made to the network need to be rolled back. Sometimes, an upgraded system will not provide the intended level of security, or may provide security but downgrade the system performance so greatly as to negate any benefits gained. If administrators need to roll back any network changes, this list will provide them with the necessary history to restore systems to their original state.

How Frequently Should Audits Be Performed?

Security audits were once performed once every three to five years. Due to the increased globalization of business, the rate of change within a corporation regarding technology, processes, and equipment is staggering. Because of the fast pace, in most cases, annual audits would be sufficient. By providing annual audits on key systems, the auditors in your corporation will be able to catch security issues as they arise, possibly heading off major security catastrophes. Other systems that don't change often, such as servers and massive portions of network cabling, do not necessarily need to be audited on a yearly basis.

Your organization will need to determine how often each system and process should be audited. Regardless of how frequently your organization audits specific systems, the security rules that are referenced during a security audit need to be kept in mind during the installation. If an intended installation could not pass the organization's audit process, either don't install the item, or modify it so that it at least meets the minimum security requirements.

18
ACCESS CONTROL

Central to the issue of protecting systems and files is the ability to properly control access to sensitive information. The topic of access control, in terms of computer security, allows a data owner to allocate specific authorities to different users. How users are verified, and what access is given each user will depend on the type of access control methodology employed on the network. In order to achieve true network security, access control is an imperative function of any security solution. The world of network security access control covers accountability, identification and authorization, and authentication.

Accountability

Accountability is created when systems log user actions. Pattern monitoring can be built into software, so that when users' actions are suspicious, the actions are logged and reported. The system administrator should be frequently reviewing such logs. Thresholds for users' suspicious activities are referred to as *clipping levels*, and behavioral variables to watch for can be programmed by an administrator. Some of the more commonly watched variables include the following.

1. Multiple failed logins to the same account
2. Users attempting to log into a decommissioned account
3. Users logging into accounts from unverified IP addresses
4. Users logging into accounts from workstations other than their own
5. Users uploading software from previously closed ports on a computer

An administrator can use these, and any other clipping levels, as a means to watch for unauthorized or suspect user behavior. Possible digital crimes can sometimes be caught before they come to fruition, and login and user history can be used as evidence in post-crime trials.

Identification and Authentication

Before users are granted any access to a system, they must be identity proofed (see Figure 18.1). This process is usually done in person, and involves the potential user physically proving to a data owner that he is who he claims to be. Government-issued photo ID is most commonly required for the "in-person" identity proofing. For other systems, users can be completely anonymous, but known only to the system. For example, many e-commerce sites allow users to log in using a unique ID and password combination known only to the user. The method of verification for many e-commerce sites is the use of a unique and verifiable e-mail address.

Once a user has been identity proofed, she is provided login credentials. Credentials allow a user access, and can include three types

---

Verifying a User

When users try to access a system, they must identify themselves, and offer proof of who they claim to be. This is called proofing, or authentication. When requiring more than one of the below methods for verification of a user's identity, the process is known as a multi-proofing Users can accomplish this proofing by providing any combination of the following:

SOMETHING THE USER KNOWS
Basically, the user must know a piece of information, along with their identfication, in order to get past the login prompt. This information can be a PIN, password or the answer to some other secret question.

SOMETHING THE USER POSSESSES
These are often referred to as "tokens." The most commonly used token is an ATM card. Used in conjunction with the cardholder's PIN, the ATM login process requires a two-factor authentication.

SOMETHING THE USER IS
Biometric locks, retina scans, and vocal recognition are all used to verify who somebody is before granting them access to some of the most secure locations.

SOMEWHERE THE USER IS
Using IP addresses and other recognizable traits contained within data transfers, some systems are now able to determine where a user is located. If a user tries to access an organization's system from inside a campus where an employee must first physically verify themselves with security personnel, it is quite a different situation than a user attempting to gain access from their home or any other remote location.

Figure 18.1 Verifying Users

of methods of authentication, including something the user has, something the user knows, and something the user is.

Something a User Has

Something the user has is always a physical item, referred to as a token. In the strictly physical world, people use keys to physically access their cars. The keys are a form of token. In computer security, a physical key is almost never used as the sole method of achieving access to a system.

Something a User Knows

Something the user knows refers to a password or personal identification number (PIN). In a secure environment, these are things only the user would know. For nonrepudiation purposes, make sure your organization doesn't maintain databases of user passwords. Although IT personnel may have the ability to force a password change, even they should not be able to access user passwords and PINs. New users can be given a single-use password. Immediately after they first log into the system, they should be asked to enter a new password. From that point forward only the user will be able to access that account.

Something a User Is

Something the user is refers to biometrics. This could include anything from fingerprints and retina scans to voice recognition software. Because of the intrinsic strength of these systems, biometric verification devices are becoming more common as the associated cost drops.

Somewhere a User Is

Some security experts include the location of the user as a fourth verification method. For example, if a user is on a computer located inside a company's firewall, the access to her account will be treated differently than had she logged in remotely. Because of the inherent risks associated with the relative ease of a hacker faking a source IP, this shouldn't be considered as a primary source of verification.

Dual Factor Authentication

Most systems require two of the three main verification methods to gain access. The most common dual factor authentication is an ATM card. The ATM card itself is a token, which is something a user has. The user's PIN number is something the user knows. Therefore, in order for a user to gain access to his bank account and withdraw money, he must go through a dual authentication process.

Some banks provide account holders with fobs for dual authentication purposes. The user can log into his bank account with just a user ID and password (something the user knows), but in order to transfer money, he must be in possession of his assigned fob (something the user has). The fob communicates wirelessly with the bank, which issues a multidigit alphanumeric code every few minutes or so. Because the bank is synched with the fob, when the user inputs the fob's current code, the bank knows the user is in possession of the fob, and authorization to transfer funds is granted.

Authorization

Authorization is provided at the operating system level and affects how much control the user has over files contained on the hard drive of the computer she is using. Depending on the assigned authorization of the user, she can perform different privileges. These privileges include read, write, and execute.

> *Read*: Users with the authorization to read files can look at the file names in a given directory, and read file contents.
> *Write*: Users with the authorization to write files can add files to a directory, create new files, delete unwanted files, and rename existing files.
> *Execute*: Users with the authorization to execute files are authorized to run executable files in accessible directories.

Different Access Control Methodologies

Three of the most commonly used access control methodologies are role-based access control, discretionary access control, and mandatory access control. Mandatory access control and role-based control are sometimes lumped together into the category of nondiscretionary access control.

Role-Based Access Control

Role-based access control (RBAC) assigns user's access at the system level. RBAC is often used in commercial networks and sometimes in government offices where many classifications of security and information are concerned. A role is essentially a set of permissions such as the OS permissions of read, write, and execute. The three rules of RBAC include role assignment, role authorization, and transaction authorization.

Role Assignment   Transactions can be made by a user, as long as the user has been assigned a required role.

Role Authorization   Each user is authorized for specific roles. Combined with role assignment, this means only roles for which the user has been authorized can be assigned to the user.

Transaction Authorization   Only transactions authorized by the user's currently active role will be allowed. This means, if a user wants to access a particular portion of a system, but his current role precludes access to that area in the system, the user must log into a role that allows access. This may simply require an administrator, currently logged in as a user, to enter her administrative password.

Mandatory Access Control

Like role-based access control, mandatory access control (MAC) is an access policy determined by the system instead of a user. This type of access control is most commonly used in systems where information is highly sensitive and classified into several different security levels, such as with the military, certain governmental systems, and some commercial entities. MAC assigns sensitivity-level labels to both users and the information in the system, and handles the import and export of data into and out of the system from and to other systems.

Sensitivity Labels   Sensitivity labels are used to classify both users and the information on the system. This type of classification does not necessarily allow a person with a higher-ranked classification level access to files with so-called lower classification levels. For instance, somebody with a top secret clearance will not necessarily have access to all pieces of information classified as secret. This is commonly referred to as a "need to know" basis. If the user is deemed as needing to know a particular piece of information, she will be granted permission, but if her function in the organization does not meet the criterion of needing to know, she will not be granted access to that information.

Import and Export of Data   The mandatory access control system doesn't just control user access to data. It constantly monitors all activity within the system to determine if every action is allowed, including incoming data to the system and exporting data from the system. For instance, if a user has permission to access and view a file on the system, he may not necessarily have permission to export the file to the printer, and the MAC system will prevent him from doing so.

The two most common methods for applying mandatory access control are lattice-based access control and rule-based access control

Lattice-Based Access Control   This access control method allows users to access only those files their level of security allows. When two users require access to the same file, such as in classified projects, the lowest common security between the two is the security level at which the project will be defined.

Rule-Based Access Control   This is a set of basic rules that determine if a piece of information can be accessed by a user. The determination is made based on a comparison of the user's sensitivity label and the piece of information's sensitivity label.

Discretionary Access Control

Discretionary access control (DAC) allows the data owner to set the access level of data instead of the system. The two main considerations of DAC include file and data ownership, and access rights and permissions.

File and Data Ownership   Each file and piece of data has a defined owner. The creator of a file, in most DAC systems, is the defined owner. That owner has the authority to set permission levels for each other user in the system.

Access Rights and Permissions   Data owners, who are usually the creators of the files in question, are authorized to assign file access permission to other users within the system.

19

SECURITY CHECKLISTS

The following checklists will help your organization toward the goal of creating a culture of security awareness throughout the organization. Each organization's needs, in terms of network security, will differ according to the scope, size, and intent of the organization's network. For instance, a small manufacturing business will have a vastly different checklist than a hospital located over several campuses. The general concepts will remain the same, however, so these checklists can be used to guide information security planners in their efforts.

Checklist for Creating a Security Policy

- Security Vision Statement
  - Clearly Defined Goals
  - Not Too Specific
  - C-Level Buy-In and Involvement
- Reporting Structure
  - C-Level Management
  - IT Management
  - IT Personnel
  - Information Security Departmental Specialists ("Techsperts")
- Network Hardware
  - Routers
    - Location of Routers
    - Types of Routers
    - Patch Update Frequency
    - Policy Regarding Logging of Patch Updates
  - Firewalls
    - Type of Firewalling Used and Reason

- Policy and Diagram Regarding How Organization's Internal Servers Will be Firewalled, and Why
- E-mail Filters
  - Type of E-mail Filter Used
  - Patch Update Frequency
  - Policy Regarding Logging of Patch Updates
- Computers
  - Inventory of Types of Computers Used
  - Quantity of Each OS Type
  - Department and Campus Location of Each Computer
  - Support Disks for Each Computer
- Peripherals
  - Inventory of Printers, Copiers, Faxes, Document Scanners
  - Driver Update Frequency
  - Policy Regarding Logging of Driver Updates
  - Support Disks for Each Peripheral
- Software Security
  - Intrusion Detection System
    - Patch Update Frequency
    - Policy Regarding Logging of Patch Updates
  - Software Firewalling
    - List of Firewall Software Implemented
    - List of Computers on Which Software is Installed
    - Configuration Policy for Each Installation
    - Patch Update Frequency
    - Policy Regarding Logging of Patch Updates
  - Network Monitoring
    - List of Network Monitoring Software Used
    - List of Software and Traffic Patterns Monitored
    - Patch Update Frequency
    - Policy Regarding Logging of Patch Updates
    - Network Packet Traffic Logging, Including Log Frequency, Log Storage, and Log Reviews
  - Authorized and Unauthorized Software
    - List of Authorized Software, Including Authorized Users Based on Level of User Access
    - Policy Regarding Removal of Unauthorized Software

- – Methods Implemented for Search and Removal of Unauthorized Software
  - – Log of Unauthorized Software Located, Including Date Software Was Found and Node
- Third-Party Software
  - Preferred Software Inventory
    - – Allowed Browsers: Mozilla Firefox, Microsoft Internet Explorer, Safari, Opera, Epiphany, Lynx, Google Chrome, Flock, etc.
    - – Allowed E-mail Clients: Microsoft Outlook, Exchange, Apple Mail, Opera Mail, Netscape Messenger, Mozilla Thunderbird, IBM Lotus Notes, etc.
  - Software Management Policy
    - – Patch Update Frequency
    - – Policy Regarding Logging of Patch Updates
    - – Support Disks and Storage
- Operating Systems
  - Operating System Inventory
    - – List of Operating System Versions Supported
    - – Locations of Each Operating System (Campus, Facility, Department)
  - Operating System Management Policy
    - – Patch Update Frequency
    - – Policy Regarding Logging of Patch Updates
    - – Support Disks and Storage
- Access Controls
  - Type of Access Control Allowed
    - – Role-Based Access Control
    - – Mandatory Access Control
    - – Discretionary Access Control
  - Access Control List
    - – Based on Whatever Access Method, List Each Employee and Associated Areas of Digital Access
    - – Tie Updates to Human Resources (Payroll) to Ensure Immediate Removal of Access Privileges upon Termination of Employment
- Human Resources

- Hiring Procedures
  - Appropriate Background Checks
  - Necessary Security Clearances
  - Drug Screening
  - Proper IT Training for Position
  - Proper Security Awareness Training for Position
  - Nondisclosure Agreement
  - Proper Security Awareness Training upon Hiring
- Termination Procedures
  - Tie-In Procedures to Payroll, to Trigger Automatic Process
  - Collection of Keys, Badges, and Any Access Tokens
  - Removal of Login and Password from Access List
  - Exit Interview
  - Contract and Consideration for Liability Protection
- Physical Access
  - Campus Location Access
    - Based on Whatever Access Method, List Each Employee and Associated Areas of Physical Access
    - Tie Into Human Resources (Payroll) To Ensure Immediate Removal upon Termination of Employment
  - Policies and Procedures for Handling External Visitors to Organization Campus
    - Will Visitors Be Escorted to Internal Locations, or Be Asked to Wait Outside Sensitive Areas?
    - Will Visitors Be Required to Wear a Badge?
    - How Will Visitors Be Logged In and Out During Their Arrival and Departure from the Organization Campus?
  - Door Locks
    - Different Types Designated for Differing Levels of Security
    - Badges, Key Cards, Proximity Cards
    - Policy for Distribution and Collection of Keys
    - List of Key Holders and Associated Accessible Areas
  - Server Room Physical Access
    - Sequestered Away from the Rest of the Campus in Low-Traffic Area
    - Type of Physical Locks Used

- Will There Exist an Access Log with a List of Who Has Accessed the Room, and When?
- Any Other Special Security-Related Policies and Procedures, Specific to Server Room Access
- Physical Computer Security
  - Are Physical Locks Used on Certain Computers When Not in Use?
  - Are CD-ROMs, Flash Drives, and Any Other External Physical Access Point to Internal Computer Operations Either Physically Locked or Removed From Certain Computers?
- Advanced Physical Security Measures
  - Guard Station
  - Cameras
  - Vehicle Access Gates for Designated Areas
  - Personnel Access Gates for Designated Areas
  - Biometric Locks: Retina Scans, Voice Recognition, Fingerprint Scanners
- Physical File Protection
  - Reasonable Locks for Each Required Access Level
  - Reasonable Fire Protection for Sensitive Documents
- Fire Protection
  - Type of Suppression Device Used
    - Dry
    - Wet
    - Chemical-Based
    - Water-Based
  - Type of Fire Detection Used
    - Ionization
    - Photoelectric
- Dissemination and Understanding of Policy
  - Clear Concise Language Used Throughout Document
    - Avoid Jargon
    - Use Language Applicable to Each Employee Function Within the Organization
  - Distribution to All Employees
    - Use Training, Meetings, Company-wide E-mails, and Brown Bag Lunches to Establish Universal

Understanding of Security Policy and Its Ramifications on Daily Operations.

- Digital or Physical Copies?
- Method of Updating: Who's Responsible, How Will the Policy Be Updated?
- Staff Is Trained on Procedures and Policies Specific to Their Functions in the Organization

- Training Program
  - Training Frequency
  - Training Methods
    - PowerPoint or Keynote Presentations
    - Training Guides and Manuals
    - Handouts
    - Concept Building Activities
  - Training Documents
    - Training Standards
    - Concept Overviews
    - Certification Records (Who Has Received Training?)
- E-mail Usage Policy
  - E-mail Filtering
    - Inbox Filtering Applications
    - E-mail Server Configurations (IP Address Filtering, Spoof Filtering)
  - File Policy
    - What Types of Files Can and Cannot Be E-mailed or Received
    - Antivirus Policy for Downloaded Software
  - Types of Allowed E-mail Protocols
    - IMAP: Files Stored on E-mail Remote Server, Accessible to Anybody with Proper Login Credentials
    - POP3: Files Retrieved from E-mail Server and Stored on Local Client Machine
    - SMTP: Files Sent from Client Machine to Remote Server for Storage or Transmission of E-mail

Network Inventory Checklist

This checklist is intended to provide you with a guide to listing all possible network assets, including hardware and software. Of course, there is always a chance something was overlooked in the creation of this list, or some new technology is not covered herein, however, this list will serve as a good basis for creating a network inventory.

- Hardware Inventory
    - Workstations
        - Desktops
        - Laptops
        - Associated Peripherals
        - Terminals (if Using Mainframe Configuration)
    - Mainframes
    - Servers
        - E-mail Servers
        - Website Servers
        - FTP Servers
        - Proxy Servers
        - Dedicated Firewall Servers
        - Lightweight Directory Access Protocol (LDAP) Servers
        - Domain Controllers
        - Domain Name System (DNS) Servers
        - File Storage Servers
    - Mobile Devices
        - PDAs
        - Mobile Phones
    - Network Equipment
        - Routers
        - Hubs
        - Bridges
        - Switches
        - Network Cabling
        - Network Cards and Interfaces
        - Modems
        - Wireless Access Points (WAPs)
        - Gateways

- Software Inventory
  - Commercial-off-the-Shelf (COTS) Software: Software Available for Purchase from a Third-Party Vendor
    - Operating Systems
    - Web-Based Software
    - Distributed Software (Installed on All Workstations Throughout the Network, or at Least a Large Portion of the Workstations)
    - Client-Based Software (Only Installed on Certain Workstations)
    - Server-Based Software
    - End User License Agreements (EULAs) for Associated Software Installations
    - Associated Usage Policy: Who Has Access to the Application and How Is Access Managed?
  - Proprietary Software: Software Developed In-House by Organization Engineers
    - Web-Based Software
    - Distributed Software (Installed on All Workstations Throughout the Network, or at Least a Large Portion of the Workstations)
    - Client-Based Software (Only Installed on Certain Workstations)
    - Server-Based Software
    - Associated Usage Policy: Who Has Access to the Application and How Is Access Managed?
- Stored File Inventory
  - Digital Documents
    - Classification
    - Storage Location
    - Allocated File Space
    - Encrypted or Plain Language
  - Physical Backups of Digital Documents
    - Location of Files
    - Quantity of Files
  - Database Files
    - Employee Records
    - Customer Records

- Company Financials
- Vendor Lists
- Sales Invoices
- Purchase Orders
- Product Inventory Lists
- Manufacturing Bill of Materials (BOM)
- Classified Files
  - Proprietary Files
  - Sealed Documents
  - Schematics
  - Research & Development Documents
  - Engineering Parts Lists
  - Miscellaneous Engineering Files
- Legal Files
  - Internal Contracts (Nondisclosure, Noncompete, etc.)
  - External Contracts (Nondisclosure, Purchase Agreements, etc.)
  - Industry Standards
  - Legal Correspondence

Physical Security Checklist

This checklist is meant to give consideration to the many facets of the physical security realm of proper network security measures. Although some of the items listed are for consideration during the construction phase, such as with external walls, the list in its entirety attempts to highlight all of the important aspects of physical security.

- Walls
  - Internal Walls
    - Ventilation into server rooms is small enough at any given point, such that an intruder cannot simply gain access to building ventilation and then drop into the server room.
    - Where drop-down ceilings are used over computer rooms and server room, walls extend upward through drop-down ceiling and into main ceiling structure above.

- External Walls and Windows
  - Workstations located on external wall do not have monitors facing outward, to ensure people passing by cannot simply look in and glean password and login information from computer screens.
  - Shatterproof, security-rated windows are used on all external walls.
  - No external cues exist that could point a possible intruder in the direction of the server room or other digitally sensitive room within the facility.
- Ceilings and Roof Access
  - At no location does access to drop-down ceilings permit easy or unguarded physical access to critical workstations or server room.
  - Any roof access is appropriately locked and secured, commensurate with the level of desired security.
  - Roof access does not immediately drop into a sensitive area, but instead is quarantined from the rest of the building, such that credentials are required to move past the point of entry.
- Doors
  - Door Materials
    - Solid-core doors are used throughout building, and industrial grade doors are used to cordon off all rooms containing sensitive files, workstations, or servers.
- Locks
  - Locks are installed on all doors leading to rooms containing any possible access point to the network including:
    - Workstations
    - Servers
    - Wireless access points
  - Biometric locks
    - Where security mandates, biometric locks are used, for added levels of protection
    - Includes
      - Voice recognition
      - Fingerprint recognition
      - Retina scanning and recognition
  - Mantraps

- If commensurate with desired security level, mantraps have been installed and are appropriately monitored in order to prohibit unauthorized individuals from piggybacking into the facility behind an authorized employee or visitor.
- Network Cabling
  - Speed of network cabling is commensurate with necessary throughputs for sizeable downloads and data transfer rates throughout the network.
  - Route network cabling separate from electrical cabling and other wiring, in order to keep it easily accessible and identifiable, as well as to avoid interference from other electrical signals.
  - In areas where possible rodent damage could occur, consider installation of metal armoring.
  - Tuck all network wiring into walls or channels, such that no person will accidentally trip over the wiring or be tempted to tamper with it.
- Workstation Physical Security
  - Remove all unnecessary external drives.
  - Physically lock workstations to desks.
  - For certain workstations that will be in public view, install "blinders" that block all viewing angles except for direct-on.
- Server Room
  - If possible, house server room in area separate from the flow of mainstream traffic.
  - If server room is located in basement, provide proper flood relief.
  - Ensure proper ventilation for air supply.
  - Fire suppression and detection systems.
  - Advanced door locks, such as keypad entry, biometrics, or digital proximity sensor locks.
  - Backup and redundant power supplies.
  - Backup and redundant server room equipment, as necessary.
- Disposal of Information
  - Cross-cut shredders for sensitive internal documents
  - Third-party, certified document destruction service

Index

About the Author

Tyler Speed lives in beautiful Bend, Oregon, with his lovely wife, Jaime, who is an award-winning teacher and an amazing mother to their big-hearted and super-smart 10-year-old son, Donavan. Tyler works as the Executive Vice President at Electronics International, an aviation company located on the Bend Airport that provides world-class engine-analyzing solutions to pilots. When not working at Electronics International or writing, Tyler teaches Kung Fu and Tai Chi at his Kung Fu studio.